Spotlight SAT

25 Lessons Illuminate
the Most Frequently Tested Topics

Kerensa Peterson
Mary Wink
Andrew Marx

PUBLISHING

New York • Chicago

SAT is a registered trademark of the College Entrance Examination Board, which neither sponsors nor endorses this product.

This publication is designed to provide accurate and authoritative information in regard to the subject matter covered. It is sold with the understanding that the publisher is not engaged in rendering legal, accounting, or other professional service. If legal advice or other expert assistance is required, the services of a competent professional should be sought.

Contributing Editors: Annette Riffle, Mark Ward, and Brandon Jones
Editorial Director: Jennifer Farthing
Senior Editor: Tonya Lobato
Production Editor: Samantha Raue
Production Artist: Virginia Byrne
Cover Designer: Carly Schnur

Published by Kaplan Publishing, a division of Kaplan, Inc.
888 Seventh Ave.
New York, NY 10106

Printed in the United States of America

February 2007
10 9 8 7 6 5 4 3 2 1

Library of Congress Cataloging-in-Publication Data
Peterson, Kerensa.
Kaplan spotlight SAT : 25 lessons illuminate the most frequently tested topics/Kerensa Peterson, Mary Wink, Andrew Marx.
    p. cm.
ISBN-13: 978-1-4195-9451-9
ISBN-10: 1-4195-9451-6
1. SAT (Educational test)--Study guides. 2. Universities and colleges--United States--Examinations--Study guides. I. Wink, Mary. II. Marx, Andrew. III. Title.
LB2353.57.P473 2006
378.1'662--dc22   2006029524

Contents

Critical Reading

Writing *Lead Role*

take time to read each question carefully!

How to Use This Book

There's no one single way to use this book. We've designed it specifically to satisfy various learning styles and to address different concerns about the SAT. You'll notice the special ranking system at the beginning of each lesson that rates the relative importance of three factors: Frequency, Difficulty, and the Surprise Factor, or chance that a relatively easy topic may catch you off guard with one or two surprisingly difficult questions. Using this ranking system, you can target your study plan to cover those topics that concern you the most.

You'll also notice a special set of colorful stickers at the back of the book that you can use to tag topics with different levels of importance. Use them to help you remember which topics to revisit (Learn Your Lines), or to call out topics you've mastered and never need to look at again (Bravo!). The four sticker choices are:

1. Learn Your Lines
2. Lead Role
3. Audition Again
4. Bravo!

Be creative and feel free to clutter up the book with these colorful sticker notes. They are intended to give you a sense of direction and progress, and to make studying a little less boring and a little more interactive.

● LESSON CONTENT

In each lesson you'll find a thorough explanation of the topic, tips on how to avoid common answer traps, rules and formulas for mastering the topic, sample questions with walk-through explanations, and a 10-item self-test quiz.

Start with any section, or any lesson—how you choose to organize your study plan is up to you. Start with the most difficult topics, or the most frequent, or the trickiest. It's important though, to read the "SAT Basics" introductions before you begin the lesson content. This will give you a bird's eye view of both the exam and each section within the exam and will be a useful foundation for mastering the most important content for each unique section of the SAT.

● DON'T FORGET ABOUT MOBILE PREP AND EXTRA PRACTICE ONLINE!

Practice doesn't end with the book. Spotlight SAT has a robust online companion that offers a complete practice test, mobile preparation—additional test items that you can download to your PDA or cell phone, SAT flashcards, and more. Since you're constantly on the move, this material is designed to let you practice almost any time and anywhere. Access the online practice materials through kaptest.com/booksonline, and make sure to have your book handy the first time you log on since a prompt will ask you a password question that is answered only in the text.

Have fun formulating your SAT plan of attack, and enjoy the creative freedom this book allows. We're confident that Spotlight SAT will give you the flexibility and the expertise you need to perform your very best on test day.

Ready?

Lights... camera... action!

SAT Basics

Before you begin the lessons, there are a few SAT basics you should know.

The SAT is 3 hours and 45 minutes long, and there are two 10-minute breaks. The exam consists mostly of multiple-choice questions, and it's divided into three sections each of Math, Critical Reading, and Writing. There is also an experimental section, but we will discuss that section later. The writing section is always first. The multiple-choice sections can appear in any order on the test. The order is random, and your test will be different from that of the person sitting next to you.

The SAT sections are broken down like this:

Section	Length	Content	Type
1. Critical Reading	25 minutes	Sentence completion and reading comprehension questions	Multiple-choice
2. Critical Reading	25 minutes	Sentence completion and reading comprehension questions	Multiple-choice
3. Critical Reading	20 minutes	Sentence completion and reading comprehension questions	Multiple-choice
4. Math	25 minutes	High school geometry and algebra, numbers and operations, statistics, probability, and data analysis	Multiple-choice questions and student-produced responses
5. Math	25 minutes	High school geometry and algebra, numbers and operations, statistics, probability, and data analysis	Multiple-choice questions and student-produced responses
6. Math	20 minutes	High school geometry and algebra, numbers and operations, statistics, probability, and data analysis	Multiple-choice questions
7. Writing	25 minutes	Student-written essay	Long-form essay
8. Writing	25 minutes	Identifying sentence errors, improving sentences, improving paragraphs	Multiple-choice questions
9. Writing	10 minutes	Improving sentences	Multiple-choice questions
10. Experimental Section	25 minutes	Math, Critical Reading, or Writing	(Anything is fair game)

● SAT SCORING

You gain one point for each correct answer on the SAT and lose a fraction of a point (¼ point, to be exact) for each wrong answer (except with Grid-ins, where you lose nothing for a wrong answer). You do not lose any points for questions you leave blank. This is important, so we'll repeat it: You do not lose any points for questions you leave blank.

The totals for the critical reading, writing, and math questions are added up to produce three raw scores. These raw scores equal the number you got right minus a fraction of the number you got wrong. These scores are converted into scaled scores, with 200 as the lowest score and 800 the highest. Each raw point is worth approximately 10 scaled points.

The three scaled scores are added together to produce your final score of 600–2400, as follows:

Scaled Scores:	Writing 200–800	Math 200–800	Critical Reading 200–800	Total 600–2400
For example:	650	710	620	1980

● ORDER OF DIFFICULTY

In the SAT, some sections will have their multiple-choice questions arranged in order of difficulty. Here's a breakdown:

		Arranged Easiest to Hardest?
Math:	Regular math	Yes
	Grid-ins	Yes
Critical Reading:	Sentence Completion	Yes
	Short Reading Comprehension	No
	Long Reading Comprehension	No
Writing:	Essay	N/A
	Identifying Sentence Errors	No
	Improving Sentences	No
	Improving Paragraphs	No

As you can see, all question sets in the Math section are normally arranged in order of difficulty, as are sentence completion questions in the Critical Reading section. As you work through a set that is organized this way, be aware of where you are in a set. When working on the easy problems, you can generally trust your first impulse—the obvious answer is likely to be right. As you get to the end of the set, you need to be more suspicious of obvious answers, because the answer should not come easily. If it does, look at the problem again. It may be one of those distracters—a wrong answer choice meant to trick you.

● IMPORTANT GROUND RULES

These are SAT rules you can use to your advantage. Knowing these rules will keep you from asking questions and wasting precious time and from committing minor errors that result in serious penalties.

- You are NOT allowed to jump back and forth between sections.
- You are NOT allowed to return to earlier sections to change answers.
- You are NOT allowed to spend more than the allotted time on any section.
- You CAN move around within a section.
- You CAN flip through your section at the beginning to see what types of questions are coming up.

That covers the SAT basics! Make sure to read about the details of each individual section, Math, Critical Reading, and Writing, in the three section introductions.

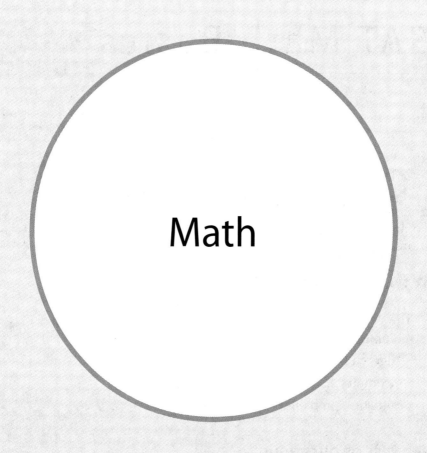

Math

SAT Math Basics

Questions in the math sections are arranged to increase gradually in difficulty. Be aware of the difficulty level as you go through a question set. The harder the question seems, the more traps you will have to avoid.

● MATH COVERED IN THE SAT

The math concepts tested on the SAT are:

- Numbers and operations
- Algebra I, II, and functions
- Geometry
- Statistics, probability, and data analysis

● TYPES OF QUESTIONS

Multiple-Choice Questions

The multiple-choice question setup in the Math section is the same as in the other two sections. You will be asked to select the best answer from five choices. Thus, certain techniques will help you eliminate answer choices and make the problems more manageable.

Grid-in Questions

The grid-in section on the SAT is more like the math tests you're used to taking at school. Rather than choosing from the five answer choices provided, you have to work through the problem and enter your answer in the grid boxes on the answer sheet. Some grid-in questions only have one correct answer, whereas others have several correct answers. There are no penalties for wrong answers on the grid-in section.

Each grid-in question provides four boxes and a column of ovals, or bubbles, in which to write your answer. The elements of your answer, that is, the digits, decimal points, or fraction signs, should be written in a separate box for each part. The corresponding bubbles underneath should be shaded in to match the box at the top of the column. There are limitations to what you may grid and what will not be counted.

You cannot grid:

- Negative answers
- Answers with variables (x, y, w, etc.)
- Answers greater than 9,999
- Answers with commas (write 1000, not 1,000)
- Mixed numbers (such as 2½)

● USING YOUR CALCULATOR (OR NOT)

You've read about all of our techniques for finding the answers to math questions using just your pencil and your mind. However, there are times when you can get some extra help and make life a little easier.

You are allowed to use a calculator on the SAT. However, that doesn't mean that you should always use your calculator on the SAT. Yes, you can do computations faster, but you may be tempted to waste time using a calculator on questions that shouldn't involve lengthy computations. Remember, no SAT question requires a calculator. If you ever find yourself doing extensive calculations—elaborate division or long drawn-out multiplication, stop. You probably missed a shortcut.

Should I Just Leave My Calculator at Home?

No. Bring it. By zeroing in on the parts of problems that need calculation, you can increase your score and save yourself time by using your calculator.

What Kind of Calculator Should I Bring?

You should bring a calculator that you're comfortable with. If you don't have a calculator now, buy one right away and practice using it between now and test day. You can use just about any small calculator; however, there are a few restrictions you must abide by. You may not bring:

- Calculators that print out your calculations
- Handheld minicomputers or laptop computers
- Any calculator with a typewriter keypad
- Calculators with an angled readout screen
- Calculators that require a wall outlet
- Calculators that make noise

When Should I Use My Calculator?

Calculators help the most on grid-ins. Because grid-ins don't give you answer choices to choose from, it's especially important to be positive about your results, and calculators can help you check your work and avoid careless errors.

Remember, a calculator can be useful when used selectively and strategically. Not all parts of a problem will necessarily be easier with a calculator. Consider this problem:

If four grams of peanuts can make 32 Peanut Joy candy bars, how many Peanut Joy candy bars could be produced from 86 grams of peanuts?

This word problem has two steps. Step one is to set up the following proportion:

4 g of peanuts = 32 bars

A little algebraic engineering tells you that:

1 g of peanuts = 8 bars

Here's where you whip out that calculator. This problem has now been reduced down to pure calculation:

$86 \times 8 = 688$

When Should I Avoid My Calculator?

You may be tempted to use your calculator on every problem, but many questions will be easier without it. Look at this example:

If $x \neq 1/3$ and $51/3x - 1 = 51/29$, then what is the value of x?

One way of answering this question would be to cross-multiply and then isolate x:

$$(51)(29) = (3x - 1)(51)$$
$$1,479 = 153x - 51$$
$$1,530 = 153x$$
$$1,530/153 = x$$
$$10 = x$$

Notice how much more quickly you'll arrive at the answer if, rather than reflexively reaching for your calculator, you invest a few moments in thinking about the question—specifically what you're given and what you're asked for. Notice that after you cross-multiplied the equation above, you were left with $(51)(29) = (3x - 1)(51)$. Simply cancel out (51) from both sides. You are now left with the following equation:

$$3x - 1 = 29$$
$$3x = 30$$
$$x = 10$$

● GOOD GUESSING ON SAT MATH

The scoring system for the SAT's Multiple-Choice Math sections, like its Critical Reading and Writing Multiple-Choice sections, is meant to discourage random guessing. For every correct answer, you earn a whole point. For every wrong answer, you lose a fraction of a point. So, if you guess at random on a number of questions, the points you lose on incorrect guesses could cancel out the points you gain from correct guesses. So, leaving a blank on the response form might be better for your score than a wild guess.

But you can and should make educated guesses. If you can eliminate one or more wrong answer choices, then your odds of guessing correctly go way up. That will increase your score, which is a good thing. We'll show you how.

The exception to the guessing penalty rule is the grid-in section. You lose no points for wrong answers on grid-in questions; therefore, you should ALWAYS fill something in the grid on these questions.

Now you're ready to begin the lessons. Good luck!

Symbols

DIFFICULTY: ★ ★ ★

FREQUENCY: ★ ★

SURPRISE FACTOR: ★ ★

● INTRODUCTION TO SYMBOL QUESTIONS

These questions probably won't be the *most* difficult ones on the test, but they can be quite hard. Answering them could involve solving complicated equations. As you'll see, they often involve multiple substitutions, which are sometimes tricky to organize. You'll see a lot of weird-looking symbols. They add to the surprise factor, and they make questions seem more difficult than they really are. In fact, they are meant to confuse and unnerve you. These questions come up pretty regularly on the SAT, so you'll want to be ready to handle them.

You're familiar with the symbols for the basic operations of arithmetic: $+$, $-$, $\times$, and $\div$. Symbol questions introduce new operations with unusual symbols. Actually, these new symbols just combine operations you're already familiar with to make new ones. In fact, the questions usually define the symbols in terms of operations you know. For instance, a question might begin by telling you that $a \ \square \ b = a + 2b$. Here, finding the value of an expression with two numbers and the $\square$ sign is a just a matter of adding twice the second number to the first number.

Now, different Symbol questions present different problems. Some of the most straightforward ones just ask you to find the value of an expression where the symbol combines two numbers. Here's an example:

If $b \sqcup c = b + \sqrt{c}$, then $9 \sqcup 16 =$

(A) 5

(B) 7

(C) 13

(D) 19

(E) 25

The correct choice is (C). We get that answer by substituting 9 for b and 16 for c:

$$b \sqcup c = 9 + \sqrt{16} = 9 + 4 = 13$$

Such Symbol questions get a little more difficult when the special symbol appears more than once. Still, it's just a matter of evaluating an algebraic expression.

Other Symbol questions require something different: equation solving. A question might define a symbol, and then require you to solve an algebraic equation involving the symbol. Here's an example:

If $g \phi h = 2g - h$ and $3 \phi x = 4$, then $x =$

(A) 1

(B) 2

(C) 3

(D) 4

(E) 5

The correct answer is (B). We substitute 3 for g and x for h to get:

$$3 \phi x = 2(3) - x = 4$$

So $6 - x = 4$

Solving this equation, we find that $x = 4$

● THE TRAP DOOR
Steering Clear of Answer Traps

There are two common kinds of traps to look out for in Symbol questions:

1. Order of substitution
2. Double negatives

Many students are led to an incorrect answer by making errors in substitution. Look at this question:

If $x \Delta y = y - 2x$, what is the value of $5 \Delta 10$?

To answer this question, you must substitute numbers for variables in $y - 2x$. Many students will substitute the first number in $5 \Delta 10$ for the first variable in $y - 2x$, but that is a trap! The definition of the symbol has the variables in the reverse order. Since the symbol is introduced in the expression $x \Delta y$, you need to substitute 5 for x and 10 for y. If you avoid the trap and do just that, you will get $5 \Delta 10 = 10 - 2(5) = 0$. A student who doesn't avoid the trap might get $5 \Delta 10 = 5 - 2(10) = -15$.

The key to avoiding the trap, then, is to take the original formula, $x \Delta y$, and make sure to pair the variables up correctly with the numbers in the expression you have to evaluate, $5 \Delta 10$. Until you've finished that step, don't let the order of the variables in $y - 2x$ distract you.

Another troublesome trap involves double negatives. Remember, $-(-4) = 4$, $-(-10) = 10$, and so on. Many Symbol questions are written with double negatives in mind, and it is up to you keep track of them. Let's look at another question featuring a different symbol we just used:

If $x \Delta y = 2x - y$, what is the value of $\overset{x}{4} \Delta \overset{y}{-2}$?

To answer this question, we substitute 4 for x and -2 for y in $2x - y$, and simplify the result:

$$x = 4$$
$$y = -2$$
$$2x - y = 2(4) - (-2)$$
$$= 8 + 2$$
$$= 10$$

We were careful to keep the minus sign in place as we substituted for *y*. Many students fall into a trap by losing track of the minus sign, thinking that the negative takes its place. It doesn't. Here is the work behind a common *incorrect* response to this question.

$$x = 4$$
$$y = -2$$
$$2x - y = 2(4) - 2$$
$$= 8 - 2$$
$$= 6$$

Remember that you need to subtract –2, and not just put –2 after 2(4). The minus sign and the negative sign are not the same thing!

● PERFORMANCE TECHNIQUES
Key Formulas and Rules

When it comes to Symbol questions, there are no key formulas. Most Symbol questions introduce brand new formulas. In many cases, they are very unusual.

There are a couple of steps to start with in Symbol questions, no matter what the ultimate objective of the question might be.

First, you need to match values with the variables in the original formula. Suppose we're told that $p @ r = \dfrac{p - r}{2}$ and are then asked to evaluate 19 @ 11. You should start by matching the numbers with corresponding letters: *p* and 19 come first in their respective expressions, so *p* = 19; *r* and 11 each come second, so *r* = 11.

Keeping track of values this way is very important, especially when the definitions use the variables out of order.

Now that we have *p* = 19 and *r* = 11, we can evaluate 19 @ 11 by substituting the number values for the variables in $\dfrac{p - r}{2}$:

$$\frac{p-r}{2} = \frac{19-11}{2} = \frac{8}{2} = 4$$

Pairing variables with their values before substituting is the key to setting up almost every Symbol question. Once you've made your substitutions, it's best to leave the original expressions with the strange symbols out of the picture altogether. You don't need them; just work with the expressions or equations you got by substitution. From that point on, working through the Symbol question is a matter of using your algebra skills.

● **DRESS REHEARSAL**
Sample Questions And Detailed Explanations

Now that we've gone over the important points, let's tackle some questions step-by-step.

1. If $c \lozenge d = \dfrac{c}{c+d}$ for all numbers greater than zero, then what is the value of $4 \lozenge 18$?

(A) $\dfrac{2}{11}$

(B) $\dfrac{2}{9}$

(C) $\dfrac{9}{11}$

(D) $1\dfrac{2}{11}$

(E) $1\dfrac{2}{9}$

This question calls for you to evaluate an expression with a new symbol, based on its definition.

If $c \lozenge d = 4 \lozenge 18$, then $c = 4$, and $d = 18$.

We can substitute these values into the expression $\dfrac{c}{c+d}$. So $c \lozenge d = \dfrac{4}{4+18} = \dfrac{4}{22}$.

This fraction can be simplified to $\dfrac{2}{11}$, and so **choice (A) is the correct answer.** Choice (B) is just the value of $\dfrac{c}{d}$. Be careful not to leave out any terms.

2. $a \blacktriangleright b = a - 2b$. What is the value of $10 \blacktriangleright (4 \blacktriangleright 3)$?

(A) 6

(B) 8

(C) 10

(D) 12

(E) 14

This is another evaluation problem, but there is a new twist here: the symbol appears twice in the expression to be evaluated. Don't let this confuse or discourage you. You can handle this in much the same you handle any expression with multiple operations: combine one pair of terms at a time.

As always, you start with the terms inside parentheses. So let's evaluate $4 \blacktriangleright 3$:

If $a \blacktriangleright b = 4 \blacktriangleright 3$, then $a = 4$ and $b = 3$. So $a \blacktriangleright b = a - 2b = 4 - 2(3) = 4 - 6 = -2$

So $4 \blacktriangleright 3 = -2$. Therefore, $10 \blacktriangleright (4 \blacktriangleright 3) = 10 \blacktriangleright -2$. All we have to do is evaluate this last expression, and we're done.

If $a \blacktriangleright b = 10 \blacktriangleright -2$, then $a = 10$ and $b = -2$. So $a \blacktriangleright b = a - 2b = 10 - 2(-2) = 10 + 4 = 14$

Since $10 \blacktriangleright (4 \blacktriangleright 3) = 14$, **choice (E) is the correct answer.**

Notice that we had to deal with a double negative when simplifying $10 - 2(-2)$. Someone who doesn't let the negative and minus signs cancel each other out might get $10 - 4$ instead of $10 + 4$ as the simplified expression and then wind up selecting the incorrect choice (A).

3. If $w \bowtie z = \sqrt{w} - \sqrt{z}$, then $169 \bowtie 144 \bowtie 4 =$

(A) −2

(B) −1

(C) 1

(D) 2

(E) 3

Here is another evaluation question where the symbol appears twice. Since this one has no parentheses, you need to work through the operations from left to right. Unlike the two previous questions, this one involves a more advanced operation in the form of radicals.

Our first step, then, is to rewrite 169 ¤ 144. 169 is the value of w, and 144 is the value of z, such that w ¤ $z = \sqrt{w} - \sqrt{z} = \sqrt{169} - \sqrt{144} = 13 - 12 = 1$.

So 169 ¤ 144 ¤ 4 = 1 ¤ 4. Now we can say that $w = 1$ and $z = 4$. Thus,

$$\sqrt{w} - \sqrt{z} = \sqrt{1} - \sqrt{4} = 1 - 2 = -1.$$

Choice (B) is the correct answer.

Choice (C), 1, is the result of using $\sqrt{w-z}$ instead of $\sqrt{w} - \sqrt{z}$ as the definition of the symbol. Using that to evaluate 169 ¤ 144 ¤ 4 gets $\sqrt{\sqrt{169-144}-4} = \sqrt{\sqrt{25}-4} = \sqrt{5-4} = \sqrt{1} = 1$

4. $m \square n = 3n - 2m$. If $5 \square 4 = 11 \square x$, then $x =$

   (A) 3
   (B) 6
   ((■)) 8
   (D) 12
   (E) 13

#try problem again# Bravo!

Here is an equation-solving Symbol question to work through. You'll want to write both sides of the equation in terms of how the symbol is defined. Let's work through the question one step at a time, then, and evaluate $5 \square 4$.

Start by pairing the variables with the values: $m = 5$ and $n = 4$. As you substitute those values in $3n - 2m$, watch out for the trap! The variables don't appear in the same order as they do on the other side of the equation. n comes first, and so we have to substitute 4, and not 5, for the first variable:

$$3n - 2m = 3(4) - 2(5) = 12 - 10 = 2$$

So we can rewrite $5 \square 4 = 11 \square x$ as $2 = 11 \square x$. Rewrite the right side of the equation, and you'll have an equation to solve.

$11 \square x = 3(x) - 2(11) = 3x - 22$, so we can write $2 = 11 \square x$ as $2 = 3x - 22$. Let's solve that equation.

Turning the equation around and adding 22 to both sides gets us $3x = 24$. After we divide both sides by 3, we have a solution of 8. **Choice (C) is the correct answer.**

Choice (E), 13, might be the result of mixing up the variables in the definition. That's the trap we warned about. By working with $m \; \square \; n = 3m - 2n$, you could wind up with the equation $7 = 33 - 2x$, which has a solution of 13.

5. $w \blacksquare z = 4w - \dfrac{z}{2}$. If $7 \blacksquare x = x \blacksquare 34$, then what is the value of x?

   (A) 7

   (B) 8

   (C) 9

   (D) 10

   (E) 11

This is another equation-solving Symbol question, but it throws in a new twist. There are variables on both sides of the equation. Not to worry; it may look complicated, but we'll take the same basic steps to set things up. The key is to substitute each side of the equation with another expression.

The left side of the equation has $7 \blacksquare z$. There, $w = 7$ and $z = x$.

So $w \blacksquare z = 4w - \dfrac{z}{2} = 4(7) - \dfrac{x}{2} = 28 - \dfrac{x}{2}$.

That's as far as we can go on that side.

The left side of the equation has $x \blacksquare 34$. Now, $w = x$ and $z = 34$.

So $w \blacksquare z = 4w - \dfrac{z}{2} = 4(x) - \dfrac{34}{2} = 4x - 17$.

Now we can rewrite this equation with new terms and operations, and without the $\blacksquare$ symbol.

If $7 \blacksquare x = x \blacksquare 34$, $28 - \dfrac{x}{2} = 4x - 1$. Now finding the value of x is just a matter of solving a more standard equation. By adding 17 to both sides, and then adding $\dfrac{x}{2}$ to both sides, we get $45 = \dfrac{9x}{2}$. Multiplying both sides by 2 gets us $90 = 9x$. Finally, we can divide both sides by 9 to get $x = 10$. **Choice (D) is the correct answer.**

● **THE FINAL ACT**
  Self-Check Quiz

1. If $x \, \S \, y = \dfrac{3x}{2y}$, then $22 \, \S \, 15 =$

   $\dfrac{3(22)}{30} = \dfrac{66}{30} = \dfrac{33}{15} = \dfrac{11}{5}$

   (A) $\dfrac{45}{44}$

   (B) $\dfrac{11}{5}$

   (C) $\dfrac{22}{5}$

   (D) $\dfrac{33}{10}$

   (E) $\dfrac{33}{5}$

2. If $a \, \# \, b = a(a + b)$, then $-10 \, \# \, 5 =$

   (A) -75

   $-10(-10 + 5)$

   (B) -50

   $100 - 50$

   (C) 50 $= 50$

   (D) 75

   (E) 105

3. $r \, \clubsuit \, s = s^2 + \sqrt{r}$. What is the value of $36 \, \clubsuit \, 16$?

   (A) 10 $16^2 + \sqrt{36}$

   (B) 262 $256 + 6$

   (C) 292 262

   (D) $1,300$

   (E) $1,552$

4. If $b \top c = b + bc$, then what is the value of $7 \top 4 \top 9$? Order of OP.

   (A) 43 $7 + 28$

   (B) 64 $35 + 315$

   (C) 252

   (D) 315

   (E) 350

5. If $c \blacktriangledown d = \dfrac{\sqrt{d} - c}{d^2}$, then $(-12 \blacktriangledown 9) \blacktriangledown 4 =$

   (A) $\dfrac{17}{432}$

   (B) $\dfrac{29}{144}$

   (C) $\dfrac{49}{432}$

   (D) $\dfrac{17}{144}$

   (E) $\dfrac{19}{144}$

6. $x \neg y = 3x + 2y$. If $a \neg 3 = 18$, what is the value of a?

   (A) 4

   (B) 6

   (C) 8

   (D) 10

   (E) 12

7. $u \# v = 5u + 2v$. What is the solution of $y \# 6 = 12 \# y$?

   (A) 4

   (B) 8

   (C) 12

   (D) 16

   (E) 18

8. If $s \phi t = \dfrac{2s}{3t}$ and $5 \phi y = \dfrac{5}{12}$, then $y =$

9. $q \blacksquare r = 2q - \sqrt{r}$. What is the solution of $14 \blacksquare 9 \blacksquare x = 43$?

10. $h \uparrow j = j^2 - h$. If $x \uparrow 14 = -64 \uparrow \sqrt{x}$, then $x =$

● ANSWERS AND EXPLANATIONS

1. **B** $x = 22$ and $y = 15$, so $\dfrac{3(22)}{2(15)} = \dfrac{66}{30} = \dfrac{11}{5}$. Choice (A), $\dfrac{45}{44}$, is the value of $\dfrac{3y}{2x}$. Choice (C), $\dfrac{22}{5}$, is the value of $\dfrac{3x}{y}$.

2. **C** Here, $a = -10$ and $b = 5$. So $a \# b = a(a + b) = -10(-10 + 5) = -10(-5) = 50$. Choice (B), -50, is the result of not letting the negative signs cancel out. Choice (E), 75, is the result of getting -15 instead of -5 when adding 5 to -10.

3. **B** Since $r = 36$ and $s = 16$, $s^2 + \sqrt{r} = 16^2 + \sqrt{36} = 256 + 6 = 262$. Be careful about substituting in the right order; r and s appear in the reverse order. The wrong substitution would result in choice (D), 1,300.

4. **E** The special symbol appears twice in this question, so we'll carry out one operation at a time. $7 \top 4 = 7 + 7(4) = 7 + 28 = 35$. So $7 \top 4 \top 9 = 35 \top 9$. That expression equals $35 + 35(9)$, or 350. Choice (D) is the result of evaluating bc instead of $b + bc$ in the second step.

5. **C** $-12 \blacktriangledown 9 = \dfrac{\sqrt{9} - (-12)}{9^2} = \dfrac{3 + 12}{81} = \dfrac{15}{81} = \dfrac{5}{27}$. So $-12 \blacktriangledown 9 \blacktriangledown 4 = \dfrac{5}{27} \blacktriangledown 4$. That expression is $\dfrac{\sqrt{4} - \dfrac{5}{27}}{4^2} = \dfrac{2 - \dfrac{5}{27}}{16} = \dfrac{\dfrac{49}{27}}{16} = \dfrac{49}{432}$.

Choice (D), $\dfrac{17}{144}$, is the result of evaluating $\dfrac{\sqrt{9} - (12)}{9^2}$ instead of $\dfrac{\sqrt{9} - (-12)}{9^2}$. Choice (E) is the result of ignoring the double negative when subtracting in the second step.

6. **A** Since, $x \neg y = 3x + 2y$, $a \neg 3 = 3(a) + 2(3) = 3a + 6$. Substituting this expression into our equation gets us $3a + 6 = 18$. The solution of that equation is 4. Choice (C), 8, is the solution of $3a - 6 = 18$. Choice (E), 12, is the solution of $a + 6 = 18$.

7. **D** $y \text{ \# } 6 = 5y + 12$, and $12 \text{ \# } y = 60 + 2y$. Therefore, we need to solve the equation $5y + 12 = 60 + 2y$. After subtracting terms from both sides, we get $3y = 48$, and so the solution is 16.

8. **8** $5 \phi y = \dfrac{2(5)}{3(y)} = \dfrac{10}{3y}$. So $\dfrac{10}{3y} = \dfrac{5}{12}$. We can solve this equation by cross-multiplying, such that $15y = 120$. Dividing both sides by 15 gets us $y = 8$.

9. **49** $14 \blacksquare 9 = 2(14) - \sqrt{9} = 28 - 3 = 25$. So the equation can be rewritten as $25 \blacksquare x = 43$. $25 \blacksquare x = 50 - \sqrt{x}$, so $50 - \sqrt{x} = 43$. $\sqrt{x} = 7$, and so $x = 49$.

10. **66** Given the definition of $\uparrow$, $x \uparrow 14 = 196 - x$, and $-64 \uparrow x = (\sqrt{x})^2 - (-64) = x + 64$. So $196 - x = x + 64$. $2x = 132$, and so $x = 66$.

Multiple Figures

DIFFICULTY: ★ ★

FREQUENCY: ★ ★ ★ ★

SURPRISE FACTOR: ★ ★ ★

● INTRODUCTION TO MULTIPLE FIGURES

Multiple Figure questions are the single most common kind of geometry question on the SAT. The unusual characteristics of the figures you'll encounter tend to make them more surprising than difficult.

These questions combine common geometric figures, such as circles, rectangles, and triangles, to form unusual geometric figures. Most Multiple Figure questions will ask you to apply area or perimeter formulas to these uncommon shapes.

Multiple Figure questions come in two varieties. Some present several figures together. Here's an example:

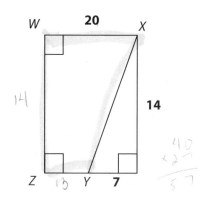

In the figure above, what is the area of quadrilateral *WXYZ*?

(A) 42

(B) 91

(C) 182

(D) 231

(E) 283

The correct answer is (D). We get that answer by subtracting the area of the triangle, 49, from the area of the rectangle, 280.

Applying the formulas is more straightforward in this question than in many others because all of the figures appear clearly.

Other questions are a little more tricky because the shapes you need to recognize aren't highlighted. Look at this question:

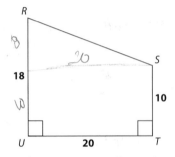

In the figure above, what is the area of quadrilateral *RSTU*?

(A) 200

(B) 220

(C) 240

(D) 260

(E) 280

The correct answer is (E). Again, we find the answer by subtracting the area of a triangle from the area of rectangle. In this question, you need to visualize the figure as a rectangle with a triangular piece cut away. You then need to use the information you have to fill in missing measurements. Here, a triangle with an area of 80 is cut away from a rectangle with an area of 360. It can also be treated as a rectangle with an area of 200 (20 x 10), combined with a triangle with an area of 80 [(20 × 8) ÷ 2].

● THE TRAP DOOR
Steering Clear of Answer Traps

One major trap involves "double counting." It means just what it sounds like: counting the same area or length twice when doing area or perimeter calculations. This trap can show up in a few different ways.

Suppose a question asks for the area of this figure:

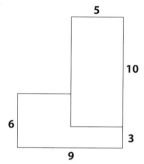

This figure includes a 5 by 10 rectangle overlapping a 6 by 9 rectangle. You might think about getting the area by multiplying each pair of dimensions and adding the products. If you did that, you would be double counting: the area where the rectangles overlap would be counted twice. To avoid the trap, you need to find a way to subtract the area of overlap, so it gets counted only once, or find a different way to calculate the areas of the multiple figures. The sum of the areas of the rectangles is $(6 \times 9) + (5 \times 10) = 104$. However, the area of overlap is $5 \times 3 = 15$, so the area of the figure is $(6 \times 9) + (5 \times 10) - 15 = 89$.

Another trap involves "too much subtraction." Suppose a question gives you the figure below, says that rectangle $ABCD$ has a perimeter of 28, and asks you for the perimeter of $ABCDE$.

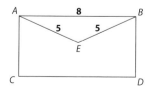

You might start by adding the two side lengths of 5. That's fine, but what do you do next? It might be tempting to subtract the perimeter of the triangle, because you would do something similar for an area question. In this case it's too much subtraction! You would subtract the side lengths of *AE* and *BE* that you just added. Here, all you need to do is subtract the length of the one side that is not part of *ABCDE*, which is *AB*, for an answer of 28 − 8 + 2(5) = 30.

● PERFORMANCE TECHNIQUES
Key Formulas and Rules

In order to succeed with Multiple Figure questions, you'll need to be able to use the basic area and perimeter formulas. Let's run through them.

Rectangles

The area of a rectangle is the product of its length, *l*, and width, *w*:

Area = *lw*

The perimeter of a rectangle is the sum of the lengths of its four sides:

Perimeter = 2*l* + 2*w*

Triangles

The area of a triangle is one-half the product of the length of its base, *b*, and its height, *h*:

Area = $\frac{1}{2}bh$

The perimeter of a triangle is the sum of the lengths of its three sides:

Perimeter = $l_1 + l_2 + l_3$

Circles

The area of a circle is the product of π (approximately 3.14) and the square of the radius, *r*:

Area = πr^2

The perimeter of a circle, also called the *circumference,* is twice the product of π the radius:

Circumference = 2πr

Remember that the radius is half of the diameter, *d.* The diameter is the length of a line segment passing right through the circle's center, connecting two edges.

The Pythagorean Theorem

You may also need to find the missing length of sides. The Pythagorean Theorem is useful when it comes to finding the lengths of diagonal sides.

In a right triangle, the square of the hypotenuse *c* (the side opposite the right angle) equals the sum of the squares of the other two sides, *a* and *b*:

$a^2 + b^2 = c^2$

● DRESS REHEARSAL
Sample Questions and Detailed Explanations

Now that we've reviewed the important points, let's tackle some questions step-by-step.

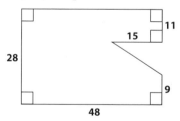

1. What is the perimeter of the above figure?

   (A) 111

   (B) 159

   (C) 167

   (D) 176

   (E) 182

The perimeter of an irregular polygon is the sum of the lengths of the sides. Notice that this figure is basically a rectangle, with a triangular piece missing. So the top side has the same length as the bottom side, 48. That leaves us with one missing length, the length of the diagonal side.

Labeling the vertices of the figure when they are not already labeled helps in setting things up:

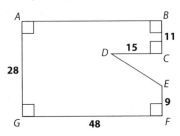

To find the length of the diagonal *DE*, use the Pythagorean Theorem. *DE* is the hypotenuse of a right triangle. The other sides are *cd*, with length 15, and the imaginary segment *ce*. How long is *ce*? The opposite side *ag* has length 28. Since *bc* = 11 and *ef* = 9, *ce* = 28 − (11 + 9) = 28 − 20 = 8.

Now let's apply the Pythagorean Theorem, where $a = 8$, $b = 15$:

$$8^2 + 15^2 = 64 + 225 = 289$$

So $c^2 = 289$, and $c = 17$

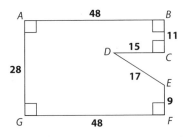

Perimeter = 28 + 48 + 9 + 17 + 15 + 11 + 48 = 176, and **(D) is the correct answer.** Choice (B) is the total perimeter, not including *DE*. Remember to include each and every side! Choice (E) is the result of getting 23 instead of 17 for *DE* (15 + 8).

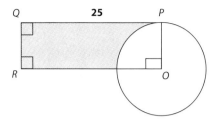

2. In the figure above, the circle with center O has a diameter of 20. What is the area of the shaded figure?

    (A) 250 – 25π

    (B) 250 – 100π

    (C) 500 – 5π

    (D) 500 – 100π

    (E) 625 – 25π

The shaded figure is the part of the rectangle that doesn't overlap with the circle. Your strategy should involve finding that area of overlap and subtracting it from the area of the rectangle. First of all, the segment PO has length 10, because that side of the rectangle also represents the radius of the circle, which is half of the diameter, 20. So rectangle OPQR has an area of 250. You can also use the value of the radius to find the circle's area. Here, $\pi r^2 = \pi(10)^2 = 100\pi$. The area of overlap is a quarter of the circle, which has an area of 25π. So the shaded region has an area of 250 – 25π, and **(A) is the correct choice.** Choice (B) treats the whole circle, not just a quarter of it, as the area of overlap. Choice (D) is the answer you'd get if you used 20 as the radius rather than the diameter.

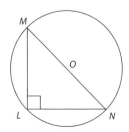

3. In the figure above, the center O of the circle lies on the hypotenuse of the isosceles right triangle LMN. If the circle has a circumference of 36π, then what is the area of LMN?

(A) 36

(B) 72

(C) 144

(D) 288

(E) 324

Here is a question where you won't combine or subtract the area of the figures. Instead, you need to use the properties of one figure to find the area of the other. We need to find the area of triangle *LMN*. The diameter of the circle happens to be the hypotenuse of the triangle. You aren't told the length of the diameter, but you are given the circumference of the circle:

$2\pi r = 36\pi$

Solving this equation gets you $r = 18$. So the diameter of the circle, which is the hypotenuse of *LMN*, is 36.

Now you can use the Pythagorean Theorem to find the lengths of the sides of the triangle. Since the right triangle is isosceles, *LM* and *LN* have the same length, *a*:

$2a^2 = 36^2 = 1{,}296$, and $a^2 = 36^2 = 648$

So *LM* and *LN* each have a length of the square root of 648, or $\sqrt{648}$. Instead of finding the value of that number, you can use the area formula of the triangle with this expression. The base and height of the triangle are both $\sqrt{648}$, so the area is

$$\frac{\sqrt{648} \times \sqrt{648}}{2} = \frac{648}{2} = 324$$

So **(E) is the correct answer.** You might have gotten (B), 72, if you began by using 36π as the area of the circle rather than the circumference.

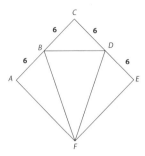

4. The above figure includes a square *ACEF* and triangle *BDF*. What is the area of triangle *BDF*?

(A) 36

(B) 54

(C) 72

(D) 90

(E) 108

To answer this question, you'll need to subtract areas. Notice that this combination of figures actually includes four triangles: three right triangles—*ABF*, *BCD*, and *DEF*—and one isosceles triangle, *BDF*. If you can find the area of the square and the right triangles, you can find the area of *BDF*. Its area is the difference between the area of *ACEF* and the sum of the right triangle area.

The two sides of the square with labeled measurements have lengths of 12 (the sum of 6 and 6). So the area of ACEF is 12^2, or 144. *ABF* and *DEF* each have bases of length 12 and heights of 6. So the area of each is $\frac{12 \times 6}{2} = \frac{72}{2} = 36$. The area of

BCD, with a base of 6 and height of 6 is $\frac{6 \times 6}{2} = \frac{36}{2} = 18$.

Now we have all the areas we need to set things up for the solution:

Area of *BDF* = Area of *ACEF* – (Area of *ABF* + Area of *BCD* +
Area of *DEF*) =
144 – (36 + 36 + 18) = 144 – 90 = 54

So **(B) is the correct choice.** You would have gotten choice (C) if you forgot to include the area of *BCD* when subtracting. You would have gotten choice (D) if you included only one of the right triangles with a base of 12 when subtracting.

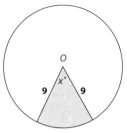

5. The shaded region of the above circle is formed by the intersection of the line segments at the center *O*. Which of the following expressions can be used to find the perimeter of the shaded region?

(A) $18 + \dfrac{\pi x}{20}$

(B) $18 + \dfrac{9\pi x}{40}$

(C) $18 + \dfrac{6480\pi}{x}$

(D) $81 + \dfrac{6480\pi}{x}$

(E) $81 + \dfrac{\pi x}{20}$

In this question, you need to find the perimeter of a fraction of the circle. You aren't told how large this fraction is, but you can figure out the formula you could use with a given value of *x*. The perimeter of the section must include the two radii, each with a length of 9, and the length of the *arc*, the section of the circle between the radii.

The perimeter of a circle is $2\pi r$. Since a circle has $360°$, a section with a $x°$ angle is $\dfrac{x}{360}$ of the entire circle. For example, if the section had a $60°$ angle, then it would be $\dfrac{60}{360}$, or $\dfrac{1}{6}$, of the whole circle (note: this is true only if the angle is at the center of the circle).

So the length of the arc created by a section with an $x°$ angle is $\dfrac{x}{360} \times 2\pi r = \dfrac{(2)(9)\pi x}{360} = \dfrac{\pi x}{20}$. Adding 18 to that gets you $18 + \dfrac{\pi x}{20}$, and **(A) is the correct choice.** Choice (B) includes the area of the section, rather than the arc length.

● **THE FINAL ACT**
  Self-Check Quiz

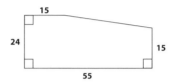

1. What is the perimeter of the above figure?
    (A) 109
    (B) 135
    (C) 148
    (D) 149
    (E) 150

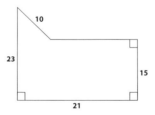

2. What is the area of the above figure?
    (A) 315
    (B) 339
    (C) 345
    (D) 363
    (E) 387

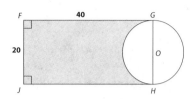

3. In the above figure, side *GH* of the rectangle passes through the center *O* of the circle. What is the area of the shaded part of the figure?

(A) 400 – 50π

(B) 400 – 200π

(C) 800 – 50π

(D) 800 – 100π

(E) 800 – 200π

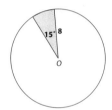

4. The above circle with center *O* has a radius of 8. What is the area of the shaded part of the circle?

(A) $\dfrac{8\pi}{3}$

(B) $\dfrac{16\pi}{5}$

(C) $\dfrac{32\pi}{9}$

(D) $\dfrac{16\pi}{3}$

(E) $\dfrac{32\pi}{5}$

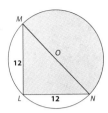

5. The above figure includes right triangle *LMN* inscribed in a circle. The hypotenuse passes through the center, *O*, of the circle. What is the area of the shaded region?

   (A) 36 + 24π

   (B) 36 + 72π

   (C) 72 + 24π

   (D) 72 + 36π

   (E) 72 + 72π

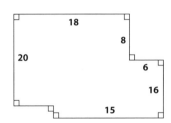

6. What is the area of the above figure?

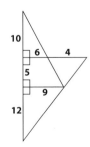

7. What is the area of the above figure?

   (A) 84

   (B) 99

   (C) 105

   (D) 115

   (E) 124

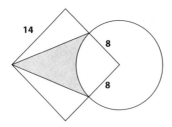

8. In the above figure, the square has one vertex at the exact center of the circle. What is the area of the shaded part of the figure?

(A) $98 - 4\pi$

(B) $112 - 16\pi$

(C) $120 - 4\pi$

(D) $148 - 16\pi$

(E) $196 - 16\pi$

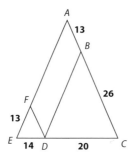

9. In the figure above, the three isosceles triangles *ACE*, *BCD*, and *DEF* are similar. What is the area of quadrilateral *ABDF*?

(A) 90

(B) 120

(C) 150

(D) 180

(E) 240

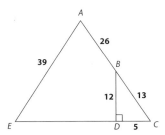

10. In the above figure, what is the area of *ABDE*?

● ANSWERS AND EXPLANATIONS

1. **E** This figure is a rectangle with a right triangular section missing. To find the area of the missing side, apply the Pythagorean Theorem. You can visualize the missing right triangle, and subtract the known side lengths to find its dimensions:

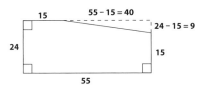

So the length of the diagonal is the square root of $40^2 + 9^2$ = $1600 + 81 = 1681$, which is 41. The perimeter is $24 + 15 + 41 + 15 + 55 = 150$. (A) is just the sum of the labeled dimensions, and (C) is the result of getting 39 instead 41 for the length of the diagonal side.

2. **B** This figure is composed of a rectangle and a right triangle, and its area is the sum of the areas of the two. The rectangle is 21 by 15, so the area is 315. The right triangle has a hypotenuse of 10. Its height must be 8, the difference between 23 and 15.

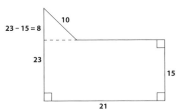

The base of the right triangle is the square root of $10^2 - 8^2$, which is 6. So the area of the triangular section is 24, and the whole figure has an area of 339. Choice (D) is the result of not halving the product of the triangle's base and height.

3. **C**   Rectangle *FGHJ* has an area of 40 x 20 = 800. The circle, with diameter of 20, has an area of $\pi\left(\dfrac{20}{2}\right)^2 = 100\pi$. The rectangle overlaps with half of the circle, which has an area of 50π. So the area of the shaded figure is $800 - 50\pi$. Choice (E) is the result of using the diameter length instead of the radius in finding the circle's area.

4. **A**   Since the circle has radius 8, the area is 64π. The section of the circle has an angle of 15°. $\dfrac{15}{360} = \dfrac{1}{24}$, so the section is $\dfrac{1}{24}$ of the circle. The area is $64\pi \times \dfrac{1}{24} = \dfrac{8\pi}{3}$. Choice (B) is the result of taking the section to be $\dfrac{1}{20}$ of the circle, rather than $\dfrac{1}{24}$. Choice (D) is the result of dividing 15 by 180 instead of 360.

5. **D**   The area of the shaded region is the sum of the triangle's area and half of the circle's area. The area of triangle *LMN* is $\dfrac{12 \times 12}{2} = 72$. To find the area of the circle, we'll need the length of the triangle's hypotenuse. Using the Pythagorean Theorem, you can find that it is $\sqrt{12^2 + 12^2} = \sqrt{288}$. So the radius of the circle is $\dfrac{\sqrt{288}}{2}$, making the area of half the circle 36π. The area of the shaded figure is $72 + 36\pi$. Choice (E) is the result of taking $\dfrac{288}{8}$ to equal 24 instead of 36. Choice (E) is the result of adding the area of the whole circle, instead of just half.

6. **492**   This figure is a rectangle with two rectangular sections missing. Adding labeled dimensions gets a width of 24 and a height of 24 for the rectangle, for an area of 576. One

rectangular section has an area of 48 (8 x 6), and the other has an area of 36 (4 x 9).

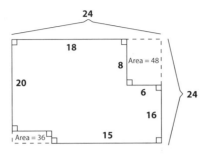

So the area of the figure is 576 – 48 – 36 = 492.

7. **D** Be careful which figures you use when you combine areas here. It would help to label every vertex:

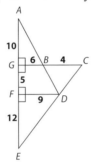

You can add the areas of triangles *ABG* and *CEG* to get the answer. Combining *AFD* and *CEG* won't get you the right answer unless you subtract areas of overlap. *ABG* has an area of 30 $\left(\dfrac{10\times6}{2}\right)$, and *CEG* has an area of $\left(\dfrac{(6+4)\times(5+12)}{2}=\dfrac{10\times17}{2}=85\right)$. So the combined area is 115. Choice (A) is what you get by combining the areas of *ABG* and *DEF*, but that leaves out *BCD*. Choice (B) is the sum of the areas of *ADF* and *DEF*. Choice (C) is the sum of the areas of *ADF* and *CEG*.

8. **B** The shaded figure is a section of a square, missing two right triangular sections and a quarter of a circle. The square has an area of 196, as one side has a length of 14. Each of the

right triangles has an area of 42. The circle has an area of 64π. So a quarter of the circle is 16π. So the shaded part has an area of $196 - 42 - 42 - 16\pi = 112 - 16\pi$.

Choice (A) divided the area of the square in half, and uses the perimeter formula for the circle instead of the area. Choice (D) is the result of subtracting only one right triangle area.

9. **E** To find the area of the quadrilateral, it's best to find the area of ACE and subtract the areas of the other two triangles. We can find the height of one triangle and use the similarity property to get the heights of the rest. Triangle DEF, being isosceles, can be described as two right triangles, and we can use the Pythagorean theorem to find a missing side length:

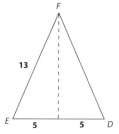

The vertical side has a length of 12. That's the height of DEF. So the area is $\frac{1}{2}(10)(12) = 60$. Triangle BCD has dimensions of twice the length, so the area is 240. ACE has an area of 540. So the area of $ABDF$ is $540 - 240 - 60 = 240$.

Choice (D) is the area of $ABDE$.

10. **510** The sum of the side measurements indicate that ACE is isosceles. Draw a line dividing ACE in half:

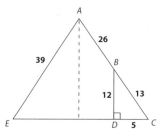

These large right triangles are similar to BCD. BCD has an area of 30. The bigger triangles have dimensions three times as long. So the area of ACE is 540, and the difference between them is 510. That's the area of $ABDE$.

Functions

DIFFICULTY: ★ ★

FREQUENCY: ★ ★ ★

SURPRISE FACTOR: ★

● INTRODUCTION TO FUNCTIONS

Function questions are common on the SAT. There are a number of important concepts to master in connection with them, and they can make some of these questions fairly difficult.

Functions are special kinds of relations. A function relates every member of a given set to a value. The members, or elements, of the first set make up the domain. The elements of the second set, the values the function puts out for the different members of the domain, make up the range. So a function is a relation where each element of the domain is paired with just one element of the range.

Some questions on the test might explore domains and ranges. Unless a question states otherwise, the domain of a function f is the set of all real numbers x, such that $f(x)$ is a real number.

You should think of the domain as the set of values for which the function is defined. The function is defined when it has a value. The expression $\dfrac{1}{4-x}$ is undefined or has no value when the denominator $4 - x$ equals 0 and has a value for all other values of x. So the domain of $f(x) = \dfrac{1}{4-x}$ is all values of x other than 4.

The range of a function is the set of outputs or values of the function. Take the expression x^2. No matter what value x has, the expression cannot have a negative value. So the range of $f(x) = x^2$ is all numbers greater than or equal to 0

Another common type of Function question involves evaluation. This might sound complicated, but it's really just a matter of substitution. You evaluate a function by substituting the variable for a given number.

For example, to evaluate the function $f(x) = 3x - 2$ for $f(2)$, substitute 2 for x and simplify:

$f(2) = 3(2) - 2 = 6 - 2 = 4$

Some Evaluation questions might have you evaluate a compound function. Such questions have you evaluate a function where the value you plug in is another function. Here's an example:

If $f(x) = 4x$ and $g(x) = x + 3$, what is the value of $f(g(2))$?

To answer this question, you need to evaluate one function at a time, starting with the one inside the parentheses. $g(2) = 2 + 3 = 5$. So $f(g(2)) = f(5) = 4(5) = 20$. Note that $g(f(2))$ has a different value.

Other function questions are based on graphs. You might be asked to identify a function or its features from a graph. You might be asked to identity a transformation of a function.

● **THE TRAP DOOR**
Steering Clear of Answer Traps

Confusing the Domain and the Range

A question that asks you to find the domain of a function might include the range among the answer choices, and vice versa. Even if you understand the difference between the domain and the range, you should be careful to avoid certain traps. Function questions don't always ask for the domain or range by name. Look at this example:

If $f(x) = \sqrt{x+1}$, what are the possible values of $f(x)$?

   (A) All real numbers greater than or equal to -1

   (B) All real numbers greater than or equal to 0

   (C) All real numbers greater than or equal to 1

   (D) All real numbers other than -1

   (E) All real numbers other than 1

The correct choice is (B). This question is asking for the range of the function. Here, since the function is a radical, the value cannot be negative. Choice (A) actually represents the domain of the function. When asked about values of $f(x)$, you are being asked about the range. The question would be asking instead about the domain if it asked about possible values of x, rather than $f(x)$.

To avoid this kind of trap, read the question carefully so that you can connect the terms it uses to either the domain or the range.

Order of Evaluation

When it comes to compound functions, be sure to take the right series of steps to evaluate them. A question might give you two functions but then put them together in the opposite order. Look at this example:

$f(x) = x + 1$ and $g(x) = 2x$. What is the value of $f(g(3))$?

   (A) 6

   (B) 7

   (C) 8

   (D) 9

   (E) 10

The correct choice is (B). You should first find that $g(3) = 6$. $f(6) = 6 + 1 = 7$. Without giving the question a closer look, it might be tempting to plug 3 into $x + 1$ first, and then plug the result into $2x$. If you did that, you'd be evaluating $g(f(3))$, rather than $f(g(3))$, and you would incorrectly reach choice (C), 8.

To avoid this trap, make sure you begin with the function inside the parentheses, and make sure that you match the letter of the function with the right expression.

● **PERFORMANCE TECHNIQUES**
Key Formulas and Rules

There are some rules you'll need to know when you encounter some common function types on the test. The two most common kinds are linear functions and quadratic functions. You're likely to see some questions that deal with one or both of these in graphs.

The graph of a linear function is a straight line. The direction or steepness of the line is described by the value of its slope. The slope m of a line that includes the points (x_1, y_1) and (x_2, y_2) is given by the formula:

$$m = \frac{y_2 - y_1}{x_2 - x_1}$$

So the slope of a line including the points (3, 1) and (6, 3) is $\frac{2}{3}$. Remember that a line that goes upward as you move from left to right on the graph has a positive slope. A line that goes down has a negative slope. A horizontal line has a slope of 0, and a vertical line has an undefined slope.

The y-intercept, the point where the line crosses the y-axis, is important. Many linear functions are given in the form $f(x) = mx + b$, where m is the slope and b is the y-intercept. So the function $f(x) = 4x - 2$ represents a line with slope 4 and a y-intercept of –2 (the x-coordinate of the y-intercept is always zero, so there's no need to give it).

Quadratic functions have a form $f(x) = ax^2 + bx + c$. The graphs of quadratic functions are U-shaped curves. If the value of a is positive, the curve is like a right side up U. If a is negative, then the curve is like an upside down U. If the curve crosses the x-axis, then you can use the coordinates where it intersects to get the function. If the curve has x-intercepts j and k, then the function $f(x)$ is the product of $(x - j)$ and $(x - k)$.

For functions presented graphically, you'll need to know how different transformations affect that graph. A transformation is an operation performed on a given function. Suppose the function $f(x)$ is a diagonal line on a graph. The function

$f(x + h)$ is that same line, with each point shifted h units *to the left* on the original. The function $f(x - h)$ has each point shifted h units *to the right* on the original. The function $f(x) + h$ shifts the original h units up, and $f(x) - h$ shifts it h units down. Note that you get different answers depending on whether the number is inside or outside the parentheses. Also, be sure to know the difference between addition and subtraction in these situations.

● **DRESS REHEARSAL**
   Sample Questions and Detailed Explanations

   1. If $f(x) = 2x^2 - 5x + 8$, then $f(-4) =$

      (A) −30

      (B) −4

      (C) 20

      (D) 36

      (E) 60

Evaluating this function is just a matter of plugging −4 into the expression $2x^2 - 5x + 8$ and simplifying. You'll want to be careful about squaring negative numbers; the square of a negative is a positive. Also, remember that subtracting a negative number is the same as adding its opposite: subtracting −20 is the same as adding 20. So let's substitute −4 for x and simplify:

$f(-4) = 2(-4)2 - 5(-4) + 8 = 2(16) - (-20) + 8 = 32 + 20 + 8 = 60$

So (E) is the correct choice. Choice (B) is the result of getting −16 instead of 16 for the value of x^2. Choice (C) is the result of subtracting 20 instead of adding.

   2. What is the value of $g(h(11))$ if $g(x) = \sqrt{x - 2}$ and $h(x) = 3x + 5$?

      (A) 4

      (B) 6

      (C) 11

      (D) 14

      (E) 18

To evaluate this compound function, you must first work through the function inside the parentheses: $h(11)$. Since $h(x) = 3x + 5$, $h(11) = 3(11) + 5 = 33 + 5 = 38$.

The next step is to take that value, and plug it into $g(x)$. Since $g(x) = \sqrt{x-2}$, $g(38) = \sqrt{38-2} = \sqrt{36} = 6$. So $g(h(11)) = 6$, and **choice (B) is the correct answer.**

Choice (D) is the value of $h(g(11))$, since $\sqrt{11-2} = 3$, and $3(3) + 5 = 14$. So choice (D) is a trap you could avoid by carefully evaluating this compound function in order.

3. If $j(x) = \dfrac{2-x}{\sqrt{x-5}}$, what is the domain of $j(x)$?

   (A) All real numbers other than 2

   (B) All real numbers greater than or equal to 2

   (C) All real numbers greater than or equal to 5

   (D) All real numbers greater than 5

   (E) All real numbers other than 5

Remember that the domain is the set of elements for which $f(x)$ is a defined real number. A fraction is undefined when the denominator equals zero or is not a real number. Since the denominator is $\sqrt{x-5}$, x cannot equal 5; that would make the denominator zero. Also, x cannot be less than 5, for then $x - 5$ would be negative. The square root of a negative number is not real. **This makes (D) the correct answer choice.**

Choice (C) overlooks the requirement that the denominator cannot equal zero. Choice (A) confuses an undefined fraction with one that equals zero. A fraction with a numerator of zero equals 0.

4.

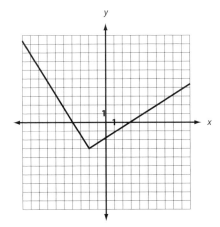

The above graph represents the function $g(x)$. Which of the following shows $g(x + 3)$?

(A)

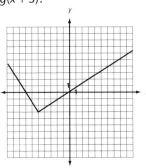

(B)

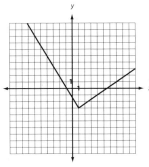

(C)

(D)

(E)

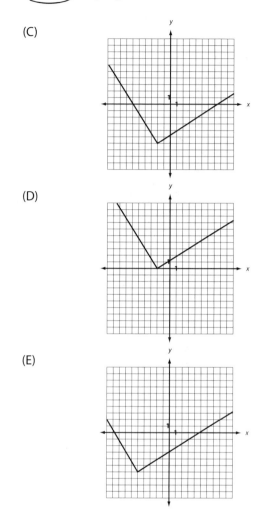

This is a Function Transformation question. Given the original function $g(x)$, the function $g(x + 3)$ will have every point on the original moved 3 units to the left. If you look at the original graph, you can see that $g(1) = 1$ and $g(-2) = -3$. So, when $x = -2$, $g(x + 3)$ will be 1. That is exactly what you see in **(A), which is the correct choice.**

Choice (B) is actually $g(x - 3)$, as every point there is shifted 3 units to the right of the original function. It might be tempting to move right when you add a number to the variable inside a function, but you should remember to do just the opposite.

Choice (D) has every point shifted 3 units up. That is actually the graph of $g(x) + 3$.

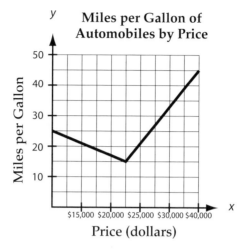

Miles per Gallon of Automobiles by Price

5. Several automobiles are available for sale at a dealership. The graph above represents the number of miles per gallon of gasoline each of them gets. Based on this information, what is the price of the car that gets the fewest miles per gallon?

(A) $17,500

(B) $20,000

(C) $22,500

(D) $30,000

(E) $32,500

This question relates a function to a real-world situation. By looking at the graph, you need to find the element in the domain that is paired with the element in the range with the smallest value. That value is the lowest point on the graph, which has a y-value of 15. If you then look at the vertical gridline, you can see that $f(x)$, 15, corresponds to the x-value of 22,500; that's the value halfway between 20,000 and 25,000. So the car with the worst gas mileage costs $22,500. **Choice (C) is the correct answer.**

● THE FINAL ACT
Self-Check Quiz

1. If $f(x) = \dfrac{x^2 - 7}{5 - x^2}$ what is $f(-3)$?

    (A) $-\dfrac{8}{7}$

    (B) $-\dfrac{1}{2}$

    (C) $-\dfrac{1}{3}$

    (D) $\dfrac{1}{7}$

    (E) $\dfrac{5}{7}$

2. If $g(x) = \dfrac{3x^2}{4}$, what is $g(-6)$?

    (A) -81

    (B) -27

    (C) 18

    (D) 27

    (E) 81

3. If $g(x) = 3x - 5$ and $h(x) = 4 - 2x$, what is the value of $g(h(-8))$?

4. If $f(x) = \dfrac{x - 9}{x^2 - 25}$, which of the following cannot be the value of x?

    (A) -9

    (B) -3

    (C) -5

    (D) 3

    (E) 9

5. If $f(x) = 5 - 4x^2$, which of the following cannot be the value of $f(x)$?

    (A) 8

    (B) 5

    (C) 4

    (D) -2

    (E) -6

6.

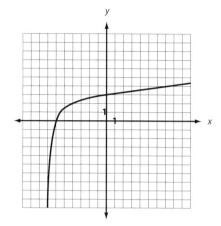

The above graph represents $f(x)$. Which of the following graphs represents $f(x - 3)$?

(A)

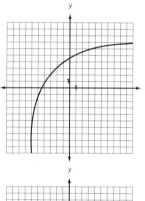

(B)

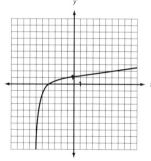

(C)

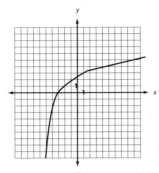

(D)

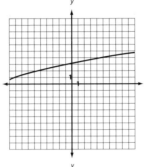

(E)

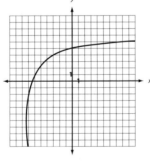

7.

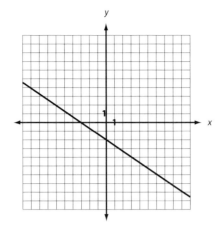

Which of the following functions appears above?

(A) $f(x) = -\dfrac{3}{2}x - 3$

(B) $f(x) = -\dfrac{3}{2}x - 2$

(C) $f(x) = -\dfrac{2}{3}x - 2$

(D) $f(x) = \dfrac{2}{3}x - 3$

(E) $f(x) = \dfrac{3}{2}x - 2$

8.

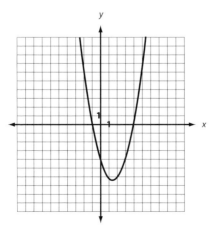

The above curve best represents which of the following equations?

(A) $y = x^2 - 4x - 3$

(B) $y = x^2 - 4x + 3$

(C) $y = x^2 - 3x - 4$

(D) $y = x^2 - 3x + 4$

(E) $y = x^2 + 3x - 4$

9.

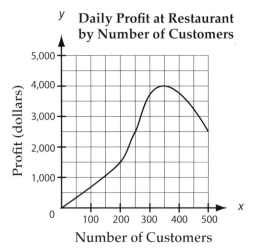

Daily Profit at Restaurant by Number of Customers

The above graph represents the amount of profit a restaurant earned according to the number of customers over a two-month period. Based on this information, how many customers can the restaurant serve in order to make the highest profit?

(A) 200

(B) 250

(C) 300

(D) 350

(E) 400

10. The amount of the water bill for an apartment is given by the function $f(x) = 0.002x + 5.25$, where x is the number of gallons of water used. If $f(x) = 7.75$, what is the value of x?

● ANSWERS AND EXPLANATIONS

1. **B** Plug −3 into the function:

$f(-3)=\dfrac{(-3)^2-7}{5-(-3)^2}=\dfrac{9-7}{5-9}=\dfrac{2}{-4}=-\dfrac{1}{2}.$ Choice (A) is the result of

getting −9 instead of 9 in both the numerator and the denominator, and Choice (D) is the result of getting that incorrect value in just the denominator.

2. **D** Plug −6 into the function:

$g(-6)=\dfrac{3(-6)^2}{4}=\dfrac{3(36)}{4}=\dfrac{108}{4}=27$. Choice (E) is the result of

squaring $3x$ instead of multiplying x^2 by 3.

3. **55** To evaluate this compound function, first plug −8 into $h(x)$:

$h(-8)=4-2(-8)$
$=4-(-16)=4+16$
$=20$

Since $h(-8)=20$, we next evaluate $g(20)$:

$g(20)=3(20)-5$
$=60-5$
$=55$

4. **C** This question asks you to find a number that is not part of the domain of the function. No number that makes $f(x)$ undefined can be a value of x. The fraction $\dfrac{x-9}{x^2-25}$ is undefined when the denominator x^2-25 equals 0, so x cannot equal −5.

5. **A** This question asks you to identify a number that is not part of the range of the function. Since $4x^2$ must have a positive value, $5-4x^2$ must have a value of 5 or less. So, the range is all real numbers less than or equal to 5. 8 is the only number among the answer choices with a value greater than 5.

6. **C** The transformation $f(x-3)$ moves every point in the graph of the original function 3 units to the right. The graph in

choice (C) represents that shift. Choice (D) represents $f(x + 2)$, and choice (E) represents $f(x) + 2$.

7. **C** This question asks you to identify a linear function. You can do that by identifying the slope and the y-intercept of the line. The line has a slope of $-\dfrac{2}{3}$ and a y-intercept of -2. So the function is $f(x) = -\dfrac{2}{3}x - 2$. Choices (A) and (D) use the x-intercept instead of the y-intercept. Choice (D) also gives the slope of a line that is perpendicular to the one shown.

8. **C** This is a quadratic function with x-intercepts at -1 and 4. So the equation is $f(x) = (x + 1)(x - 4) = x^2 - 4x + x - 4 = x^2 - 3x - 4$. Choice (E) is the function you would get if you multiplied $(x - 1)$ and $(x + 4)$ instead of $(x + 1)$ and $(x - 4)$.

9. **D** This is another question relating a function to a real-world situation. You need to use the graph to find the element in the domain that is paired with the element in the range with the greatest value. That value is the highest point on the curve, which has a y-value of 4,000. If you then look at the vertical gridline, you can see that $f(x)$, 4000, corresponds to the x value of 350. So the restaurant's profits are highest when it has 350 customers.

10. **1,250** Since you are given $f(x) = 0.002x + 5.25$, and a value of $f(x)$ of 7.75, you need to solve the equation $0.002x + 5.25 = 7.75$. Subtract 5.25 from both sides to get $0.002x = 2.5$. Dividing both sides by 0.002 gets you 1,250.

Fractions

DIFFICULTY: ★ ★ ★

FREQUENCY: ★ ★ ★

SURPRISE FACTOR: ★ ★

● INTRODUCTION TO FRACTIONS

Questions involving fractions cover a lot of ground on the SAT. They have a high frequency because they come up in many different forms. Some Fraction questions are relatively simple; they might involve basic addition or multiplication. Others are more complicated, involving ratios and proportions. Other questions involve polynomial fractions, also known as rational expressions. Some of them can be especially difficult.

On test day, you should be ready to work with fractions. You should know how to carry out arithmetic operations on them and how to simplify them. You may need to do these things when algebraic variables are involved.

Since decimals and percentages are kinds of fractions, you should be ready to work with those as well. You'll probably need to know how to convert these numbers from one form to another, since many questions combine them.

You should also be ready to work with ratios and proportions. While fractions give quantities in terms of parts of wholes, many ratios express relations of parts to parts. Suppose a class has 10 boys and 12 girls. The ratio of boys to girls is 10 to 12. We can simplify a ratio much as we would a fraction, and state this one as 5 to 6 instead of 10 to 12. You might see a question that asks you to find a fraction, based on a ratio.

What fraction of the class do the boys make up? It might be tempting to say $\frac{10}{12}$ or $\frac{5}{6}$, but you need to keep in mind that 12 is the size of another part of the whole. The size of the whole is actually 10 + 12, so the correct fraction is $\frac{10}{22}$ or $\frac{5}{11}$.

Many Fraction questions involve proportions, which are equations involving fractions or ratios. The equation $\frac{50}{100} = \frac{1}{2}$, for instance, gives a proportion. Many proportions involve an unknown. You have to find this unknown by solving an algebraic equation.

Rational expressions are fractions where the numerator and denominator are polynomials, such as

$$\frac{x^3 - 4x^2 + 5x - 7}{2x^2 + 6x - 9}$$

The test may ask you to simplify a fraction like this one. A fraction like this one is simplified when the numerator and denominator are both divided by all their common factors.

● THE TRAP DOOR
Steering Clear of Answer Traps

Many traps related to fractions take advantage of mistakes in conversion. Remember that when you convert a fraction, you must multiply the top and bottom by the same number, and that the number multiplies every term in the numerator and denominator.

Some SAT question traps take advantage of confusion about ratios. Some questions involve two related ratios. The parts of these ratios probably won't refer to the same whole. In a common ratio trap, separate ratios will have a common part represented by two different numbers. Since the ratios refer to different wholes, the proportions might be off.

Suppose a question tells you that a coin collection consists of pennies, dimes, and quarters. The ratio of pennies to dimes is 4:1 and the ratio of dimes to quarters is 4:2. What is the ratio of pennies to quarters? Hint: It's not 4:2. To avoid this trap, restate the ratios so that the quantity of the common part is the same in each ratio. Then the ratios for all of the parts can be compared.

Another ratio trap involves confusion over the relation between parts and wholes. If the ratio of A's to B's is 4:7, then

ᴀ ′)n of $\dfrac{4}{11}$ of the total, not $\dfrac{4}{7}$. The denomi-

vhole, which is the sum of the parts. It is

u can avoid this trap by carefully taking

make up the whole.

● PERFORMANCE TECHNIQUES
Key Formulas and Rules

Converting a fraction to a decimal is straightforward. Just divide the numerator (the top number) by the denominator (the bottom number).

You can also convert decimals to fractions. If the decimal you are given to work with doesn't go on forever, you can always convert it to a fraction with a whole number *numerator* and a denominator that is a factor of 10.

Take 0.789. The first digit to the right of the decimal point, 7, is the *tenths* place; the next digit is in the *hundredths* place; and the last digit is in the *thousandths* place. Take the last place of the decimal. The numbers on the right of the decimal point stand for that many thousandths. So 0.789 is 789 thousandths, or $\dfrac{789}{1,000}$.

Many fractions can be *simplified*. A simplified fraction has the same value, but a smaller numerator and a smaller denominator. To simplify a fraction, divide the numerator and denominator by a common factor. If there are no common factors (other than 1), then the fraction is fully simplified.

To multiply two fractions, simply multiply the numerators and the denominators.

$$\frac{1}{2} \times \frac{3}{4} = \frac{1 \times 3}{2 \times 4} = \frac{3}{8}$$

When you multiply fractions, you're finding a fraction *of* a fraction. When you evaluate $\frac{1}{2} \times \frac{3}{4}$, you find the value of one half of $\frac{3}{4}$. It turns out that one half of $\frac{3}{4}$ is $\frac{3}{8}$.

You can divide a fraction by another fraction by multiplying the first by the reciprocal, or multiplicative inverse, of the second. So $\frac{1}{2} \div \frac{3}{4} = \frac{1}{2} \times \frac{4}{3} = \frac{1 \times 4}{2 \times 3} = \frac{4}{6} = \frac{2}{3}$

You can add or subtract fractions if they have the same denominator. To combine such fractions, just add or subtract the numerators. The value of the denominator stays the same.

$$\frac{2}{7} + \frac{3}{7} = \frac{2+3}{7} = \frac{5}{7}$$

$$\frac{8}{11} - \frac{5}{11} = \frac{8-5}{11} = \frac{3}{11}$$

If the two fractions don't have the same denominator, don't give up. You can rewrite one or both of them so that they have the same denominator. To do that, find the least common multiple (LCM) of the denominators. If you are asked to evaluate $\frac{3}{4} + \frac{5}{6}$, you must rewrite both of the fractions so that they have the same denominator. Since the LCM of 4 and 6 is 12, you know that you can rewrite $\frac{3}{4}$ and $\frac{5}{6}$ as fractions with denominators of 12.

$$\frac{3}{4} + \frac{5}{6} = \frac{3(3)}{4(3)} + \frac{5(2)}{6(2)} = \frac{9}{12} + \frac{10}{12} = \frac{19}{12}$$

Now let's go through ratios and proportions. If you have a ratio of a to b, where a and b represent parts of a whole, then a represents the fraction $\frac{a}{a+b}$ of the whole.

Suppose a question indicates that the ratio of A to B is equivalent to the ratio of x to D. You could work to find the value of x by setting up a proportion:

$$\frac{A}{B} = \frac{x}{D}$$

Next, "cross-multiply" to set up a new equation. When you have a proportion like this, the product of the first numerator and the second denominator equals the product of the second numerator and the first denominator:

$AD = Bx$. So $x = \dfrac{AD}{B}$.

Finally, let's go through a technique for simplifying rational expressions. On the test, you'll want to use the "picking numbers" technique to find the simplified form of a rational expression. To find the expression that equals the rational expression you are given, start by evaluating the rational expression for a given value. Then evaluate each expression in the answer choices. The correct answer will have the same value as the rational expression.

● **DRESS REHEARSAL**
Sample Questions and Detailed Explanations

1. $\dfrac{2}{5} \times 0.3 - 0.04 =$

   (A) $\dfrac{1}{50}$

   (B) $\dfrac{7}{200}$

   (C) $\dfrac{7}{100}$

   (D) $\dfrac{2}{25}$

   (E) $\dfrac{4}{5}$

This is an arithmetic question involving fractions and decimals. Fractions can be written as decimals, and vice versa. Here, you could convert the fraction $\dfrac{2}{5}$ to a decimal, simplify the expression, and convert the result to a fraction. You could instead convert 0.3 and 0.04 to fractions and then simplify, but the first approach is likely to require fewer steps.

Since $\dfrac{2}{5} = 0.4$, $\dfrac{2}{5} \times 0.3 - 0.04 = 0.4 \times 0.3 - 0.04 = 0.12 - 0.04 =$ $0.08 = \dfrac{8}{100} = \dfrac{2}{25}$. **So choice (D) is the correct answer.** Choice (A) equals 0.02, the result of converting $\dfrac{2}{5}$ to 0.2 instead of 0.4.

Choice (B) is the value of 0.035 which is what you might get if you converted $\frac{2}{5}$ to 0.25 instead of 0.4.

2. What is the sum of $\frac{5}{8x}$ and $\frac{7}{6y}$?

(A) $\dfrac{21x+10y}{16xy}$

(B) $\dfrac{25}{16xy}$

(C) $\dfrac{28x+15y}{24xy}$

(D) $\dfrac{43}{24xy}$

(E) $\dfrac{20x+21y}{24xy}$

To add these fractions, you'll need to find common denominators. You can't add fractions unless the denominators are the same. Don't be intimidated by the presence of variables in the denominators. You can find a common multiple of terms with variables. Just remember that you must multiply the numerator of each fraction by whatever you multiply each denominator by to get the common multiple.

The least common multiple of 8 and 6 is 24. So the least common multiple of $8x$ and $6y$ is $24xy$. $24xy$ is $8x$ multiplied by $3y$, and $6y$ multiplied by $4x$.

$$\frac{5(3y)}{8x(3y)}=\frac{15y}{24xy}$$
$$\frac{7(4x)}{6y(4x)}=\frac{28x}{24xy}$$
$$\frac{28x}{24xy}+\frac{15y}{24xy}=\frac{28x+15y}{24xy}$$

So (C) is the correct answer choice. Choice (A) is the result of taking 16 to be the product of 6 and 3. That error could lead someone to add $\dfrac{21x}{16xy}$ and $\dfrac{10y}{16xy}$. Choice (E) is the result of multiplying the numerator of each fraction by the wrong factor.

3. All of the vehicles in a lot are cars or vans. The ratio of cars to vans is 7:2. What fraction of the vehicles are cars?

(A) $\dfrac{2}{9}$

(B) $\dfrac{2}{7}$

(C) $\dfrac{2}{5}$

(D) $\dfrac{5}{7}$

⬤ $\dfrac{7}{9}$

A fraction gives the ratio of parts to the whole. The ratio you're given to start with gives the ratio of parts to parts: cars to vans. The ratio indicates that there are 7 cars for every 2 vans. Since each vehicle is a car or a van, there are 7 cars for every 9 vehicles. 7 out of every 9 vehicles is a car, so $\dfrac{7}{9}$ of the vehicles are cars. **(E) is the correct choice.** Choice (D) would be the correct ratio if 7 was the total number of vehicles for every 2 vans, rather then the number of cars for every two vans.

4. A jar of mixed nuts contains almonds, cashews, and pecans. The ratio of almonds to cashews is 3:2, the ratio of cashews to pecans is 3:1. What fraction of the nuts in the jar are almonds?

(A) $\dfrac{6}{17}$ $9/6$ $9/2$

(B) $\dfrac{7}{15}$

(C) $\dfrac{1}{2}$

(D) $\dfrac{9}{17}$

(E) $\dfrac{3}{5}$

In order to find the fraction represented by the number of almonds, you'll have to find a common term for the two ratios. Since both ratios include cashews, you could rewrite them so that the number of cashews is the same in each. This is similar to rewriting fractions to get common denominators.

6 is a common multiple of 2 and 3, so you can write each ratio in terms of that number of cashews. The ratio of almonds to cashews is 9 to 6, and the ratio of cashews to pecans is 6 to 2. So, for every 9 almonds, there are 6 cashews and 2 pecans. For every 9 almonds, then, there are 9 + 6 + 2 nuts altogether. **That makes choice (D) the correct answer.** Choice (C) might be tempting, since it is the ratio of 3 to 3 + 2 + 1. Remember that you can't combine two ratios unless they have a common part with the same value in each.

5. For all values of x not equal to −6 or 1, $\dfrac{x^3 + x^2 - 26x + 24}{x^2 + 5x - 6}$ is equal to

   (A) $x - 8$

   (B) $x - 4$

   (C) $x - 2$

   (D) $x + 3$

   (E) $x + 9$

This question asks you to simplify a rational expression. Picking numbers is the easiest way to the correct answer. The first step is to evaluate $\dfrac{x^3 + x^2 - 26x + 24}{x^2 + 5x - 6}$ for a number of your choosing. Say $x = 2$. In that case,

$$\frac{x^3 + x^2 - 26x + 24}{x^2 + 5x - 6} = \frac{2^3 + 2^2 - 26(2) + 24}{2^2 + 5(2) - 6} = \frac{8 + 4 - 52 + 24}{4 + 10 - 6} = \frac{-16}{8} = -2$$

Now you need to evaluate each of the answer choices for the very same value of x:

$$x - 8 = 2 - 8 = -6$$
$$x - 4 = 2 - 4 = -2$$
$$x - 2 = 2 - 2 = 0$$
$$x + 3 = 2 + 3 = 5$$
$$x + 9 = 2 + 9 = 11$$

$x - 4$ has a value of −2 when $x = 2$. **So choice (B) is the correct answer.**

If you evaluated $x^3 + x^2 + 26x + 24$ instead of $x^3 + x^2 - 26x + 24$ in the numerator, then you would have gotten a value of 11 for the value of the rational expression. That would have led you to the incorrect choice (E).

● THE FINAL ACT
Self-Check Quiz

1. $\left(0.36 + \dfrac{3}{5}\right) \div \dfrac{3}{8} =$

   (A) $\dfrac{54}{25}$

   (B) $\dfrac{59}{25}$

   (C) $\dfrac{64}{25}$

   (D) $\dfrac{69}{25}$

   (E) $\dfrac{74}{25}$

2. $\left(\dfrac{2}{7} - 0.25\right) \times \dfrac{4}{5} =$

   (A) $\dfrac{1}{20}$

   (B) $\dfrac{1}{25}$

   (C) $\dfrac{1}{30}$

   (D) $\dfrac{1}{35}$

   (E) $\dfrac{1}{40}$

3. For all values of a other than 0, $\dfrac{2}{3a} + \dfrac{a+5}{4a^2} =$

   (A) $\dfrac{3a+23}{12a^2}$

   (B) $\dfrac{9a+5}{12a^2}$

   (C) $\dfrac{9a+15}{12a^2}$

   (D) $\dfrac{11a+5}{12a^2}$

   (E) $\dfrac{11a+15}{12a^2}$

4. If $\frac{2}{9} = \frac{x+5}{36}$, then $x =$

(handwritten: $72 = 9(x+5)$ $x = 3$ $72 = 9x + 45$ $27 = 9x$)

5. A restaurant serving breakfast, lunch, and dinner had a total of 360 customers yesterday: $\frac{1}{8}$ of them were served breakfast, and $\frac{1}{3}$ of them were served lunch. How many of the customers were served dinner?

(handwritten: $3 + 8$, $\frac{11}{24}$)

   (A) 165
   (B) 185
   (C) 195
   (D) 200
   (E) 210

(handwritten: $\frac{240}{4}$)

6. On a school field trip, there is a student to adult ratio of 11:4. If 60 people went on the trip, how many students went?

7. A baking recipe calls for 3 ounces of flour for every 2 cups of water. If 24 ounces of flour are used, how many cups of water should be used?

(handwritten: $\frac{3}{2}$ $\frac{24}{x}$ $3x = 48$ $x = 16$)

   (A) 12
   (B) 16
   (C) 18
   (D) 30
   (E) 36

8. An automobile dealership sells cars, trucks, and vans. It has a car to truck ratio of 7:2, and a truck to van ratio of 4:3. What fraction of the total number of vehicles at the dealership do the vans represent?

   (A) $\frac{1}{7}$
   (B) $\frac{3}{16}$
   (C) $\frac{3}{13}$
   (D) $\frac{3}{7}$
   (E) $\frac{2}{3}$

For all values of x not equal to 0, $\dfrac{2x^4 - 9x^3 - 35x^2}{x^2 - 7x}$ is equal to

(A) $x^2 + 5$

(B) $x^2 + 5x$

(C) $2x + 5$

(D) $2x^2 + 5$

(E) $2x^2 + 5x$

10. For all values of y not equal to -3 and 7,

$\dfrac{6y^4 - 22y^3 - 116y^2 - 114y - 378}{2y^2 - 8y - 42}$ equals

(A) $3y^2 + y + 9$

(B) $3y^2 + 2y + 9$

(C) $3y^2 + 3y + 9$

(D) $3y^2 + 2y + 14$

(E) $3y^2 + 3y + 14$

● ANSWERS AND EXPLANATIONS

1. **C**   Here, you can convert 0.36 to a fraction, $\dfrac{36}{100}$, and evaluate:

$$\left(0.36 + \frac{3}{5}\right) \div \frac{3}{8} = \left(\frac{36}{100} + \frac{3}{5}\right) \div \frac{3}{8} =$$

$$\left(\frac{36}{100} + \frac{60}{100}\right) \div \frac{3}{8} = \frac{96}{100} \div \frac{3}{8} =$$

$$\frac{96}{100} \times \frac{8}{3} = \frac{32}{25} \times 2 = \frac{64}{25}$$

2. **D**   Convert 0.25 to a fraction, $\dfrac{1}{4}$, and evaluate:

$$\left(\frac{2}{7} - 0.25\right) \times \frac{4}{5} = \left(\frac{2}{7} - \frac{1}{4}\right) \times \frac{4}{5} = \left(\frac{8}{28} - \frac{7}{28}\right) \times \frac{4}{5} = \frac{1}{28} \times \frac{4}{5} = \frac{4}{140} = \frac{1}{35}$$

3. **E**   To add these fractions, you'll need common denominators. Multiply the top and bottom of $\dfrac{2}{3a}$ by $4a$ to get $\dfrac{8a}{12a^2}$. Multiply the top and bottom of $\dfrac{a+5}{4a^2}$ by 3 to get $\dfrac{3a+15}{12a^2}$.

$$\frac{2}{3a} + \frac{a+5}{4a^2} = \frac{8a}{12a^2} + \frac{3a+15}{12a^2} = \frac{11a+15}{12a^2}.$$

Choice (A) is the result of getting $\dfrac{8}{12a^2}$ instead of $\dfrac{8a}{12a^2}$ when converting $\dfrac{2}{3a}$. Choice (D) is the result of getting $\dfrac{3a+5}{12a^2}$ instead of $\dfrac{3a+15}{12a^2}$ when converting $\dfrac{a+5}{4a^2}$.

4. **3**   To answer this question, you could convert $\dfrac{2}{9}$ to a fraction having a common denominator with $\dfrac{x+5}{36}$. Then you could solve an equation with the numerators of the fractions. $\dfrac{2}{9} = \dfrac{8}{36}$, so $\dfrac{8}{36} = \dfrac{x+5}{36}$. So $8 = x + 5$, and $x = 3$.

5. **C** $\dfrac{1}{8}$ of 360 is $\dfrac{360}{8}$, or 45. $\dfrac{1}{3}$ of 360 is $\dfrac{360}{3}$, or 120. So 165 people had breakfast or lunch. Since $360 - 165 = 195$, the number of people who had dinner at the restaurant is 195. You might have gotten choice (A) if you didn't carry out the subtraction in the last step.

6. **44**   If the student to adult ratio is 11 to 4, then the student to total ratio is 11 to 15. For every 15 people, there are 11 students. Set this up as a proportion: $\dfrac{11}{15} = \dfrac{x}{60}$. So, $15x = 660$, and $x = 660 \div 15 = 44$. 60 is 15 x 4, so there are 11 x 4 or 44 students on the field trip.

7. **B**   You can set the solution up as a proportion, with the amounts of water in the numerators and the amounts of flour in the denominators. Since the amount of water used with 24 ounces of flour is the unknown, the proportion is $\dfrac{2}{3} = \dfrac{x}{24}$. So $48 = 3x$, and $x = 48 \div 3 = 16$.

8. **A** A 7 to 2 ratio is the same as a 14 to 4 ratio. So, for every 14 cars, there are 4 trucks and 3 vans. There are 21 vehicles for every 3 vans, and so vans are $\frac{1}{7}$ of the total. Choice (B) is the ratio of 3 to 7 + 2 + 4 + 3. Choice (E) is actually the fraction of the total that are cars. Be careful about keeping track of the objects of the ratios.

9. **E** You can find the right simplified form of this expression with the picking numbers technique. You can evaluate this expression for $x = 2$:

$$\frac{2x^4 - 9x^3 - 35x^2}{x^2 - 7x} = \frac{2(2)^4 - 9(2)^3 - 35(2)^2}{(2)^2 - 7(2)} = \frac{32 - 72 - 140}{4 - 14} = \frac{-180}{-10} = 18$$

Only $2x^2 + 5x$ also equals 18 when $x = 2$.

10. **A** Use the picking technique to find the simplified form of the rational expression. If $y = 2$, then

$$\frac{6y^4 - 22y^3 - 116y^2 - 114y - 378}{2y^2 - 8y - 42} =$$
$$\frac{6(2)^4 - 22(2)^3 - 116(2)^2 - 114(2) - 378}{2(2)^2 - 8(2) - 42} =$$
$$\frac{6(16) - 22(8) - 116(4) - 114(2) - 378}{2(4) - 8(2) - 42} =$$
$$\frac{96 - 176 - 464 - 228 - 378}{8 - 16 - 42} = \frac{-1150}{-50} = 23$$

Out of all of the answer choices, only $3y^2 + y + 9$ has a value of 23 when $y = 2$.

Roots and Exponents

DIFFICULTY: ★ ★ ★

FREQUENCY: ★ ★

SURPRISE FACTOR: ★ ★

● INTRODUCTION TO ROOTS AND EXPONENTS

Roots and exponents can be confusing. They come up frequently in the SAT, but not as often as some other major algebra topics do. We focus on them here because of their difficulty. There are a number of rules that need to be followed, and those rules open the door for several traps.

Some of the algebraic equations you see on the test might include radicals. A radical expression, one that includes the operator $\sqrt{}$, represents a positive square root. $\sqrt{9} = 3$, for instance and $\sqrt{25} = 5$. It is also important to know that the square of a radical is the number inside the sign. So $\left(\sqrt{25}\right)^2 = 25$, and $\left(\sqrt{30.6}\right)^2 = 30.6$. That relationship is very important to know when it comes to solving equations that include radicals.

Exponents frequently appear in questions that require you to perform operations on them. You'll need to be familiar with the rules for multiplying and dividing terms with exponents. Also, you need to know how to handle exponents that are negative numbers or fractions. Not all exponents are positive integers. The expression $x^{\frac{1}{2}}$ is the square root of x. We can rewrite that expression with a radical sign as $\sqrt{x}$. The cube root of x is $x^{\frac{1}{3}}$, which can also be written as $\sqrt[3]{x}$. In general, the expression $\sqrt[n]{x}$ represents the nth root of x, and can also be written as $x^{\frac{1}{n}}$. Remember that $\left(\sqrt[n]{x}\right)^n = x$ for any number n. You'll be expected to know how to convert a root expression like $\sqrt[n]{x}$ to an expression with an exponent.

Exponents are also likely to appear on the test in questions involving geometric sequences. A geometric sequence is one where the ratio between consecutive terms is constant. The ratio of the first term to the second is the same as the ratio of the second term to the third, and so on. Therefore, the rate at which the values of the terms change can be described using exponents. Exponential Growth questions usually require you to determine the rate of growth, the value of a term in the sequence, or both.

● **THE TRAP DOOR**
Steering Clear of Answer Traps

As we mentioned above, some questions might involve terms with negative or fractional exponents. It is important to avoid getting the effects of such exponents confused. Some SAT questions include traps meant to take advantage of that confusion. In the expressions 8^{-3} and $8^{\frac{1}{3}}$, -3 and $\frac{1}{3}$ are the additive and multiplicative inverses of 3, respectively. They do very different things to numbers, though: $8^{-3} = \dfrac{1}{512}$ and $8^{\frac{1}{3}} = 2$. You shouldn't be surprised to see 2 as an answer choice in a question asking you for the value of 8^{-3}. Know the difference between negative and fractional exponents to avoid the trap.

Another trap might target another kind of confusion: the difference between 8^{-3} and -8^3. One is the multiplicative inverse of 8^3 and the other is the additive inverse. So if a question on the test asks you to evaluate 5^{-2}, don't be surprised to see -25 as one of the incorrect choices. Remember that 5^{-2} is not even a negative number, even though it has a negative exponent.

Another common Exponent question trap targets confusion in multiplying or dividing exponents. To simplify an expression like $b^7 \times b^5$, you add the exponents. You would want to look out for an incorrect choice of b^{35}, which one might get by multiplying the exponents. Likewise, dividing terms with exponents requires you to subtract them.

● PERFORMANCE TECHNIQUES
Key Formulas and Rules

Solving a rational equation involves a step not often found in most other kinds of equation-solving: squaring both sides of the equation. It is necessary to square a radical in order to get rid of the sign. This will be the last step in solving a radical equation if the variable is the only thing inside a radical sign. Other steps, no matter whether they are taken before or after you square both sides, are common to many other kinds of equation-solving.

When a question involving the manipulation of exponents comes up, you'll need to recall how exponents behave when multiplied or divided. Remember that when two powers with the same base are multiplied, you need to add the exponents. When one power is divided by another, you must subtract the exponents.

$$x^a \cdot x^b = x^{a+b}$$
$$x^a \div x^b = x^{a-b}$$

When one power is raised to another power, you must multiply the exponents.

$$\left(x^a\right)^b = x^{a \cdot b}$$

A number raised to a negative power is equivalent to the reciprocal, or multiplicative inverse, of that number raised to a positive power. For instance, $4^{-3} = \dfrac{1}{4^3} = \dfrac{1}{64}$. In general, $x^{-n} = \dfrac{1}{x^n}$.

When dealing with rational exponents, remember that a fractional exponent represents a root. For instance, $x^{\frac{1}{2}} = \sqrt{x}$, and $x^{\frac{1}{3}} = \sqrt[3]{x}$. $x^{\frac{3}{2}} = \left(x^3\right)^{\frac{1}{2}} = \sqrt{x^3}$. In general, $x^{\frac{1}{n}} = \sqrt[n]{x}$, so $x^{\frac{1}{n}}$

represents the nth root of x. If p and q are integers, $x^{\frac{p}{q}} = \sqrt[q]{x^p}$.

In a geometric sequence where r is the ratio between consecutive terms, a_1 is the first term, and a_n is the nth term, then $a_n = a_1 r^{n-1}$.

So if the first term in a series is 4 and the ratio is 3, then the fifth term is

$$a^5 = 4(3)^{5-1} = 4(3)^4 = 4(81) = 324$$

You might see a question on the test that gives you the first term and the nth term, and then asks you to find the ratio. To do that, you can work with the formula we just used. Since $a_n = a_1 r^{n-1}$, $r^{n-1} = \dfrac{a_n}{a_1}$.

Once you have the value of $\dfrac{a_n}{a_1}$, you'll have to find its $(n-1)^{\text{th}}$ root to get the ratio r.

● **DRESS REHEARSAL**

Sample Questions and Detailed Explanations

1. If $30 + 3\sqrt{x} = 42$, then what is the value of x?

(A) 2
(B) 4
(C) 8
(D) 12
(E) 16

You can solve this rational equation by performing standard operations of subtraction and division, until you have the radical alone one side of the equation:

$$30 + 3\sqrt{x} = 42$$
$$\underline{-30 \quad -30}$$
$$3\sqrt{x} = 12$$
$$\underline{\div 3 \quad \div 3}$$
$$\sqrt{x} = 4$$

Now you need to square both sides of the equation to get the variable x outside of the radical sign:

$$\left(\sqrt{x}\right)^2 = 4^2 = 16$$

Since $\left(\sqrt{x}\right)^2 = x$, $x = 16$, and **choice (E) is the correct answer.**

You might have gotten choice (A), 2, if you took x to be the square root of 4, based on $\sqrt{x} = 4$. This equation actually shows that 4 is the square root of x.

2. $a^6 \cdot a^9 \div a^3 =$ $\quad a^{15-3}$

$\quad\quad\quad\quad\quad\quad\quad\quad\quad\quad a^{12}$

(A) a^5

(B) a^9

(C) a^{12}

(D) a^{27}

(E) a^{51}

To answer this question correctly, you'll need to recall that multiplication and division of powers involves the addition and subtraction of exponents. The trap in this question involves confusion with multiplication and division.

Since we add exponents when multiplying, $a^6 \cdot a^9 = a^{6+9} = a^{15}$. Next, you divide by a^{15} by a^3. That involves the subtraction of exponents:

$$a^{15} \div a^3 = a^{15-3} = a^{12}$$

Choice (C) is the correct answer. Choice (A) is the result of a correct multiplication in the first step that is followed by a mistake in dividing. 15 is divided by 3 to get an exponent of 5. Choice (D) is the result of multiplying and then dividing exponents.

3. $x^2 \div x^{2.5} =$

(A) $-\sqrt{x}$

(B) $-\dfrac{1}{\sqrt{x}}$

(C) $\dfrac{1}{x^2}$

(D) $\dfrac{1}{\sqrt{x}}$

(E) $\sqrt{x}$

This question requires you to divide exponents and eventually work with negative, fractional powers. To carry out this division, you need to subtract the exponents.

$$x^2 \div x^{2.5} = x^{2-2.5} = x^{-0.5}$$

An expression with a negative exponent is the multiplicative inverse of the number raised to the absolute value of that exponent. So $x^{-0.5} = \dfrac{1}{x^{0.5}}$. Now, $x^{0.5} = x^{\frac{1}{2}} = \sqrt{x}$, so $\dfrac{1}{x^{0.5}} = \dfrac{1}{\sqrt{x}}$, and **(D) is the correct answer choice.**

Choice (A), $-\sqrt{x}$, could be the result of taking $x^{-0.05}$ to equal $-x^{-0.05}$. Don't forget the meaning of a negative exponent!

4. Which expression is equivalent to $y^{\frac{2}{3}} \times y^3$?

Shortcut: just add $\frac{2}{3} + 3$ together!

(A) $\sqrt[11]{y^6}$

(B) $\sqrt[11]{y^3}$

(C) $\sqrt[6]{y^3}$

(D) $\sqrt[3]{y^6}$

(E) $\sqrt[3]{y^{11}}$

This question brings together several topics in Roots and Exponents. You'll need to convert an expression with an exponent to one with a root sign. Before that, however, you have to carry out the multiplication. Remember that you add exponents when multiplying. That's a little more complicated here, since one of the exponents is a fraction.

$$y^{\frac{2}{3}} \cdot y^3 = y^{3+\frac{2}{3}}$$

In order to add the 3 and $\frac{2}{3}$, we'll need numbers with common denominators. Convert 3 to $\frac{9}{3}$ and add:

$$y^{3+\frac{2}{3}} = y^{\frac{9}{3}+\frac{2}{3}} = y^{\frac{11}{3}}$$

Now we must convert $y^{\frac{11}{3}}$ into an expression with a root sign. Recall the formula $x^{\frac{p}{q}} = \sqrt[q]{x^p}$. Applying that here tells us that $y^{\frac{11}{3}}$ is the cube root of y^{11}, or $\sqrt[3]{y^{11}}$. **So, choice (E) is the correct answer.**

Be careful to apply the formula $x^{\frac{p}{q}} = \sqrt[q]{x^p}$ carefully. If you got it backwards, you might have picked choice (B). Choice (D) is the result of multiplying the exponents instead of adding.

5. If the first term of a geometric sequence is 5 and the fifth term is 1,280, then what is the value of the seventh term?

(A) 2,560

(B) 5,120

(C) 6,400

(D) 20,480

(E) 32,000

The sequence in the question involves exponential growth. Before we can find a later term in the sequence, we must determine the ratio. We can use the formula $r^{n-1} = \frac{a_n}{a_1}$ where $a_1 = 5$ and $a_5 = 1,280$: $r^{5-1} = \frac{1,280}{5} = 256$. So $r^4 = 256$. Since $4^4 = 256$, $r = 4$. Now we can plug the values of r into the formula $a_n = a_1 r^{n-1}$ to get the value of the seventh term:

$a_7 = 5(4)^6 = 5(4,096) = 20,480$.

So (D) is the correct choice. Choice (B), 5,120, would be the seventh term if r had a value of 2 instead of 4. Choice (E), 32,000, is the result of using a value of 5 for r.

● THE FINAL ACT
Self-Check Quiz

(handwritten: $4\sqrt{x} = 44$)

1. If $4\sqrt{x} - 7 = 37$, then $x =$ *(handwritten: $\sqrt{x} = 11$ $x = 121$)*

2. If $6\sqrt{2y-3} + 9 = 51$, then $y =$

   (handwritten: $6\sqrt{2y-3} = 42$ $\sqrt{2y-3} = 7^2$ $2y-3 = 49$ $2y = 52$)

   (A) 19.5

   (B) 23

   (C) 26

   (D) 42

   (E) 51.5

3. If $2\sqrt{2x} = \sqrt{11x - 54}$, then what is the value of x? *(handwritten: 18)*

4. $\sqrt{x} \div \sqrt[3]{x} =$ *(handwritten: $\frac{1}{2} - \frac{1}{3}$ $\frac{3}{6} - \frac{2}{6} = \frac{1}{6}$)*

   (A) $\sqrt[6]{x}$

   (B) $\sqrt[6]{x^2}$

   (C) $\sqrt[3]{x^2}$

   (D) $\sqrt{x^3}$

   (E) $\sqrt{x^6}$

5. Which of the following is equal to $y^4 \cdot y^{-7}$?

   (handwritten: y^{-3} $\frac{1}{y^3}$)

   (A) $\dfrac{1}{y^{28}}$

   (B) $\dfrac{1}{y^3}$

   (C) $\sqrt[28]{y}$

   (D) $\sqrt[3]{y}$

   (E) $\sqrt{y^{28}}$

6. What is the sum of $16^{\frac{3}{2}}$ and $16^{\frac{3}{4}}$?

$\sqrt{16^3}$ $\sqrt[4]{16^3}$
64 8

   (A) 64

   (B) 72

   (C) 136

   (D) 192

   (E) 320

7. $27^{\frac{2}{3}} - 4^{\frac{5}{2}} =$

$\sqrt[3]{27^2} - \sqrt{4^5}$
9 32

   (A) -23

   (B) -7

   (C) -5

   (D) 8

   (E) 12

8. $\sqrt[3]{x} \div x^{\frac{5}{4}} =$

$\frac{4}{12} - \frac{15}{12} = \frac{-11}{12}$

   (A) $-\sqrt[12]{x}$

   (B) $-\dfrac{1}{x^{12}}$

   (C) $\dfrac{1}{\sqrt[12]{x}}$

   (D) $\dfrac{1}{\sqrt[12]{x^{11}}}$

   (E) $\sqrt[12]{x}$

9. The first term in a geometric sequence is 3 and the second term is 12. What place in the sequence does 3,072 have?

   (A) Fourth

   (B) Fifth

   (C) Sixth

   (D) Seventh

   (E) Eighth

10. The fourth term in a geometric sequence is 135 and the fifth term is 405. What is the second term in the sequence?

● ANSWERS AND EXPLANATIONS

1. **121** Solve this equation by getting the radical alone on one side of the equation:

$$4\sqrt{x} - 7 = 37$$
$$\underline{+7 \quad +7}$$
$$4\sqrt{x} = 44$$
$$\underline{\div 4 \quad \div 4}$$
$$\sqrt{x} = 11$$

Now you can square both sides of the equation to find x:

$$\left(\sqrt{x}\right)^2 = \left(11\right)^2$$
$$x = 121$$

2. **C** You'll need to get the radical expression alone on one side:

$$6\sqrt{2y-3} + 9 = 51$$
$$\underline{-9 \quad -9}$$
$$6\sqrt{2y-3} = 42$$
$$\underline{\div 6 \qquad \div 6}$$
$$\sqrt{2y-3} = 7$$

Now square both sides of this radical equation. Since $7^2 = 49$, $2y - 3 = 49$. So $2y = 52$, and $y = 26$.

Choice (E), 51.5 is the result of adding 9 to the right side of the equation in the first step, instead of subtracting, so as to get $6\sqrt{2y-3} = 60$.

3. **18** This radical equation is a little different, in that there are no operations to perform before squaring. Here, squaring both sides will get rid of all of the radicals.

Remember that the 2 outside of the radical on the left side of the equation gets squared as well.

$$\left(2\sqrt{2x}\right)^2 = \left(\sqrt{11x - 54}\right)^2$$
$$4(2x) = 11x - 54$$
$$8x = 11x - 54$$

Now you can take the basic steps needed to solve the equation for x. $3x = 54$, and $x = 18$.

4. **A** You can work this one out by converting the radical expressions to ones with exponents. Rewrite $\sqrt{x} \div \sqrt[3]{x}$ as $x^{\frac{1}{2}} \div x^{\frac{1}{3}}$. Since $\frac{1}{2} - \frac{1}{3} = \frac{1}{6}$, $x^{\frac{1}{2}} \div x^{\frac{1}{3}} = x^{\frac{1}{6}}$. That is the sixth root of x, which can be rewritten as $\sqrt[6]{x}$. Choice (D) represents an attempt to divide the exponents. $\frac{1}{2} \div \frac{1}{3} = \frac{3}{2}$, and $x^{\frac{3}{2}} = \sqrt{x^3}$.

5. **B** $y^4 \cdot y^{-7} = y^{4-7} = y^{-3}$. y^{-3} is the multiplicative inverse of y^3, which can be written as $\frac{1}{y^3}$. Choice (A) is the result of multiplying the exponents instead of adding. Choice (D) is the result of confusing the exponent -3 with the exponent $\frac{1}{3}$.

6. **B** You need to evaluate each expression before adding. $16^{\frac{3}{2}}$ is the cube of the square root of 16, or $4^3 = 64$. $16^{\frac{3}{4}}$ is the cube of the fourth root of 16, which is 2. $4^3 = 64$ and $2^3 = 8$, so $16^{\frac{3}{2}} + 16^{\frac{3}{4}} = 64 + 8 = 72$. Choice (C) is the result of getting 128 instead of 64 for the value of $16^{\frac{3}{2}}$.

7. **A** Here, again, you need to evaluate each expression before combining. $27^{\frac{2}{3}}$ is the square of the cube root of 27. 3 is the cube root of 27, so $27^{\frac{2}{3}} = 9$. $4^{\frac{5}{2}}$ is the square root of 4, raised to the fifth power. The square root of 4 is 2, and $2^5 = 32$. So $27^{\frac{2}{3}} - 4^{\frac{5}{2}} = 9 - 32 = -23$.

Choice (B) is the result of taking 2^5 to equal 16, instead of 32, since $9 - 16 = -7$.

8. **D** In order to carry out this division, you can convert the first term to one with an exponent.

$\sqrt[3]{x} = x^{\frac{1}{3}}$, so $\sqrt[3]{x} \div x^{\frac{5}{4}} = x^{\frac{1}{3}} \div x^{\frac{5}{4}} = x^{\frac{1}{3} - \frac{5}{4}} = x^{\frac{4}{12} - \frac{15}{12}} = x^{-\frac{11}{12}}$.

$x^{-\frac{11}{12}}$ is the multiplicative reciprocal of $x^{\frac{11}{12}}$, which equals $\sqrt[12]{x^{11}}$. So $x^{-\frac{11}{12}} = \dfrac{1}{\sqrt[12]{x^{11}}}$

Choice (C) is what you would get if you simplified $x^{\frac{4}{12} - \frac{5}{12}}$ instead of $x^{\frac{4}{12} - \frac{15}{12}}$. Remember to convert your fractions carefully when finding common denominators.

9. **C** Since 3 and 12 are consecutive terms in the sequence, we can find the ratio by dividing them. $12 \div 3 = 4$, so we can plug in 4 for the value of r in $a_n = a_1 r^{n-1}$. The first term is 3. So, here are the values for the terms lists in the answer choices:

$a_4 = 3(4)^3 = 3(64) = 192$
$a_5 = 3(4)^4 = 3(256) = 768$
$a_6 = 3(4)^5 = 3(1,024) = 3,072$
$a_7 = 3(4)^6 = 3(4,096) = 12,288$
$a_8 = 3(4)^7 = 3(16,384) = 49,152$

10. **15** This question asks you to find an earlier term in the sequence, given two later terms. Here, 135 and 405 are consecutive terms. So the ratio r is 405 divided by 135, which is 3. So the third term is 135 divided by 3, 45. The second term is 45 divided by 3, 15.

LESSON 6

●

Probability

DIFFICULTY: ★ ★ ★ ★

FREQUENCY: ★

SURPRISE FACTOR: ★ ★ ★

● INTRODUCTION TO PROBABILITY QUESTIONS

Probability questions are not very common on the SAT. When they do appear, however, they could be rather difficult. It can be challenging to make sense of the event or events the question describes, and setting up the solution can be tricky. Probability questions are fraught with traps, as you'll see. There is also a pretty big surprise factor when it comes to Probability questions. You might get a question that describes a very unusual situation. That can make setting up the solution more challenging.

The probability of an event is the likelihood that a given event will happen. Probabilities are expressed as fractions or decimals between 0 and 1, or between 0% and 100%. An event with a probability of 0 or 0% definitely *won't* happen. An event with a probability of 1 or 100% definitely *will* happen. Events with higher probabilities are more likely to occur than events with lower probabilities.

SAT questions usually focus on activities with several possible random outcomes. It could be something like flipping a coin, rolling dice, picking a name out of hat, and so on.

At this stage, the basic formula to apply is:

$$\text{probability} = \frac{\text{\# of desired outcomes}}{\text{\# of possible outcomes}}.$$

So think about the probability of getting tails on a single coin toss. There are only two possible outcomes: heads and tails. Therefore, the probability of getting tails is:

$$\frac{\text{\# of desired outcomes}}{\text{\# of possible outcomes}} = \frac{1}{2}.$$

You could also express that probability as 0.5 or 50%.

When it comes to activities like rolling dice, on the other hand, there might be several different ways to get a particular outcome. If the outcome is a total of 5 on a roll of a pair of dice, you could get it by rolling a 1 and 4, a 4 and 1, a 2 and a 3, or a 3 and a 2. You would have to take all of those desired outcomes into account when finding the probability of getting a total of 5.

A question on the test might involve compound probability: the probability that two or more events will occur. Those events might be dependent or related. For instance, suppose you have a jar full of marbles of different colors, and you want to know the probability that the first two marbles you take from the jar will both be red. The probability that the second marble is red depends on whether the first one is red, since that will affect that number of red marbles remaining.

While many Probability questions involve activities in real-world situations, some involve what is called *geometric probability*. Geometric Probability questions are geometry questions that require a probability calculation in the final step. They usually ask for the probability that a given point on a portion of area or length will be selected if one is chosen at random from an entire figure. Think about a dart that is thrown wildly at a dartboard. If the dart will definitely land on the board, but at a completely different point, then you might wonder about the probability that it will land in the bull's-eye, the innermost circle. That probability is the ratio of the area of the bull's-eye to the area of the rest of the board.

● THE TRAP DOOR
Steering Clear of Answer Traps

There are several major Probability question traps to watch out for. One of them has to do with the difference between "and" and "or." A question might involve two separate events, A and B, and ask you for the probability of "A or B." Typically, that one of the events will happen is more likely than both of them happening. Many questions play on the confusion between "A and B" and "A or B." Different calculations are needed for each of those.

Another probability question trap involves the independent events. Recall the example we gave earlier with the jar of marbles. The outcome of the first marble-picking affects the outcome of the second, as long as the first marble is not put back immediately. If it is put back, then the events really are independent. Most questions involving compound probability won't come out and tell you whether the events are independent. You'll have to figure that out from the context and set up the solution accordingly.

Another basic trap involves the total number of possible outcomes. This is not always stated, and you may have to use careful addition to find it. Be careful to avoid confusing the number of "undesired" outcomes with the total number of possible outcomes. Some questions have answer choices that are meant to take advantage of just that confusion!

● PERFORMANCE TECHNIQUES
Key Formulas and Rules

Setting up the solution properly is vital when it comes to Probability questions. Again the general formula is:

$$\text{Probability} = \frac{\text{\# of desired outcomes}}{\text{\# of possible outcomes}}.$$

Finding the probability of one of two kinds of desired outcomes occurring is a matter of addition:

Probability of A or B =

$$\frac{\text{\# of desired outcomes } A}{\text{\# of possible outcomes}} + \frac{\text{\# of desired outcomes } B}{\text{\# of possible outcomes}} - \frac{\text{\# of desired outcomes } A \text{ and } B}{\text{\# of possible outcomes}} =$$

$$\frac{\text{\# of desired outcomes } A + \text{\# of desired outcomes } B}{\text{\# of possible outcomes}} - \frac{\text{\# of desired outcomes } A \text{ and } B}{\text{\# of possible outcomes}}$$

This can be illustrated with a Venn diagram:

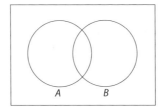

If the area of the rectangle represents a probability of 1, and the areas of the circles represent the probabilities of events *A* and *B*, then the probability of the both *A* or *B* occurring is sum of the areas of the circles, minus the area of the region of overlap.

So the probability of *A* or *B* is the sum of the probability of *A* and the probability of *B*, minus the probability that both will occur. In many cases, there is only one actual outcome, and so you won't have to bother with the subtraction part.

Finding the probability of two independent events both occurring is a matter of multiplication:

Probability of *A* and *B* =

$$\frac{\text{\# of desired outcomes } A}{\text{\# of possible outcomes}} \times \frac{\text{\# of desired outcomes } B}{\text{\# of possible outcomes}}.$$

In the case of dependent events, you need to keep track of the number of how the outcome of the first event affects the second event:

Probability of *A* and *B* (dependent) =

$$\frac{\text{\# of desired outcomes } A}{\text{\# of possible outcomes}} \times \frac{\text{\# of desired outcomes } B \text{ remaining}}{\text{\# of possible outcomes}}.$$

In order to answer Geometric Probability questions, you'll need to be able to apply the basic geometric area and perimeter formulas to probability. We reviewed those formulas in Lesson 2.

● **DRESS REHEARSAL**
  Sample Questions and Detailed Explanations

1. A box filled with a mixture of bottled drinks contains 25 lemonades, 20 juices, and 35 sodas. All of the bottles are the same shape. What is the probability that the next bottle taken at random will be lemonade?

   (A) $\dfrac{5}{18}$

   (B) $\dfrac{5}{17}$

   (C) $\dfrac{5}{16}$

   (D) $\dfrac{5}{14}$

   (E) $\dfrac{5}{11}$

This question involves a simple probability in the sense that there is one event with one kind of desired outcome. There are a total of 80 bottles (25 + 20 + 35), and 25 of them are the of "desired" kind, lemonade. So, if the selection of the next bottle is random, then the probability that it is lemonade is $\dfrac{25}{80} = \dfrac{5}{16}$. **(C) is the correct answer choice.**

Choice (E) is actually the ratio of desired outcomes to undesired outcomes: $\dfrac{25}{20+35} = \dfrac{25}{55} = \dfrac{5}{11}$. Remember that the total number of outcomes, the sum of the desired and undesired outcomes, belongs in the denominator.

2. Jane and Stephanie are part of a group of 10 students who will deliver speeches. One of the 10 students will be picked at random to give the first speech. What is the probability that Jane or Stephanie will be picked to give the first speech?

   (A) $\dfrac{1}{100}$

   (B) $\dfrac{1}{50}$

   (C) $\dfrac{1}{20}$

   (D) $\dfrac{1}{10}$

   (E) $\dfrac{1}{5}$

Since there are 10 students, and 1 will be selected at random, each one has a $\frac{1}{10}$ chance of being picked. The probability of one of two events happening in this kind of situation is the sum of the individual probabilities. Since Jane and Stephanie each have a $\frac{1}{10}$ chance, the probability that one or the other will be picked is $\frac{1}{10} + \frac{1}{10} = \frac{2}{10} = \frac{1}{5}$. **(E) is the correct choice.** You would get choice (A) if you multiplied the probabilities instead of adding them.

3. 4 out of the 120 tickets sold in a raffle will earn prizes. What is the probability that 2 tickets bought at random will both earn prizes?

(A) $\dfrac{1}{1200}$

(B) $\dfrac{1}{1190}$

(C) $\dfrac{1}{990}$

(D) $\dfrac{1}{900}$

(E) $\dfrac{1}{750}$

This question involves dependent probability. The likelihood that the second ticket is a winner depends on whether the first one was a winner. The probability that the first ticket wins is simply 4 out of 120, or $\frac{1}{30}$. That's not the probability of the second ticket being a winner, though. Once a winner is drawn, there are three winning tickets left, out of a total of 119. Therefore, the probability is $\frac{3}{119}$, and the probability that both tickets will earn prizes is $\frac{1}{30} \times \frac{3}{119} = \frac{3}{3570} = \frac{1}{1190}$. **Choice (B) is the correct answer.**

Choice (D) is the result of treating the events as independent ones, such that the probability of each is $\frac{1}{30}$. That's a trap you'll want to avoid!

4. One student from a class of 24 will be picked at random to read aloud. There is a 0.625 probability that the student selected will be a girl. How many boys are in the class?

(A) 8

(B) 9

(C) 12

(D) 15

(E) 16

This question gives you a probability and asks you to use it to find other information. Watch out for a little trap here: the question gives you the probability of picking a girl, but then asks for the number of boys. Since the probability of picking a girl is 0.625, the probability of picking a boy is $1 - 0.625 = 0.375$. That probability is the ratio of x, the number of boys, to the total of 24.

$$0.375 = \frac{x}{24}$$

So, $x = 0.375(24) = 9$, and **(B) is the correct choice.** Choice (D), 15, is the number of girls in the class.

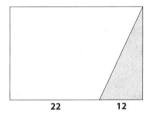

22   12

5. What is the probability that a point selected at random from the interior of the above rectangle will be in the shaded region?

(A) $\frac{3}{17}$

(B) $\frac{3}{14}$

(C) $\frac{3}{11}$

(D) $\frac{6}{17}$

(E) $\frac{6}{11}$

If a point is picked at random from within the rectangle, then the probability that it will be inside the shaded triangle is the ratio of the area of the triangle to the area of the rectangle. Here, you aren't given the height of the rectangle (or the triangle, for that matter), but you needn't worry. Since that dimension is the same for both figures, you just use a variable that will cancel out when you divide.

So, let's say that the vertical dimension is h. In that case, the triangle has an area of $\dfrac{12h}{2}$, or $6h$. To get the area of the rectangle, first find the length by adding the two labeled dimensions. Since $22 + 12 = 34$, the area is $34h$. So, the ratio of the triangle's area to the rectangle's area is $\dfrac{6h}{34h} = \dfrac{3}{17}$. So, $\dfrac{3}{17}$ is the probability of randomly picking a point in the shaded figure, and **choice (A) is the correct answer**.

Choice (B) is the result of using 22 instead of 34 as the length of the triangle. Choice (C) represents the ratio of the area of the shaded portion of the figure to the area of the unshaded portion. Remember that the range of possible outcomes includes the entire rectangle. Choice (D) is the result of using twice the triangle's ratio. Remember that the triangle's area is half of the product of the base and height.

● **THE FINAL ACT**
  Self-Check Quiz

1. A gumball machine contains 28 grape, 36 cherry, and 56 orange gumballs, mixed randomly. What is the probability that the next gumball taken from the machine will be cherry?

(A) $\dfrac{7}{30}$

(B) $\dfrac{3}{10}$

(C) $\dfrac{7}{15}$

(D) $\dfrac{9}{25}$

(E) $\dfrac{9}{20}$

2. If a number between 1 and 5 is picked at random, what is the probability that it will NOT be 3?

   (A) 0.25

   (B) 0.4

   (C) 0.6

   (D) 0.75

   (E) 0.8

3. A single six-sided die will be rolled twice in a row. What is the probability that it will land on 1 or 2 on both rolls?

4. A pack of ballpoint pens holds 6 blue and 6 black pens. If the pack is opened and two are taken at random, what is the probability that they will both be blue?

   (A) $\dfrac{1}{4}$

   (B) $\dfrac{3}{22}$

   (C) $\dfrac{5}{24}$

   (D) $\dfrac{5}{22}$

   (E) $\dfrac{3}{11}$

5. Twelve of the televisions assembled at a factory yesterday are defective. Any one television selected at random from those assembled yesterday has a 2.5% chance of being defective. How many televisions were assembled at the factory yesterday?

   (A) 300

   (B) 480

   (C) 540

   (D) 600

   (E) 720

6. If a coin is flipped four times in a row, what is the probability that it does not land on heads twice in a row?

    (A) $\dfrac{1}{8}$

    (B) $\dfrac{1}{4}$

    (C) $\dfrac{3}{8}$

    (D) $\dfrac{1}{2}$

    (E) $\dfrac{3}{4}$

7. Jim will roll a pair of six-sided dice twice. What is the probability that he will roll a combined total of 5, and then a combined total of 8?

    (A) $\dfrac{1}{108}$

    (B) $\dfrac{5}{432}$

    (C) $\dfrac{5}{324}$

    (D) $\dfrac{1}{54}$

    (E) $\dfrac{5}{216}$

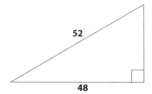

8. What is the probability that a point selected at random from the perimeter of the above right triangle will be on the side with the unlabeled dimension?

    (A) $\dfrac{1}{10}$

    (B) $\dfrac{1}{8}$

    (C) $\dfrac{1}{6}$

    (D) $\dfrac{1}{5}$

    (E) $\dfrac{1}{3}$

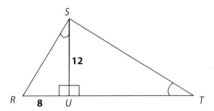

9. What is the probability that a point selected at random from the interior of the triangle *RST* will be also be in the interior of *RSU*?

(A) $\dfrac{4}{13}$

(B) $\dfrac{1}{3}$

(C) $\dfrac{4}{11}$

(D) $\dfrac{4}{9}$

(E) $\dfrac{2}{3}$

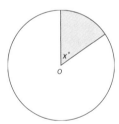

10. In the above figure, the two line segments intersect at the center of the circle *O*. The probability that a point selected at random from the interior of the circle will be in the shaded region is $\dfrac{4}{45}$. What is the value of *x*?

● ANSWERS AND EXPLANATIONS

1. **B** There are 36 desired outcomes, one for each cherry. There are 120 possible outcomes, one for each gumball in the machine. Thus, the probability is just the ratio of those two numbers, $\dfrac{36}{120} = \dfrac{3}{10}$. Choice (C) is the probably of getting an orange gumball. Be careful when identifying the real desired outcome. You might have gotten choice (D) if you took 100 to be the total number of gumballs, rather than 120. Be careful when figuring those totals!

2. **E** The probability that 3 will be picked is $\frac{1}{5}$, or 0.2. So, the probability that this outcome won't occur is 1 – 0.2, or 0.8. You could also get that result by counting the desired outcomes: 1, 2, 4, and 5. There are 4 desired outcomes, and that number divided by the total, 5, gets you 0.8. Choice (D) would be the probability of not picking 3 out of the numbers 1 – 4.

3. $\frac{1}{9}$ This question involves two independent events. The probability of getting 1 on a roll is $\frac{1}{6}$. The same goes for getting 2. So, the probability of getting one or the other is $\frac{1}{6}+\frac{1}{6}=\frac{2}{6}=\frac{1}{3}$. The probability of getting that outcome twice in a row, then, is $\frac{1}{3}\times\frac{1}{3}=\frac{1}{9}$.

4. **D** This is a Dependent Probability question. The probability that the first pen will be blue is $\frac{6}{12}$, or $\frac{1}{2}$. If that outcome occurs, then there are 5 blue pens remaining, and 11 pens left altogether. Thus, the probability that the second pen is blue is $\frac{5}{11}$, and the probability that both are blue is $\frac{1}{2}\times\frac{5}{11}=\frac{5}{22}$. You might have gotten $\frac{1}{4}$, choice (A), if you treated the second outcome as independent. Choice (C) is the result of taking into account that there is one less blue pen for the second draw, but not figuring one less pen in the total. Choice (E) does the reverse of that. $\frac{3}{11}$ is the probability that the first is blue and the second is black.

5. **B** This question requires you to solve an equation. The unknown is the number of televisions assembled. We know that 2.5% of them are defective, and that number is 12. So, $0.025x = 12$. Dividing both sides by 0.025 gets $x = 480$, and that is the number of televisions assembled. Choice (A) is the result of multiplying 25 by 12.

6. **D** There are 2^4 or 16 possible outcomes of four coin flips. Eight of those don't have heads landing consecutively:

T, T, T, T   H, T, T, T   T, H, T, T   T, T, H, T
T, T, T, H   H, T, T, H   H, T, H, T   T, H, T, H

Since there are eight desired outcomes out of 16 possible ones, the probability is the fraction $\frac{8}{16}$, or $\frac{1}{2}$. You would have gotten choice (C) if you counted only 6 desired outcomes.

7. **C** There are 6^2 or 36 possible outcomes of a roll of a pair of dice. There are four ways to roll a total of 5 [(1,4), (4,1), (2,3), (3,2)]. So, the probability of rolling a total of 5 is $\frac{4}{36}$ or $\frac{1}{9}$. There are five ways to roll a total of 8 [(4,4), (2,6), (6,2), (3,5), (5,3)]. Therefore, the probability of rolling a total of 5 is $\frac{5}{36}$. The product of rolling 5 and 8 on consecutive rolls is

$$\frac{1}{9} \times \frac{5}{36} = \frac{5}{324}$$

Choice (B) is actually the probability of getting 8 and 10. Choice (C) is the probability of getting 5 and 7, and (D) is that of getting 7 and 8.

8. **C** In order to apply the probability formula, you must first find the length of the third side. You can use the Pythagorean theorem by plugging in the length of the hypotenuse and the base.

$$C^2 - B^2 = A^2$$
$$A = \sqrt{C^2 - B^2}$$
$$\sqrt{(52)^2 - (48)^2} = \sqrt{2704 - 2304} = \sqrt{400} = 20$$

The third side has a length of 20, and the whole perimeter is $20 + 48 + 52 = 120$. The probability of picking a point on that smallest side is $\frac{20}{120} = \frac{1}{6}$. You might have gotten (D) instead of (C) if you did not add 20 to the value in the denominator.

9. **A** Your first step should be to find the length of TU. Since $\angle RSU = \angle STU$, the two right triangles are similar. You can set up the following proportion to solve for the length of TU:

$$\frac{RS}{SU} = \frac{SU}{TU}$$
$$\frac{8}{12} = \frac{12}{x}$$
$$8x = 144$$
$$x = 18$$

TU has a length of 18. The area of *RSU* is $\frac{8 \times 12}{2} = 48$, and the area of *STU* is $\frac{12 \times 18}{2} = 108$. The area of *RST* is 156, the sum of those two areas. The ratio of *RSU*'s area to *RST*'s is $\frac{48}{156} = \frac{4}{13}$.

10. **32** *x* represents the degree measure of the angle in the shaded region. Since the ratio of the area of the shaded region to the area of the circle is $\frac{4}{45}$, that is also the ratio of the angle measure to 360, the total number of degrees in a circle. To get the angle measure, then, you need only multiply 360 by $\frac{4}{45}$:

$$360 \times \frac{4}{45} = \frac{1140}{45} = 32$$

So, the angle measure is 32°, and *x* = 32.

LESSON 7

Word Problems

DIFFICULTY: ★ ★

FREQUENCY: ★ ★ ★

SURPRISE FACTOR: ★ ★ ★

● INTRODUCTION TO WORD PROBLEMS

Word problems are fairly common, and they can relate to virtually any SAT topic. That adds to the surprise factor, since a word problem could involve something you're not used to dealing with in a verbal form. So, obviously, we can't cover every kind of word problem you could possibly encounter on the test. Instead, we'll go through some common word problem topics. As you gain experience in setting up such problems, you'll be better prepared to handle whatever comes up on test day.

Many word problems involve percentages. Percentages come up in many real-world situations, such as taxes and interest on loans. A percentage is a special way of expressing a fraction or decimal. One percent, or 1%, is equal to $\frac{1}{100}$ or 0.01; 100% is equal to one. The value of any percentage, in fraction or decimal form, is the number divided by 100. So 57% is $\frac{57}{100}$ or 0.57. So to find a certain percent of a number, we multiply it by the corresponding decimal or fraction:

$$x\% \text{ of } y = y \times \frac{x}{100}$$

Area and perimeter are important concepts in geometry-related word problems. Many of these questions will require you to apply standard formulas to solve for unknowns.

Averages are also a common subject of algebra word problems. The average of a set of numbers, a, is the sum of the numbers, s, divided by the number of members, n, in the set: $a = \dfrac{s}{n}$.

A question on the test might give you the value of the average and then ask you to find the number of members or the value of one of the numbers, based on other information provided.

One of most common types of algebra word problems deals with rates. A rate is basically a comparison of two measurements. Usually, one of the measurements is time. Velocity, for example, is a rate, as it compares a distance traveled to time elapsed. That is why velocity is described in terms of units such as miles per hour or feet per second. Another rate might be that of the speed of a photocopier or printer, which might be described in terms of copies per second or pages per minute.

● **THE TRAP DOOR**
Steering Clear of Answer Traps

One kind of answer trap that comes up in any kind of word problem involves hidden instructions. A small clue or detail can mean the difference between the right answer and a wrong one. For instance, a question might tell you that someone who earns $800 per week received a 10% pay raise, and then ask how much *more* the person now earns per week. If you overlook the word *more*, you might select the answer choice that gives his current pay rate, rather than the increase. To avoid the trap, read the question carefully so you can be sure that you understand precisely what is being asked. A single word can change the meaning of a question, so watch out!

Since percentages are often used in word problems, let's take note of another trap. One involves situations where a quantity undergoes multiple percentage increases or decreases. When you have such a series of changes, you can't simply add or subtract the percentages to get the answer. The first change is a percentage of the starting amount, but the second change is a percentage of the new amount. To avoid the trap, remember that you must calculate these changes one at a time.

Now let's look at a trap frequently encountered in Rate questions. Some Rate questions will give you the rates for two parts of a trip (or some other process) and ask for the average overall rate. To get such an average rate, you shouldn't just average the two rates you are given. A common trap presents that result as an answer choice. Instead, use the information provided (as well as information you can provide yourself) to come up with a total distance and a total time. You can use that to compute the average rate.

It's not just with average rates that you need to on the look-out for traps; other kinds of questions involving averages may have traps. Some averages, such as test score averages, average payments, and so on, are weighted. Be aware that you cannot combine averages of different quantities by averaging those original averages. For instance, if a question says that the average weight of a litter of 6 puppies is 5 pounds, and the average weight of another litter of 8 puppies is 7 pounds, you would be wrong to take the average of both litters to be 6 pounds. Instead, you must find the total weight of both litters and divide that amount by the total number of puppies.

● **PERFORMANCE TECHNIQUES**
Key Formulas and Rules

Since percentages are used frequently in word problems, you should be prepared to calculate percentage changes. If you are given an "old value" and a "new value" in a question, you can find the percentage increases and decreases as follows:

$$\% \text{ increase} = \frac{\text{new value} - \text{old value}}{\text{old value}} \times 100$$

$$\% \text{ decrease} = \frac{\text{old value} - \text{new value}}{\text{old value}} \times 100$$

The standard rate formula is *rate* × *time* = *distance*, or $rt = d$. It is also common to give the rate in a formula in terms of the distance and time: $r = \dfrac{d}{t}$.

Many questions involving rates do not involve distances, strictly speaking, but you can just think of distance as the total done in a given period. If we were talking about a photocopier, for instance, the "distance" might be the number of copies made in a given period.

When the question involves a familiar relationship, such as rates, times, and distances, you should be ready to apply the appropriate formula. If the question describes a new situation, where none of the formulas we reviewed earlier apply, then you need to work with the question to restate what is said there in terms of a formula. What operations does the question describe? In what order are they performed? As you answer those questions, you should be in a better position to state the equation or inequality presented in the question.

After you have identified the equation that correctly captures the relationship, you need to identify the stated values and the unknown values. Those variables with no stated values are the unknowns. They are ones you must solve for.

When writing equations, use letters that will help you to keep track of variables. There's a reason why we use the letters r, t, and d in the rate formula—we'd be more likely to plug the value of the rate in the wrong place if we used letters such as x, y, and z.

When you deal with averages, remember that $a = \dfrac{s}{n}$, where a is the average, s is the total, and n is the number of members. You can manipulate this formula to find unknown quantities: s is the product of a and n, and n is s divided by a.

● **DRESS REHEARSAL**
Sample Questions and Detailed Explanations

1. A rectangular room has a perimeter of 54 feet and a width of 12 feet. What is the area of the room?

    (A) 27 sq. ft.

    (B) 33 sq. ft.

    (C) 180 sq. ft.

    (D) 252 sq. ft.

    (E) 504 sq. ft.

This question involves both the perimeter and the area formulas. You'll first need to solve an equation with the perimeter formula. Since the width, w, is 12,

$P = 2l + 2w = 2l + 2(12) = 2l + 24 = 54$
So, $2l = 30$, and $l = 15$.

The area of the room is the product of the dimensions. Since the length of the room is 15 feet, the area is $12 \times 15 = 180$. **Choice (C) is the correct answer.**
Remember that the perimeter of a rectangle is the sum of the lengths of all four sides, and not just the sum of the two dimensions. Choice (B) is the answer you'd get if you made that mistake, so it's a trap you'll want to avoid. Be sure not to confuse the area and perimeter formulas. Choice (A) is what you'd get if you took 54 to be the product of the dimensions and used that value to find the sum of the side lengths.

2. After his first year his job, Jed received a 10% salary raise. After another year, he received an 8% raise. If his starting salary was x dollars, how many dollars is his current salary?

(A) $1.008x$

(B) $1.018x$

(C) $1.188x$

(D) $1.18x$

(E) $1.8x$

In order to find the result of these percentage changes in terms of x, the starting salary, you should work with one change at a time. After a year, Jed's salary is x plus 10% of x, which is $0.1x$. That sum is $1.1x$. So a 10% raise results in a salary that is 110% of what it was before. So the following year's increased salary is 108% of $1.1x$. To find 108% of 1.1, multiply 1.1 by 1.08. The product is 1.188, and the salary is $1.188x$. **(C) is the correct answer choice.**
In this question, choice (D) represents a trap. The choice gives a salary that is 18% higher than the original. 18% is the sum of 10% and 8%. But you cannot simply add percentages, as we explained earlier. Here, that's because the 8% increase applies to the extra 10%, as well as the original salary.

3. A car rode at a speed of 42 miles per hour on a stretch of highway. It then turned around and returned to its starting point at a speed of 56 miles per hour. What was the average speed of the car for this entire time?

   (A) 47 miles per hour

   (B) 48 miles per hour

   (C) 49 miles per hour

   (D) 50 miles per hour

   (E) 51 miles per hour

To find the overall average speed, we need to divide the total distance traveled by the overall time. Although the question doesn't tell us about the distance traveled, you can just assume a number. Since the distance is the same for each leg of the trip, the proportions will be the same.

So let's say that the trip was 42 miles in each direction. This means that the first part of the trip took exactly 1 hour. In the second part, when the car is moving at 56 miles per hour, $t = \dfrac{d}{r} = \dfrac{42}{56} = 0.75$. Therefore, the car traveled 84 miles in 1.75 hours. The average rate, then, is $\dfrac{84}{1.75} = 48$ miles per hour. **(B) is the correct answer choice.**

Choice (C) might be tempting because 49 is the average of 42 and 56. It's a trap, however. You cannot get an average rate by averaging the rates you are given unless the times are the same. If the times are different, then you need to use our approach, even if the distances traveled are the same.

4. The average height of one class of 14 students is 5.2 feet. The average height of another class of 21 students is 5.3 feet. What is the average height of the students in both classes?

   (A) 5.22

   (B) 5.23

   (C) 5.24

   (D) 5.25

   (E) 5.26

This is a Weighted-Average question, and one of the choices is a trap! Although choice (D), 5.25, is the average of 5.2 and 5.3, it is not the average of the group. That's because there are fewer students in the group with an average height of 5.2 feet. To find the real overall average, multiply each class average by the number of students in the class, and add the products. Since an average amount in a group is the sum of the amounts, divided by the number of objects, the sum is the product of the average and the number of objects.

So, the sum of the students' heights in the first class is 5.2 x 14 = 72.8, and the sum for the second class is 5.3 x 21 = 111.3. Thus, the grand sum for all 35 students is 72.8 + 111.3 = 184.1. The average, then, is 184.1 ÷ 35 = 5.26. **The correct answer choice is (E)**.

5. Two elevators starting at the same floor at the same time each start going up. The first elevator travels at a speed of 3 feet per second, and the second one travels at a speed of 2.5 feet per second. The first elevator will travel 36 feet in how many seconds fewer than the second elevator?

    (A) 0.5

    (B) 2.4

    (C) 12

    (D) 14.4

    (E) 18

Questions requiring you to compare rates are very common on the SAT. To compare the two rates, you must calculate each of them. Since time = distance ÷ rate, the first elevator's travel time is $\frac{36}{3} = 12$ seconds, and the second elevator's travel time is $\frac{36}{2.5} = 14.4$ seconds. Since 14.4 − 12 = 2.4, the first elevator travels 36 feet 2.4 seconds quicker than the second elevator. **(B) is the correct choice**.

Because the second elevator has a travel time of 14.4 seconds, choice (D) is a trap. It will appear to be the correct choice to someone who overlooks the word *fewer* in the question. Just as we cautioned, a single word can change the entire meaning of a question.

● THE FINAL ACT
Self-Check Quiz

1. A triangle has an area of 450. If the base of the triangle is decreased by 9% and the height is increased by 12%, by how much will the area be increased?

   (A) 8.64

   (B) 13.5

   (C) 12.38

   (D) 94.5

   (E) 99.36

2. One square room has a perimeter of 44 feet, and another square room has a perimeter of 64 feet. How many more square feet of area than the smaller room does that larger room have?

   (A) 77

   (B) 121

   (C) 135

   (D) 203

   (E) 256

3. A runner jogs around a circular track with a diameter of 240 feet. If she jogged a total of 4,320π feet, how many times around the track did she go?

   (A) $\dfrac{1}{9}$

   (B) $\dfrac{3}{10}$

   (C) 3

   (D) 9

   (E) 18

4. The monthly rent for an apartment was raised from $750.00 to $795.00. If the rent is increased again by the same percentage, what will be the new rental rate?

   (A) $826.08

   (B) $834.75

   (C) $840.00

   (D) $842.70

   (E) $850.00

5. An item of clothing in a store is marked with a price of $20. The price will be discounted by a certain percentage during a store sale. A sales tax of 5% will apply to the discounted price. If the total cost, including sales tax, is $20.16, what is the percentage discount?

6. Three apples have an average weight of 2.25 ounces. If one of the apples weighs 2.35 ounces, what is the average weight in ounces of the other two apples?

7. The average daily high temperature over a 6-day period was 72°F. If the high temperature on the 7th day brought the average up to 74°F, what was the high temperature on the 7th day?

   (A) 76°F

   (B) 80°F

   (C) 84°F

   (D) 86°F

   (E) 90°F

8. A car traveled at a speed of 60 miles per hour for $\frac{3}{4}$ hours. It then traveled 25 miles in $\frac{1}{2}$ hours. What was the car's average speed for the entire time?

   (A) 53 miles per hour

   (B) 54 miles per hour

   (C) 55 miles per hour

   (D) 56 miles per hour

   (E) 57 miles per hour

9. An airplane traveled a certain distance at a speed of 520 miles per hour. If another plane traveled $\frac{9}{10}$ of that distance in $\frac{4}{5}$ of the time, what was the speed of the other plane?

   (A) 332.2
   (B) 364
   (C) 374.4
   (D) 428.8
   (E) 585

10. A car will travel 40 miles at a speed of 48 miles per hour. Once the car has traveled for 20 minutes at this speed, how many miles will it have left to travel?

   (A) 16
   (B) 18
   (C) 20
   (D) 22
   (E) 24

● **ANSWERS AND EXPLANATIONS**

1. **A** If the base of the triangle is decreased by 9%, then you can take 91% of the base by multiplying it by 0.91. Since the height is increased by 12%, you can multiply it by 1.12. So if $\frac{bh}{2} =$ 450, then $\frac{(0.91b)(1.12h)}{2} = (0.91)(1.12)450 = (0.91)504 = 458.64$. $458.64 - 450 = 8.64$.

   Choice (B) is a trap; it's the result of subtracting 9% from 12% and finding a 3% increase over 450.

2. **C** To find the area of each square room, first divide each perimeter by 4. That gives you a side length of each square. The smaller room has dimensions of 11 feet, and the larger room has dimensions of 16 feet. So the difference between the areas is $16^2 - 11^2 = 256 - 121 = 135$. Choices (B) and (D) are traps, then, since each of them is the area of a room.

3. **E**   Since the diameter of the track is 240 feet, the radius is 120 feet. You are looking for the circumference of the circle, which is $2\pi r = 2\pi(120) = 240\pi$ feet. So the number $4{,}320\pi$ feet is $4{,}320\pi \div 240\pi = 18$ times around the track.

Be careful when selecting the right formulas and dimensions. If you found the area of the circle instead of the circumference, you might have gotten (B), $\frac{3}{10}$. You most likely got choice (D) if you used 240 as the length of the radius instead of the diameter.

4. **D**   You must first figure out the rate of the first rent increase. Since $795 - 750 = 45$, the first is \$45.00. Now, $\frac{45}{750} = 0.06$, so the increase is 6%. A 6% increase over \$795.00 is $795 \times 0.06 = 47.7$. So the new rent is $795 + 47.7$, for a total of \$842.70.

Choice (C) uses a percentage increase based on the value of $795 \div 45$. At that rate of increase, the rent increases again by the very same amount, \$45.00.

5. **4**   \$20.16 is 105%, or 5% more, of the discounted price. Divide 20.16 by 1.05 to find that discounted price. $20.16 \div 1.05 = 19.2$, so the discounted price is \$19.20, \$0.80 less than the original price. $0.8 \div 20 = 0.04$, so the discount is 4%, and the answer is 4.

6. **2.2**   The combined weight of the apples is $2.25 \times 3 = 6.75$ ounces. Subtracting 2.35, the weight of the one apple, leaves a total of 4.4 ounces for the remaining 2 apples. The average weight in ounces for those two is $4.4 \div 2 = 2.2$.

7. **D**   The average for the 7-day period is the sum of the daily temperatures divided by 7. Since you have the 6-day average, you can multiply it by 6 to get the 6-day total. $72 \times 6 = 432$. The 7-day total is 518, the product of 74 and 7. The day 7 temperature is the difference between the 7-day and 6-day totals. $518 - 432 = 86$, so the high temperature on the seventh day was $86°F$.

Choice (A) is a trap because 74 is the average of 72 and 76. Keep in mind that you are working with a weighted average.

8. **D** Since $d = rt$, the distance traveled in the first part of the trip is $60\left(\dfrac{3}{4}\right) = 45$. The total distance traveled is $45 + 25$, and the total time is $\dfrac{3}{4} + \dfrac{1}{2} = \dfrac{5}{4}$. Since $r = \dfrac{d}{t}$, the overall average speed is $70 \div \dfrac{5}{4} = 56$. The speed for the second part of the trip is 50 miles per hour. Choice (C) is a trap, since it is just the average of the two rates.

9. **E** Since the question doesn't give you a travel distance or time, you'll have to assume a number. Say that the first plane traveled exactly 520 miles; at a speed of 520 miles per hour, that puts the travel time at one hour. So the second plane travels $520 \times \dfrac{9}{10}$ miles in $\dfrac{4}{5}$ hours. $520 \times \dfrac{9}{10} = 450$, and $r = \dfrac{d}{t}$. So the rate of travel of the second plane is $468 \div \dfrac{4}{5} = 468 \times \dfrac{5}{4} = 585$

Choice (C) is a trap; it's the result of multiplying 520, $\dfrac{9}{10}$, and $\dfrac{4}{5}$. Since you actually have to divide by $\dfrac{4}{5}$ in the last step, that approach won't work.

10. **E** To find the fraction of the trip represented by 20 minutes, find the total trip time. Since $t = \dfrac{d}{r}$, that time is $\dfrac{40}{48} = \dfrac{5}{6}$ hours. 20 minutes is $\dfrac{1}{3}$ hours. So, the car travels a fraction $\dfrac{1}{3} \div \dfrac{5}{6} = \dfrac{1}{3} \times \dfrac{6}{5} = \dfrac{2}{5}$ of the trip in 20 minutes. $\dfrac{2}{5}$ of 40 miles is 16 miles. That leaves 24 miles to go. Watch out for choice (A); it's a trap! 16 is the number of miles already traveled, not the number remaining. This is one instance where the question must be read carefully.

Arithmetic and Number Properties

DIFFICULTY: ★ ★

FREQUENCY: ★ ★

SURPRISE FACTOR: ★ ★ ★ ★

● INTRODUCTION TO ARITHMETIC AND NUMBER PROPERTIES QUESTIONS

Although the most basic mathematics involves arithmetic, the SAT presents Arithmetic questions that are surprisingly abstract. On the test, you'll probably need to apply knowledge of number properties, including odd and even numbers, prime numbers, absolute values, and so on.

Division is a basic operation of arithmetic, and division often leaves remainders. Remainder questions are rather common on the SAT. They may involve a variable, telling you that dividing that variable by a given number leaves a certain remainder, e.g., "n divided by 6 has a remainder of 5." It may then ask you to find the remainder when another term with that variable is divided, e.g., $2n$ by 5.

Another basic operation is subtraction, of course. You might have to use this in questions involving counting. One of the key factors in Counting questions is the difference between the range of numbers and the number of numbers in that range. We'll review that shortly.

Some Arithmetic questions involve prime or composite numbers. A *prime number* is one that has two factors, 1 and itself.

Numbers that are not prime, having more than two factors, are *composite numbers*. Most prime numbers are odd. Every even number has 2 as a factor. So 2 is the only even prime. Every odd and even composite integer is *composed* of *prime factors*. By this we mean that every number can be expressed as a product of prime numbers. You should be ready for questions on the test that draw on those relationships.

Another important number property is absolute value. The absolute value of a number is the distance from that number to zero on the number line. Since absolute values represent distances, they are always positive. The absolute value of 7 is 7. This is expressed as $|7| = 7$. Likewise, the absolute value of -7 is 7; $|-7| = 7$. So every positive number is the absolute value of two numbers: itself and its negative. Some SAT questions will test your knowledge of absolute value in the context of equations or inequalities.

● THE TRAP DOOR
Steering Clear of Answer Traps

Questions involving number counting usually have traps. It may seem that subtracting numbers is all that it takes to answer them, but that is often not the case. Suppose a question tells you that a person read pages 15 through 25 of a book, and asks you how many pages she read. Subtracting the first integer in a range from the last integer will give you difference between the two numbers. However, it won't give you the number of integers in that range. A question would probably include 10 as an incorrect answer choice. That is the value of 15 subtracted from 25, but you can count the integers in the range:

$$
\begin{array}{ccccccccccc}
15 & 16 & 17 & 18 & 19 & 20 & 21 & 22 & 23 & 24 & 25 \\
1 & 2 & 3 & 4 & 5 & 6 & 7 & 8 & 9 & 10 & 11
\end{array}
$$

To avoid this trap and find the correct total, subtract the integers and add 1 to the difference.

Many Arithmetic questions involve another kind of trap. Incorrect answer choices may be based on the assumption that only positive integers are involved. For instance, suppose that a question tells you that n is a positive number and asks you whether it is possible that n^2 is less than n. It's true that n^2 must be greater than n if n is an integer greater than 1, but what if n is a fraction, such as $\frac{1}{2}$? In that case, $n^2 = \frac{1}{4}$ and n^2 is less than n. If you overlook fractions, then you might miss the correct answer. Similar traps might play on your overlooking the properties of negative numbers. To avoid such traps, be careful to take the full range of numbers into account, unless the question specifies a certain set of numbers (integers, positives, etc.). On the other hand, when a question specifies nothing, you should be especially cautious!

● PERFORMANCE TECHNIQUES
Key Formulas and Rules

Remainder questions may appear difficult on the surface; they seem to require you to solve an equation for the variable. That's not necessary, though. You can simply pick a number that satisfies the sentence and use it as the value of the variable. Suppose you're told that "y divided by 5 has a remainder of 4." Since 9 is a number that leaves that remainder when divided by 5, you can use it to find the solution. Generally you can pick a number by taking a multiple of the number you are dividing by, and adding the remainder.

Suppose you are asked for the remainder left by dividing $3y$ by 5. Using 9 as the value of y, you'd get $3y = 27$. Divide that value by 5, and you'll get a remainder of 2. So long as the number you pick gives the right remainder when divided, the result will be the same.

When working with absolute values, remember that every absolute value equation represents two other equations. Say that A stands for a given expression. If A is positive, then $|A| = A$. If A is negative, then $|A| = -A$, since $-A$ is positive. If A is an algebraic expression with an unknown variable, then you could say that if $|A| = 5$, then $A = 5$ or $-A = 5$. You would then have two equations to solve, and there is more than one possible value of the variable.

When it comes to dealing with questions that test knowledge of number properties, you should expect to see unusual arithmetic relationships and expressions. Fortunately, there are familiar techniques you can use to work through most of these questions. Many of them involve picking numbers. If a question tells you about certain properties of a variable or algebraic expression, it will probably help to substitute a number with those properties. This will help you to determine when a given equation must be true, or when a given equation could be false. Many Arithmetic and Number Property questions are written in that way, asking you to identify necessary, possible, or impossible statements on the basis of properties they give you. You'll do well to make such abstract problems more concrete by substituting numbers for variables wherever possible.

● **DRESS REHEARSAL**
Sample Questions and Detailed Explanations

1. When a is divided by 4, the remainder is 1. What is the remainder when $2a$ is divided by 4?

   (A) 0

   (B) 1

   (C) 2

   (D) 3

   (E) 4

You can set up the solution by picking a number that satisfies the first statement, one that leaves a remainder of 1 when divided by 4. To find such a number, just add 1 to a multiple of 4. For example, $(4 \times 2) + 1 = 9$. We'll use 9 as the value of a, then, and $2a = 18$. You get a remainder of 2 if you divide 18 by 4. This means that the remainder is 2 when $2a$ is divided by 4, no matter what value a has, as long as the remainder is 1 when a is divided by 4. **(C) is the correct answer choice.**

2. Mel read two whole chapters of a textbook. One goes from page 28 to 41, and the other goes from page 61 to 82. How many pages did Mel read altogether?

   (A) 33

   (B) 34

(C) 35

(D) 36

(E) 37

This is an Integer Counting question. Several of the answer choices are traps, since they represent the result of incorrect counting in the first or second chapters, or both. Remember that you can't just subtract the highest and lowest numbers in each page range. That will leave you with one page too few in each case.

The number of pages in the first chapter is $(41 - 28) + 1$, which is 14:

28	29	30	31	32	33	34	35	36	37	38	39	40	41
1	2	3	4	5	6	7	8	9	10	11	12	13	14

The number of pages in the second chapter is $(82 - 61) + 1 = 22$.

Since $14 + 22 = 36$, **choice (D) is the correct answer.** Choice (B) is a trap, as it is the sum of the differences in each integer range. If you counted incorrectly in just one of the ranges, you might have gotten choice (C).

3. If $x - y = 5$ and $y < 0$, then which of the following could be true?

 I. $-5 < x < 0$

 II. $0 < x < 5$

 III. $x > 5$

 (A) I only

 (B) II only

 (C) III only

 (D) I and II

 (E) I, II, and III

This question tests your understanding of arithmetic involving negative numbers, as the variable y is said to be negative. To figure out which statements could be true, pick numbers to be the values of the variables. Use a different value for each of the three inequalities. Where $-5 < x < 0$, let $x = -1$. Can you subtract a negative number from -1 to get 5? Since $-1 - (-6) = -1 + 6 = 5$, statement I could be true.

Suppose $x = 1$. In that case, $1 - (n^24) = -1 + 4 = 5$, so statement II could be true.

What about $x > 5$? If you subtract a negative number from a number greater than 5, the difference will be even greater. So statement III cannot be true. **(D) is the correct choice.**

Remember that subtracting a negative integer is like adding its absolute value. The result will be a greater number. If you incorrectly subtracted negative numbers to get smaller ones, you may have concluded that statement III was the only possible one and picked (C).

4. If x and y are integers and $xy = 12$, then how many possible values of $x + y$ are there?

   (A) 3

   (B) 4

   (C) 6

   (D) 9

   (E) 12

This Arithmetic question involves a trap that is very important to be aware of. Remember that the product of two negative numbers is a positive number. Otherwise, you might overlook pairs of negative integers, such as -2 and -6, with a product of 12. Altogether, there are six pairs of integers with a product of 12: 1 and 12, 2 and 6, 3 and 4, -1 and -12, -2 and -6, and -3 and -4. **So (C) is the correct choice.**

You probably would have picked (A) if you overlooked the negative numbers. Choice (E) is the number of pairs of integers that have a product of 12 or -12. Remember that the product of a negative integer and a positive one is negative.

5. If $|x - 4| = 10$, then which of the following could be the value of x?

   I. -14

   II. -6

   III. 6

   (A) I only

   (B) II only

(C) III only

(D) I and II

(E) I and III

This question spotlights absolute value, an important number property. If the absolute value of an expression is 10, then the expression has a value of −10 or 10. Therefore, you need to solve two equations. Since $|x-4|=10$, $x-4=10$ or $-(x-4)=10$.

If $x-4=10$, then $x=14$. That's not one of the three options. If $-(x-4)=10$, then $4-x=10$, then $x=-6$. That's option II. None of the other options can be values of x, and **so (B) is the correct answer choice.** If x equaled −14, then $|x-4|$ would be $|x-4|=|-14-4|=|-18|=18$. If x equaled 6, then $|x-4|$ would be $|x-4|=|6-4|=|2|=2$.

● **THE FINAL ACT**
Self-Check Quiz

1. Dividing n by 6 leaves a remainder of 3. What remainder is left when $3n$ is divided by 6?

   (A) 0

   (B) 1

   (C) 2

   (D) 3

   (E) 4

2. m, n, and p are prime numbers, and $m \neq n \neq p$. How many factors does mnp have, other than 1 and itself?

   (A) 3

   (B) 4

   (C) 5

   (D) 6

   (E) 7

3. On a hotel floor with 40 rooms, the rooms numbered 22 through 31 are all currently unoccupied. Rooms 24 through 27 will become occupied tonight. What fraction of the currently unoccupied rooms will become occupied tonight?

(A) $\dfrac{3}{10}$

(B) $\dfrac{1}{3}$

(C) $\dfrac{2}{5}$

(D) $\dfrac{4}{9}$

(E) $\dfrac{1}{2}$

4. For integers p, q, and r, if $pq = 12$ and $pr = -18$, then which of the following could be the value of qr?

(A) -28

(B) -24

(C) -16

(D) 22

(E) 30

5. An integer r is evenly divisible by exactly two integers, s and t, other than 1 and itself. Which of the following could be true?

   I. r is even.
   II. s is composite.
   III. t is prime.

(A) I only

(B) III only

(C) I and III

(D) II and III

(E) I, II, and III

6. Amelia spent 72 minutes doing exercises on pages 17 through 25 of a workbook. If she did work on each page, what was the average number of minutes she spent on each page?

7. If a and b are positive integers such that $a > b$ and ab is prime, then which of the following must be true?

   (A) $a = ab$

   (B) $a > ab$

   (C) $a < ab$

   (D) $b = ab$

   (E) $b > ab$

8. If $fgh = 30$ and $f > g > h > 1$, then which of the following must be true?

   I. $f, g,$ and h are all prime.

   II. $fg > gh$

   III. $f, g,$ and h are all even.

   (A) I only

   (B) II only

   (C) I and III

   (D) II and III

   (E) I, II, and III

9. Which of the following has a value of 8?

   (A) $-|-2+10|$

   (B) $-|1+7|$

   (C) $|-11-3|$

   (D) $|6-2|$

   (E) $|12-20|$

10. If $|y+2| > 11$, which of the following statements are true?

   I. $y > 9$

   II. $y < -13$

   III. $y > 13$

   (A) I only

   (B) II only

   (C) III only

   (D) I and II

   (E) I and III

● ANSWERS AND EXPLANATIONS

1. **D**   15 is the sum of 3 and a multiple of 6. So 15 is a number that leaves a remainder of 3 when divided by 6. If $a = 15$, then $3a = 45$. You get a remainder of 3 when you divide 45 by 6.

2. **D**   Whatever value mnp has, it has m, n, and p as factors. If that's all you counted, you would have picked (A), but the products of these factors are also factors. This includes mn, mp, and np. That bring the total to 6. Remember that m, n, and p have no other factors, since they are primes.

3. **C**   This question requires you to count the number of integers in two ranges. The larger range is 22 to 31, and the number of integers there is $(31 - 22) + 1 = 10$. The smaller range is 24 to 27, and the number of integers in that range is $(27 - 24) + 1 = 4$. So the fraction of the currently unoccupied rooms that will become occupied tonight is $\frac{4}{10} = \frac{2}{5}$. Choice (B) is a trap; $\frac{3}{9}$ is the fraction you'd get by simply subtracting the numbers in each range. Choices (A) and (D) each involve that mistake in one part of the fraction.

4. **B**   Even though you don't know the values of p, q, and r, you can narrow the range of possibilities. They can only be numbers that are factors of 12 and -18, since those are the products pq and qr. The positive and negative factors of 12 are -12, -6, -4, -3, -2, -1, 1, 2, 3, 4, 6, and 12. The positive and negative factors of -18 are -18, -9, -6, -3, -2, -1, 1, 2, 3, 6, 9, and 18.

What numbers in the answer choices can be products of two of these numbers, one from each group? Choice (A), -28, has 7 as a prime factor. Choice (C), is the product of 4 and -4, -2 and 8, or 2 and -8. Not enough of those numbers appear. Choice (D), 22, has 11 as a prime factor. Choice (E), 30, has 5 as a prime factor. All of those choices can be eliminated, leaving (B).

Choice (B), -24, is the product of -4 and 6. So if $p = -3$, $q = -4$, and $r = 6$, then $pq = 12$, $pr = -18$, and $qr = -24$.

5. **E**   If s or t is even, r is even. One of the integers s and t must be prime, or else r would have more factors. Say that t is

prime. In that case, *s* could be composite if it is the square of *t*. Suppose *r* is 8, then. It is divisible by 8, 4, 2, and 1. Let *s* = 4 and *t* = 2. Each statement is satisfied under those conditions.

6. **8**   This Arithmetic question requires you to count correctly before dividing. Since the exercises covered a range of pages beginning with 17 and ending with 25, the number of pages in the range is (25 − 17) + 1, which is 9. So the average time per page is 72 divided by 9, which is 8. Watch out again for the counting trap; if you count 8 pages instead of 9, you'd get an average time of 8.

7. **A**   Remember that a prime number has only itself and 1 as integer factors. So if *ab* is prime, and *a* and *b* are unique integer factors, one of them must be *ab* itself and the other must be 1. Since *a* > *b*, *b* = 1, and *a* = *ab*.

8. **B**   This question has a major trap. You might see that statement II must be true. You're told that *f* > *h*. As long as *g* is positive, the inequality holds when both sides are multiplied by *g*, so *fg* > *gh*. Now, it is true that 2 x 3 x 5 = 30, and those factors are all primes. Two of them are odd, and that's enough for you to eliminate statement III. It's also true that 2, 3, and 5 are the only unique integer factors of 30 (other than 30 and 1), but that doesn't make statement I true! That's because you're not told that *f*, *g*, and *h*, are all integers. Remember that you can't rule out nonintegers unless the question tells you to. So if *f* = 1.5, *g* = 2, and *h* = 10, then *fgh* = 30. There are lots of other possibilities, but that's good enough to rule out statement I.

9. **E**   Evaluate each expression to find the one with a value of 8:

$$-\left|-2+10\right|=-\left|8\right|=-8$$
$$-\left|1+7\right|$$
$$\left|-11-3\right|=\left|-14\right|=14$$
$$\left|6-2\right|=\left|4\right|=4$$
$$\left|12-20\right|=\left|-8\right|=8$$

Remember that while absolute value expressions are always positive, the negative of an absolute expression must be negative.

10. **D**   This absolute value inequality actually represents two inequalities: $y + 2 > 11$ and $-(y + 2) > 11$. Solving the first inequality gets you $y > 9$. Solving the second inequality gets you:

$$|y+2| > 11$$
$$-(y+2) > 11$$
$$-2 - y > 11$$
$$-y > 13$$
$$y < -13$$

Since y > 9 and y < 13, $9 < y < 13$. Remember that multiplying both sides of an inequality requires you to change the direction of the inequality. You might have picked choice (E) if you didn't take that step.

Combinations and Permutations

DIFFICULTY: ★ ★ ★ ★

FREQUENCY: ★

SURPRISE FACTOR: ★ ★ ★

● INTRODUCTION TO COMBINATIONS AND PERMUTATIONS

Combination and Permutation questions usually involve counting. You'll need to count the number of ways a group of objects can be combined or ordered. There are some important differences between those two actions. Combination and Permutation questions are not very common, but they deserve your attention because they can be difficult. The variety of real-world situations these questions can involve adds to their surprise factor.

Suppose you have four people: Adam, Bob, Carol, and Diane. If you have to form a two-person group from those four, then there are a number of possibilities. You could pick Adam and Bob, Bob and Carol, Adam and Diane, and so on. There are actually six possibilities altogether. We'll explain how we got that total later.

What if you weren't just making a group, but were making one where each member had a special role? Suppose the first person you pick will drive a car, and the second one will be a passenger. In that case, the order of the selection matters. When it does, there are 12, not 6, possible groups of two that could be formed from the larger group of four.

This is an example of a permutation. Different permutations can have all the same members, in different configurations. Permutations can be tricky when the size of the configuration is smaller than the number of objects you have to work with. Another layer of difficulty is found when not all of the objects are unique. How many ways can you scramble the letters of the word *abacus*? Here's a hint: since the *a*'s are interchangeable, there are not as many ways to scramble that word as there are ways to scramble, say, *hanger*.

● THE TRAP DOOR
Steering Clear of Answer Traps

There are several traps to be aware of when Combination or Permutation questions come up on Test Day. We've already mentioned the first trap: confusing combinations with permutations. Calculating or counting the right number depends on being able to tell the difference. Usually, it comes down to a difference between an ordered group and an unordered one. The language of the question must allow you to identify what you must count, one way or another. Pay careful attention to the wording to avoid the trap.

Another trap plays on confusion about the number of objects you have to work with. Suppose a question tells you that a lock has a five-digit combination code, and each digit can be a number from 1 to 5. In that case, you're free to use the same number more than once. On the other hand, suppose a question asks you how many unique numbers you can make by scrambling the digits of the number 12,345. In that case, you can use each of the numbers 1, 2, 3, 4, and 5 only once. So, the correct answer to the first question is a number much greater than the answer to the second question. If you don't take this detail into account, you might set up the solution in the wrong way.

The last trap we'll discuss has to do with permutations. Remember the word *abacus* we used in the example above? Not every way of scrambling the letters of that word results in a new permutation. If we scrambled the word by swapping the two *a*'s, we'd still have the word *abacus*. You might fall for a trap if you don't take that kind of factor into account. You can avoid such a trap by keeping track of numbers, letters, or objects that are not unique.

● PERFORMANCE TECHNIQUES
Key Formulas and Rules

Some Combination and Permutation questions can be answered by straightforward counting. You may be able to come up and list all of the possible combinations or permutations for some simple questions.

For many questions, however, there are simply too many possibilities to list and count in the time you have. Instead, you'll have to use certain formulas. The key to answering most Combination and Permutation questions is the factorial. The factorial of a number is the product of 1 and every other integer up to that number. For instance, the factorial of 5, which we express using an exclamation point (!) as 5!, has a value equal to $5 \times 4 \times 3 \times 2 \times 1$. Likewise, $7! = 7 \times 6 \times 5 \times 4 \times 3 \times 2 \times 1$.

Factorials can help you because you can use them to describe many permutations. Suppose you want to know how many ways the string of letters ABCDE can be arranged. Since there are 5 letters, there are 5 possibilities for the first position in the string. There are 4 left over for the second position. There are then 3 remaining for the third position, and so on. So the number of possibilities overall is 5!, which equals 120.

In general, to find the number of permutations of a group of *n* objects, evaluate *n*!.

Suppose instead that you are asked to find the number of three-letter strings you could get by arranging parts of ABCDE. For a 3-letter string, there are 5 possibilities for the first position in the string, 4 for the second position, and 3 for the third position. Since $5 \times 4 \times 3 = 60$, there are 60 possible 3-letter strings. This is the value of 5! divided by 3!.

In general, to find the number of permutations of a subgroup of *r* objects taken from a group of *n*, evaluate $\dfrac{n!}{(n-r)!}$. This expression is often symbolized as $_nP_r$.

So

$$_6P_4 = \frac{6!}{(6-4)!} = \frac{6!}{2!} = \frac{720}{2} = 360$$

So 360 is the number of permutations of a four-member subgroup of a six-member group.

Now, suppose you want to know the number of possible four-member subgroups, without regard to how each group is ordered. There are fewer than 360 such subgroups. Each four-member subgroup can be ordered in 4! or 24 ways, after all. Thus, there is 1 unordered subgroup for every 24 ordered ones. The number of unordered subgroups, then, is 360 ÷ 24, which is 15. That is the value of

$$_6C_4 = \frac{6!}{4!(6-4)!} = \frac{6!}{4!2!} = \frac{720}{24(2)} = \frac{720}{48} = 15.$$

In general, the number of possible r-member unordered subgroups of an n-member group is $_nC_r = \dfrac{n!}{n!(n-r)!}$.

This is the formula to use for combinations. That's why it uses the letter C.

Some questions might call for the number combinations of objects from different groups, or the number of permutations of objects, where the number of possibilities for each place is given. In such cases, you probably won't be able to use factorials. Instead, exponents are more likely to come in handy.

Suppose a question asks you for the number of possible ordered combinations of three letters of the alphabet. You wouldn't use factorials there if any letter can be used in any place. The answer is $26^3 = 26 \times 26 \times 26 = 17,576$.

● **DRESS REHEARSAL**
Sample Questions and Detailed Explanations

1. A jukebox will play five different songs in a row. In how many different orders can the songs be played?

   (A) 24

   (B) 25

   (C) 32

   (D) 120

   (E) 125

The number of different song orders is 5!. Any of the five songs can be played first. That leaves four possible songs for the second spot in the order. So far, the number of possible combinations of songs for those two spots is 5 × 4, or 20. Any of the three remaining songs can go third, leaving two for the fourth spot. Once you get to the last spot, there is only one song remaining. The total number of orders, or permutations, is 5 × 4 × 3 × 2 × 1 = 120. **(D) is the correct choice.** Choice (B) is 5^2, and choice (C) is 2^5. Remember that factorials, not exponents, are needed to find the number of permutations when each item can be appear only once.

2. How many three-digit numbers can be made using the digits 4, 5, 6, 7, when each digit can be used more than once?

(A) 24

(B) 64

(C) 81

(D) 210

(E) 343

This is a Permutation question, one where you must find the number of ordered combinations of a given length. Unlike many other Permutation questions, this one lets you re-use numbers. It is not a matter of scrambling or arranging four digits. So there are four possibilities for each digit. That makes the total number of possibilities 4^3, or 64. So, **(B) is the correct answer choice.**

Choice (C), 81, is 3^4. If this were a standard Permutation question, where each digit could be used once, then 24, choice (A), would be the correct answer.

Don't be thrown off by the values of the digits used. The number of possibilities for a three-digit number would be the same even if you were given four unique digits other than 4, 5, 6, and 7. Choice (E), 343, is the value of 7^3.

3. From a group of six teachers, four will be selected at random to lead a field trip. How many possible selections of four teachers are there?

(A) 15

(B) 60

(C) 120

(D) 360

(E) 720

The number of possible combinations is given by the formula $_nC_r = \dfrac{n!}{r!(n-r)!}$, where n is the size of the larger group, and r is the size of the subgroup.

Here, $n = 6$ and $r = 4$, so $_6C_4 = \dfrac{6!}{4!(6-4)!} = \dfrac{6!}{4!2!} = \dfrac{30}{2} = 15$. So 15 different groups of four could be formed. **(A) is the correct choice.**

Choice (E) is the value of 6!. That represents the number of ordered six-member groups. We have to divide 6! by 2! to account for the smaller committee size. We also divided by 4! to account for the factor that the order of the selection doesn't matter. $\dfrac{6!}{2!}$ represents the number of "ordered" four-person committees, which is 360, choice (D).

4. From a group of eight people, five will be selected to give speeches, one at a time. How many possible orderings of speeches are there?

   (A) 56

   (B) 336

   (C) 720

   (D) 6,720

   (E) 8,064

The formula to use here is $_nP_r = \dfrac{n!}{(n-r)!}$, where $n = 8$ and $r = 5$. $_8P_5 = \dfrac{8!}{(8-5)!} = \dfrac{8!}{3!} = 8 \times 7 \times 6 \times 5 \times 4$.

This product represents the right number of orderings because there are eight possibilities for the first spot, seven for the second, six for the third, five for the fourth, and four for the fifth. Since $8 \times 7 \times 6 \times 5 \times 4 = 6{,}720$, **(D) is the correct choice.**

You might have gotten choice (A) if you used $_nC_r = \dfrac{n!}{r!(n-r)!}$ instead of $_nP_r = \dfrac{n!}{(n-r)!}$. Remember that that formula is used to find the number of unordered combinations. In this situation, the order counts. Choice (B) is the value of $\dfrac{n!}{r!}$. That actually represents the number of permutations of a three-person order, taken from a group of eight people.

5. How many different seven-letter configurations could be made from arranging all of the letters below?

   D, E, F, F, G, J, F

   (A) 70
   (B) 210
   (C) 840
   (D) 1,680
   (E) 5,040

The number of unique configurations of seven different letters is 7!, or 5,040. You'll have fewer than that here, however, because not all of the letters are different. There are three F's in the group of seven letters, and there are 3!, or 6, ways that those F's could be sequenced. So the number of seven-letter configurations is 7! divided by 3!:

$$\frac{7!}{3!} = \frac{7 \times 6 \times 5 \times 4 \times 3 \times 2 \times 1}{3 \times 2 \times 1} = \frac{7 \times 6 \times 5 \times 4}{1} = 840.$$

So (C) is the correct answer choice. Choice (B) is the value of $\dfrac{7!}{4!}$. That's the wrong expression to evaluate, because $_nC_r = \dfrac{n!}{r!(n-r)!}$ is not the applicable formula. Choice (D) is the value of $\dfrac{7!}{3}$. That answer might be the result of taking the number of orderings of the F's to be three, rather than six.

● THE FINAL ACT
Self-Check Quiz

1. How many three-letter sequences can you make from the letters A, B, C, D, and E, if no letter can appear in a sequence no more than once?

2. Mark must pick two different days out of the next seven to do housecleaning. How many combinations of days can he select?

   (A) 21

   (B) 28

   (C) 35

   (D) 42

   (E) 49

3. A telephone area code for one city is a three-digit number. Each digit is a number between 1 and 9. What is the total number of possible area codes for this city?

   (A) 21

   (B) 84

   (C) 243

   (D) 504

   (E) 729

4. Carrie has six books to arrange on a shelf. In how many different orders can she arrange the books?

   (A) 36

   (B) 64

   (C) 120

   (D) 360

   (E) 720

5. A salesperson must visit four of seven different cities this month. How many possible ordered lists of visits are there?

6. How many unique numbers can be made by scrambling the digits of 525,352?

   (A) 60

   (B) 120

   (C) 180

   (D) 240

   (E) 360

7. How many four-digit numbers can be formed by arranging the digits 5, 6, 7, and 8?

   (A) 12

   (B) 24

   (C) 72

   (D) 128

   (E) 256

8. Bill has nine separate errands to perform. He will pick four of them to perform today. How many different ordered lists of errands for the day can he make up?

   (A) 126

   (B) 630

   (C) 1,512

   (D) 3,024

   (E) 15,120

9. How many different numbers could be made by scrambling the digits of 1,514?

   (A) 6

   (B) 12

   (C) 18

   (D) 22

   (E) 24

10. How many different numbers ending with 4 or 5 can be made by scrambling the digits of 56,413?

(A) 12

(B) 24

(C) 48

(D) 60

(E) 72

● **ANSWERS AND EXPLANATIONS**

1. **10** Since a three-member ordered group will be formed from a five-member group, the expression for the number of possible permutations is $\dfrac{5!}{(5-3)!} = \dfrac{5!}{2!} = \dfrac{120}{2} = \dfrac{120}{2} = 60$.

2. **A** This question asks for a number of combinations, rather than permutations. The number is $\dfrac{7!}{2!(7-2)!} = \dfrac{7!}{2!5!} = \dfrac{7 \times 6}{2} = 21$. Choice (D), 42, is the number of ordered combinations, or permutations.

3. **E** Unlike many other Permutation questions, this one doesn't involve unique numbers. So there are nine possibilities for each digit. This means that there are 9^3 or 729 possible three-digit area codes. Choice (D) is the number of permutations where each number can be used only one. Choice (B) is the number of unordered combinations with that limitation.

4. **E** Since you need to find the value of $_6P_6$, the expression to evaluate is 6!. $6 \times 5 \times 4 \times 3 \times 2 \times 1 = 720$. Choice (A) is the value of 6^2, and choice (B) is the value of 2^6.

5. **840** Since the list of cities is ordered, you need to use a permutation formula:

$$_7P_4 = \dfrac{7!}{(7-4)!} = \dfrac{7!}{3!} = 7 \times 6 \times 5 \times 4 = 840.$$

6. **A** There are 6!, or 720, permutations of six unique digits. Here, one of the digits, 5, appears three times, so you divide

720 by 3!, or 6, to account for that. Divide again by 2! to account for the two occurrences of the digit 2. The result is 60 unique permutations. Choice (B), 120, accounts for the multiple occurrences of 5, but not the multiple occurrences of 2. Choice (E), 360, does just the opposite.

7. **B** Here, you are asked to find the number of possible permutations of four digits. To answer the question, all we need to do is evaluate 4!. That expression is 4 x 3 x 2 x 1 = 24. So we can arrange the digits 5, 6, 7, and 8 to make 24 different numbers, including 5,678, 7,856, etc. Choice (E) is the value of 4^4; that's how many four-digit numbers you could make if could reuse any of the four digits.

8. **D** This question requires you to find the number of permutations of four objects, out of a group of nine: $_9P_4 = \dfrac{9!}{5!} = 9 \times 8 \times 7 \times 6 = 3{,}024$. Choice (A) is the value of $_9C_4$, and choice (E) is the value of $_9P_5$.

9. **B** While a four-digit number with all unique digits has 4!, or 24, permutations, this one has half that many, or 12. The two 1's are interchangeable, and that makes half of the permutations identical to others.

10. **C** There are 5! permutations of 56,413, but only a fraction of them end with 4 and 5. In fact, $\dfrac{1}{5}$ of them end with 4, and $\dfrac{1}{5}$ of them end with 5. So $\dfrac{2}{5}$ of them end with one or the other. $\dfrac{2}{5}$ of 5! is 48. Choice (E), 72, is $\dfrac{3}{5}$ of 5!. That's the number of permutations that have neither 4 nor 5 as the last digit.

Critical
Reading

SAT Critical Reading Basics

do: ① Sentence Completion
② Reading comprehension on short passages
③ Reading Comp. on LONG passages

The Critical Reading component of the SAT is designed to test three basic skills:

1. Vocabulary—both the breadth of your vocabulary and your ability to determine meaning from context

2. Reasoning skills—including your ability to determine the relationship between words and ideas

3. Reading skills—how well you understand what you read (main idea, tone, etc.)

The Critical Reading section of the SAT includes two types of questions

1. Sentence Completion questions

2. Reading Comprehension questions

To do well on SAT Critical Reading, you need to be systematic in your approach to each question type. We'll describe each type in more detail in a moment.

do ① Sentence Completion questions are the fastest question type of the three because there is no passage to read—just a sentence with one or two blanks that you need to fill in. You can earn points faster on these questions than on Reading Comprehension questions, which require you to read anywhere from one to three paragraphs. Thus, you should do these first, even if they are the last questions in the section.

You might want to do the Reading Comprehension questions based on the shorter passages right after that. Why? It takes less time to read a short passage than it does to read a long one, so the short passage points can be accumulated faster. By working on the Long Passage questions last, you won't run the risk of getting bogged down on the longer passages and leaving yourself only a few minutes for the short passages and Sentence Completion questions.

Now that you know what order to work through the critical reading section, let's take a look at the question types.

● SENTENCE COMPLETION QUESTIONS

The Sentence Completion question sets are arranged in order of difficulty. The first few questions in a set might be fairly straightforward and manageable. The middle few questions will be a little harder, and the last few questions should be the most difficult. Keep this in mind as you work.

Sentence Completion questions look like this:

> Although this small and selective publishing house is famous for its _____ standards, several of its recent novels have appealed to the general population.
>
> (A) proletarian
>
> (B) naturalistic
>
> (C) discriminating
>
> (D) imitative
>
> (E) precarious

To answer this type of question, you must choose the word that best completes the sentence. We have specific strategies for tackling this question type in Lesson 10. In case you're curious, the answer for this question is (C), discriminating.

● READING COMPREHENSION QUESTIONS

As we mentioned, there are two kinds of Reading Comprehension passages: short and long. Short passages are approximately 100–150 words long. They are typically followed by two questions. Long passages are approximately 400–850 words long and are typically followed by 8–13 questions.

The passages and questions are predictable. The topics are drawn from the humanities, social sciences, natural sciences, and fiction. The questions ask about the overall tone and content of a passage, the details used, and what the author's overall meaning may be. You will also have one or more Paired-Passage question sets consisting of two related excerpts. Those questions will ask you to compare and contrast the two passages.

Reading Comprehension questions are not arranged by difficulty. That means easy, medium, and hard questions can appear in any order. Any time you find yourself spending too much time on a question, skip it and return to it later.

● THE TRAP DOOR
Steering Clear of Answer Traps

Traps are lurking in every set of answer choices on the SAT Reading Comprehension questions. They don't change much from question type to question type, though, so here are the classics: those wrong-answer traps you'll see time and time again in all of the Reading Comprehension questions.

Out of the Scope of the Passage

Answers that are *out of scope* are the incorrect answers that students choose most frequently on SAT Inference questions. These answers are so tempting because they look good and sound good, but go beyond what is discussed in the passage. If you should happen to read a passage of which you already have some previous knowledge, be especially careful to avoid out of scope answer traps. Some of the answer choices may be true in the real world, but if they weren't discussed in the passage, they can't be the right answer. Remember, the SAT is not testing you on any previous knowledge that you may have; instead, the test-makers want to know whether you can answer questions correctly **based only on the information in the passage**. No previous knowledge is necessary!

Extremes

Extreme answers use extreme language. They exaggerate the correct answer and often use specific language like *always, never, all, no one,* and *every.* This is by no means a complete list of extreme words—you'll see other extreme words in practice questions throughout this book.

The test-makers will also exaggerate emotional language in an extreme trap. If the author finds a fact mildly disturbing, the right answer won't say that he finds that fact "tragically flawed." The only time an extreme answer could be correct is if you can find specific support for that extreme attitude or fact in the passage.

Misused Details

Another trap that the test-makers may set is to cite a specific detail from the passage in an answer choice, but that detail will have nothing to do with the question at hand. Misused details can be especially confusing in NOT or EXCEPT questions. Always keep in mind that the correct answer must address the question being asked, not just be found in the passage.

Opposites

It has been said that opposites attract—perhaps that is one of the reasons test-makers use this trap. Opposite answers are just wrong, but if you skim them too quickly, you might miss their inherent wrongness. Those little words like NOT or EXCEPT can change the whole meaning of an answer choice—watch out for them. Remember, these words can appear in question stems as well as answer choices so pay close attention while reading through both the question stems *and* the answer choices.

Distortions

Sometimes the test-maker will take a detail from the passage but distort it to mean something different from what it means in the text. A distortion may describe an inference that could be made from the reading or cite a specific detail, but the source of the information will be incorrect. Distortions are often half right and half wrong answers, which makes them totally wrong. You must read an entire answer choice in order to determine whether or not it is correct.

All of these traps can be avoided on Test Day with a little practice at identifying them. When you look at the Final Act at the end of each lesson, be sure to think about why answers are wrong, as well as why the correct answer is right!

LESSON 10

Mapping the Sentence

DIFFICULTY: ★ ★

FREQUENCY: ★ ★

SURPRISE FACTOR: ★ ★ ★ ★

● INTRODUCTION TO SENTENCE COMPLETION QUESTIONS

Sentence Completion questions take many students by surprise because they expect these questions to be simple fill-in-the-blanks. Instead, they find lots of confusing answer choices, more than one of which could work to answer the question correctly. After spending too much time debating the answers, they run out of time for the rest of the Critical Reading questions in those sections of the SAT. You could read many of the answer choices into the blank in the sentence and rationalize why several different answers might work. But there is always only one BEST answer! With the Kaplan Method for Sentence Completions, along with some practice, you will quickly find these questions easy to tackle.

There are 19 Sentence Completions on the SAT. Once you understand how to "map the sentence" (that is, to identify and mark the clue words the test maker has given you within each question), you will shine on test day. And while there are only

19 of these questions, they represent points that you can add to your score quickly and easily.

There are two types of Sentence Completion questions: One Blank and Two Blanks. We'll focus on the One Blank questions to start, but it's important to keep in mind that what you learn about One Blank Sentence Completions can be applied to the Two Blank questions as well.

● THE TRAP DOOR
Steering Clear of Answer Traps

Traps are harder to recognize in this section of the SAT. You will certainly see *opposite* answer choices, which you should avoid. Most wrong-answer choices can be eliminated if you locate the context clues in the sentence and use your prediction. If you don't make a prediction and simply read all of the answers back into the sentence, the choices may *seem* to make sense within the sentence, but *cannot* be supported by the contextual clues in the question stem.

Making a *prediction* based on the clue words in the sentence takes the guesswork out of choosing the right answer. So don't take shortcuts here or look at the answer choices before you've made your prediction! If you skip the step of predicting your own answer, many, if not all, of the answer choices can become tempting wrong-answer traps.

There are a few ways that the SAT makes Sentence Completions appear harder than they actually are. Once you learn what the test makers are doing to create more difficult questions, you can relax and stay focused on what's really important for the test.

Wordiness

Sometimes the sentence to be completed is long and wordy. This can make it harder to locate the necessary part(s) of the sentence and identify the clue words that will help you make your prediction. If you're faced with a wordy sentence, strip the sentence down to its bare bones—clue words that help define the blank and key punctuation. Pay attention to what's truly important and leave the rest behind.

Tough Vocabulary

Tougher Sentence Completion questions often contain words that are not commonly used. If a tough vocabulary word appears in the question stem, don't panic! You don't always have to know the exact definition of a tough word to get the right answer to the question. Instead you may be able to gather the meaning of the word from the context of the sentence.

If you see lots of tough vocabulary in the answer choices, don't fret! Sometimes the one word you do know will be the right answer, so don't be swayed by complex vocabulary in the answer choices if there's a simple word that matches your prediction. Breaking up answer choices into roots, prefixes, and suffixes can help you ascertain the *basic* meaning of the word. So you may not even have to know the exact definition to answer a Sentence Completion question correctly.

You can also use word charge (positive, negative, or neutral) to help you eliminate wrong answers. For example, if you can tell from the context of a sentence that you are searching for a negative word to fill in the blank, you can eliminate any positive words immediately. Although word charge is not the *most* reliable way to eliminate answers, it can be helpful when dealing with a question that you have a prediction for, but you are not certain of the meaning of tough vocabulary words. However, if you rely only on word charge to eliminate wrong answers on a Sentence Completion question, it's probably best to skip that one and come back to it at the end of the test section, if time allows.

Unpredictable Sentences

There may be a sentence that does not contain enough clue words to enable you to make a strong prediction. In these cases, you should plug the words back into the Sentence Completion to find the best word in context. Don't worry, though. These types of questions usually only occur once per test, or sometimes not at all.

● PERFORMANCE TECHNIQUES
Key Formulas and Rules

There are three steps to the Kaplan Method for Sentence Completion that you should apply every single time you encounter one of these questions. Aim to spend only 30 to 45 seconds on each Sentence Completion question.

Step 1: Read the Sentence, Looking for Clues

The two kinds of clue words that you want to pay close attention to are words that define the blank or words and phrases that indicate the relationship of the rest of the sentence to the blank.

Relationship words can show contrast between the blank and rest of the sentence. Or they may provide clues that show similarities between the blank and the rest of the sentence. For example, if you see *but* in a sentence immediately before the blank, it's almost a sure thing that the missing word will be the opposite of whatever words or phrase preceded *but*. Similarly, *and* indicates the right answer is a synonym for something else in the sentence.

Words that indicate a definition for the blank can often be plugged into the blank as your prediction. For instance, in the sentence "The murky water was so cloudy that we couldn't see the fish," if we substituted a blank for *murky,* then the word *cloudy* would work as our prediction for the blank.

To succeed at these questions you should practice identifying clue words so you can make strong predictions for the blank. Mark these clue words by underlining them, and create a "map" of the sentence that will lead you to the correct answer choice. With a trail of marks to follow, you can use the clue words to help you with the second step of the Kaplan Method—making a prediction.

Step 2: Make a Prediction

Creating a strong map for the sentence helps you make a strong prediction. Predictions don't have to be fancy words. Often words like *good* or *bad* can be enough. As was mentioned in the explanation of the first step, there are some Sentence Completion questions in which a word from the sentence can be used as your prediction and plugged directly into the blank. Other times, several words from the rest of the sentence will help you make a prediction for the blank. On a recent SAT, one-third of the Sentence Completions contained a word that led to an immediate prediction for the blank. On that same test, another one-third of the Sentence Completions contained words that were in direct contrast to the blank. Odds are strongly in your favor for answering the question correctly if you find the clue words, which will lead to a strong prediction.

Step 3: Select the Answer that Best Matches Your Prediction

Now that you have a prediction for the Sentence Completion question, compare your prediction to the actual answer choices. Eliminate any answers that don't match your prediction and pick the one that best matches your prediction.

● DRESS REHEARSAL
Sample Questions and Detailed Explanations

Take a look at these one-blank Sentence Completion questions and practice the Kaplan Method while working through each one.

Step 1: Read the sentence, looking for clues.

Remember to underline all clues!	Since the king was usually _____ in the assessment of his warriors, many people were surprised when he rewarded them all equally for their duties in battle.

Step 2: Make a prediction. _not humble_

Step 3: Select the answer that best matches your prediction.

(A) equitable

(B) cumulative

(C) unfair

(D) adulatory

(E) moderate

There are several clue words in this sentence. After the blank and the comma, we see that *people were surprised* the king was *equally* rewarding the warriors. Therefore, we need to predict a contrasting word. One that means NOT equal. In fact, you can just use *not equal*. That would immediately eliminate (A) and (E). (B) and (D) don't make sense within the context of the sentence and don't have anything to do with not being equal, so (C) is the best choice.

If there are any words you don't recognize in the question stem or answer choices, start a list of vocabulary words so that you can look up their definitions and study them.

Step 1: Read the sentence looking for clues.

2. Although the writer earned mild praise from her critics, she felt her books deserved more _____.

Step 2: Make a prediction. _aknowledgmen_

Step 3: Select the answer that best matches your prediction.

- (A) disdain
- (B) attitude
- (C) acclaim
- (D) deliberation
- (E) publicity

Although is a huge contrast clue, which should lead you to know that the blank will be a contrast to what is contained in the first part of the sentence. You also get a straight definitional word in this sentence, *praise*. You can use that word as your prediction. Acclaim (C) is the only word that matches with *praise*.

Step 1: Read the sentence, looking for clues.

3. In ancient Greece, people did not have e-mail, telephones, or fax machines, so all forms of correspondence were _____.

Step 2: Make a prediction. _deprived_

Step 3: Select the answer that best matches your prediction.

- (A) concurrent
- (B) illusory

(C) immutable

(D) inauspicious

(E) epistolary

This sentence is not very difficult to decipher, but when faced with the answer choices, you might need to take a deep breath. Remember, tough vocabulary shouldn't hold you back from eliminating answer choices based on your prediction. Look at roots, prefixes, and suffixes. Do any of these words sound familiar? Do they contain pieces of words that are familiar to you like concurrent in (A)? Sometimes all you need is the basic meaning of the word in order to eliminate it. And if you can eliminate one or more answers, always take a guess.

Since people in ancient times did NOT have electronic ways of communicating, correspondence must have been *handwritten*. You may have chosen another word for your prediction that meant something similar. It's important not to get hung up on trying to make the "perfect" prediction. You just need to choose a word that gives a basic meaning for the blank.

Great rehearsal! Now let's try out these methods on a test-like set of questions.

● **THE FINAL ACT**
Self-Check Quiz

This quiz should take no longer than seven and a half minutes.

1. The stock market is in a constant state of _____, moving up and down throughout the day.

   (A) delay

   (B) flux

   (C) stability

   (D) saturation

   (E) union

2. Worrisome parents are often seen as controlling, while they are really just trying to _____ their children.

(A) safeguard

(B) endanger

(C) remove

(D) compose

(E) enliven

3. Laurence Olivier, a _____ actor, won many prestigious awards throughout his career.

(A) charismatic

(B) keen

(C) terrifying

(D) celebrated

(E) creative

4. The military has created a(n) _____ plane that can fly silently under radar completely undetected by enemies.

(A) benevolent

(B) express

(C) stealth

(D) ambitious

(E) lucid

5. After so many failed experiments and so many long years of research, most leaders in the pharmaceutical industry did not believe the scientists would find a cure for the pervasive disease, but the _____ scientists were relieved when the results of the arduous drug trials were deemed a complete success.

(A) strong

(B) tenacious

(C) distraught

(D) eloquent

(E) irresolute

6. The mayor's _____ accomplishments were honored during a public ceremony.

   (A) morose

   (B) notable

   (C) fragile

   (D) didactic

   (E) clandestine

7. The maple syrup's _____ aromas filled the house with a nauseatingly sweet smell.

   (A) sour

   (B) remote

   (C) pathetic

   (D) cloying

   (E) coarse

8. The professor found the student's argument in favor of gun control _____ because it flew in the face of established reason.

   (A) sound

   (B) untenable

   (C) wicked

   (D) nefarious

   (E) predicated

9. The super villain's _____ plot to destabilize the government was so treacherous and subtle that it nearly caused a national disaster.

   (A) ostentatious

   (B) tolerable

   (C) eccentric

   (D) insidious

   (E) drab

10. Our club president has created feelings of acrimony between himself and the members with his _____ remarks during committee meetings.

(A) disparaging

(B) bleak

(C) diffident

(D) verbose

(E) affable

● ANSWERS AND EXPLANATIONS

1. **B**   The stock market *is* in a *constant state* of _____, *moving up and down throughout* the day.

The big clue words here are *moving up and down*. If you just put that phrase into the blank for your prediction, you can easily eliminate many of the answer choices. *Flux* is the word that best matches your prediction.

2. **A**   Worrisome parents *are* often *seen as controlling, while* they are really just trying to _____ their children.

You get a relationship clue in this sentence, as well as a definitional clue. *Worrisome* is in direct contrast to the blank because *while* is a contrast word. Your prediction might be something like *protect*, which would lead you to *safeguard*.

3. **D**   Laurence Olivier, a _____ actor, *won many prestigious awards* throughout his career.

If you simply read through the answers, there are several words that might seem like they could readily fit into the blank. However, if you map out the sentence, you will see the phrase *won many prestigious awards* and then make a prediction that has something to do with winning. Don't be fooled by other words that are often used to describe celebrities! The correct answer must make sense within the context of the sentence, meaning there must be some clue words to back up what is being said.

4. **C** The military has created a(n) _____ plane *that* can fly *silently* under radar, *completely undetected* by enemies.

Ask yourself what is a word that means *silently* and *completed undetected*? Or just put those words into the blank since this blank is asking for a straight definition. If there are any words contained in these answer choices that you are unfamiliar with, add them to your vocabulary list.
Benevolent—kind
Lucid—clear

5. **B** *After* so many *failed* experiments and so many *long years* of research, most leaders in the pharmaceutical industry did not believe the scientists would find a cure for the pervasive disease, but the _____ scientists were relieved when the results of the *arduous* drug trials were deemed a complete success.

The scientists were able to find a cure because they worked long and hard on the drug trials. Even if you're not sure what *arduous* means, you could come up with a prediction that means "working at something for a long time." This would help you eliminate several answers. Ask yourself does *strong* mean "working at it for a long time?" Does *distraught, eloquent,* or *irresolute* match "working at something for a long time?" If the answer is no, that answer can't be the **correct** answer.
Tenacious—stick firmly to a decision or opinion without changing or doubting it

6. **B** The mayor's _____ *accomplishments were honored* during a public ceremony.
What kind of *accomplishments* would be *honored*? Good ones! So look for a word that means good.
Morose—withdrawn and gloomy
Didactic—give instruction or advice, even when not wanted
Clandestine—secret, usually illegal

7. **D** The maple syrup's _____ aromas filled the house *with a nauseatingly sweet smell.*
Maple syrup is described as nauseatingly sweet in this sentence. Even if you don't know what cloying means, you can eliminate all the other words.

8. **B** The professor found the student's argument in favor of gun control _____ *because* it *flew in the face of established reason.* You get a strong relationship clue in *because* and definitional clues in the phrase *flew in the face of established reason.* You can predict "indefensible" or "ridiculous" once you've identified these clue words. *Sound* (A) is the opposite. *Wicked* (C) and *nefarious* (D) are distortions. And *predicated* means based on something that must come before it (E).

9. **D** The super *villain's* _____ plot to destabilize the government *was* so *treacherous and subtle* that it nearly caused a national *disaster.*

All of the clue words in this sentence point to something "very bad." You are faced with lots of tough vocabulary, so break the words down into roots, prefixes, and suffixes. Use word charge to help you, too.

Ostentatious—vulgar display of wealth
Eccentric—unconventional
Insidious—slowly and subtly destructive or harmful
Drab—dull, uninteresting

10. **A** Our club president *has created* feelings of *acrimony between* himself *and* the members *with* his _____ remarks during committee meetings.

Your clue word in this sentence is a tough vocabulary word, as are the answer choices. If you aren't sure of the vocabulary, use word charge, and roots, prefixes, and suffixes to help you. If you can't eliminate any answer choices, skip answering the question on the test.

Acrimony—bitterness and resentment in speech, attitude, or tone
Disparaging—disapproving
Bleak—without hope
Diffident—shy
Verbose—too long-winded or complicated
Affable—likable, friendly

LESSON 11

Two Blanks

DIFFICULTY: ★ ★

FREQUENCY: ★ ★

SURPRISE FACTOR: ★ ★ ★

● INTRODUCTION TO TWO BLANKS QUESTIONS

Two Blanks questions sound like what they are—Sentence Completions that are asking you to fill in two blanks instead of just one. On a recent SAT, just over half of the Sentence Completion questions had two blanks. Many students find Two Blanks questions easier than One Blank questions, but it's still important to take the time to find the clue words in each sentence. If you're not conscious of the relationship between the blanks, these questions could take you by surprise. Once you have a firm grasp on the Kaplan Method for Sentence Completions and see how it applies to Two Blanks, you will be able to gain points on these questions with ease.

In Two Blanks questions, the missing words sometimes appear right next to each other or on opposite ends of the sentence completion. In this chapter you will continue to work on mapping the sentence. By mapping the sentence, or marking clue words in the sentence, you focus your attention on the structural and definitional clues so you don't get lost.

These common relationships include: **similar** meaning, **contrasting** meaning, and **combined** meaning. Each type of relationship uses typical clue words that signal the kind of relationship the blanks share.

● THE TRAP DOOR
Steering Clear of Answer Traps

All of the answer traps that were discussed for One Blank Sentence Completions apply to Two Blanks, too. However, with Two Blanks you have added a blank, which means you have *double* the chances to eliminate wrong answers based on your prediction. You've doubled your odds at getting to the correct answer!

Since both blanks must be correct within the context of the sentence, you *must* pay attention to both words in the answer choices. One may work well while the other is completely wrong. Again, this just means you have two shots at eliminating the wrong answers, so always pay attention to both words in the answer choices.

● PERFORMANCE TECHNIQUES
Key Formulas and Rules

The Method

The three-step Kaplan Method for Sentence Completion is the same for two blanks as for one blank, but when it comes to predicting, there are a few things to be aware of.

First, if you can only make a prediction for one blank, that's OK. You can still eliminate answers based on the blank for which you've made a prediction. If one of the words in an answer choice pair is incorrect, then the whole answer must be wrong and therefore can be eliminated.

Next, you may feel more confident with your prediction for one of the blanks than the other. There's no obligation to look at the blanks in the order they appear, so feel free to first look at the blank for which you have a better prediction. Again, eliminate answers based on that blank and then plug the remaining choices back into the sentence to see which answer choice works best. There have been Two Blanks questions on the SAT that you answer correctly by only predicting and eliminating answer choices for one of the blanks.

Vocabulary Study

Studying vocabulary for the SAT may seem like a daunting challenge. First, let's determine some of the ways that you learn vocabulary best. Are you taking a foreign language right now? Think about how you study vocabulary for your French or Spanish class. Do you make flashcards, write word lists, group words together with similar meanings, write each word into a sentence? Maybe you do a combination of these techniques. And certainly your foreign language teacher assigns you reading material with the new vocabulary terms in context to help you remember the new words. All of these things can be applied to learning new words for the SAT.

As you work through the practice problems, write down words that you don't know and create a word list or flashcards to study those words. You can also look at the flashcards that are part of the online component of this book. Another way to learn new words is by getting definitions in context or using words in context, so read texts with challenging words or use vocabulary words to help cement new words into your vocabulary. Finally, try memorizing groups of roots, prefixes, and suffixes; with these vocabulary building blocks you will be able to understand the basic meaning of many words even if you don't know the exact definition. Studying Greek and Latin word roots and common prefixes and suffixes can make deciphering tough vocabulary words much easier on Test Day.

Sound daunting? It doesn't need to be. You don't need to study millions of new vocabulary words. Pick 15 to 20 new words to work on each week from now until two weeks before Test Day. Then use the two weeks before the SAT to review all of the words you've learned. Try using them when writing papers or speaking and that will help you cement these new words into your vocabulary quickly.

● DRESS REHEARSAL
Sample Questions and Detailed Explanations

The Kaplan Method remains the same here, but you get twice as many chances to eliminate wrong answers. Make and use your predictions quickly and watch your score increase.

Step 1: Read the sentence, looking for clues.

1. To an outsider, my friend's behavior may seem _____, but since I _____ his motives for behaving strangely in public, I don't find his behavior out of the ordinary.

Step 2: Make a prediction.

Blank 1: _rediculous_   Blank 2: _know_

Step 3: Select the answer that best matches your prediction.

(A) ~~ordinary~~..~~misinterpret~~

(B) peculiar..understand

(C) terrifying..guess

(D) ~~dull~~..create

(E) cautious..abhor

You get a terrific structural clue in *but since* which sets up a contrast between the blanks. You also get lots of definitional clues in this sentence—*outsider, friend, strangely, don't find out of the ordinary*. You could put strange directly into the first blank and then eliminate every choice except (B) just by looking at the first blank.

> Remember to cross off any answer that has a word in it that does not match your prediction!

Step 1: Read the sentence, looking for clues.

2. In our speech class, we all had to _____ a three-minute speech and then _____ it from memory for a grade.

Step 2: Make a prediction.

Blank 1: _create / learn_   Blank 2: _preform_

Step 3: Select the answer that best matches your prediction.

(A) interpret..learn

(B) recall..label

(C) evict . . verbalize

(D) memorize . . recite

(E) write . . mumble

These blanks are working together with similar meanings. Your biggest clue comes in the phrase *from memory*. Even if your predictions are simple like "do . . say," those predictions along with recognizing the clue from memory (do from memory...say from memory) will get you to eliminate the incorrect choices until you are left with (D), which matches your prediction well.

Great work! Let's try some sentences with tougher vocabulary.

Step 1: Read the sentence, looking for clues.

3. Despite the _____ behavior of the antihero in the story, he saves the community by making a(n) _____ donation to the community fund in the end.

Step 2: Make a prediction.

Blank 1: ___bad___   Blank 2: ___large___

Step 3: Select the answer that best matches your prediction.

(A) malevolent . . munificent

(B) altruistic . . enormous

(C) condescending . . meager

(D) obdurate . . insane

(E) unequivocal . . puny

Despite immediately alerts us to a contrast between the blanks. We get definitional clues in words like *antihero, saves,* and *donation*. These clues lead us to simple predictions like "bad" and "large." When we look at the blanks, we see there's tougher vocabulary that might stand in our way. If we take the first blank, we might only be able to get rid of one answer if you're unfamiliar with these vocabulary words. Maybe you were able to cross off more! However, if we consider the second blank with our prediction, we can easily get rid of (C), (D), and (E) since none of these words mean "large." Then you're left with (A) and (B).

Break down the roots in these words and you see that *mal*=bad and *vole*=wishing. If you didn't know this before, you'll know it now for Test Day, and that is what's most important. Even if you're not certain of any of the words in the two choices left, you're down to a 50/50 guess, which are great odds for guessing the correct answer.

Malevolent—having or showing a desire to harm others
Munificent—characterized by generosity
Altruistic—unselfishly concerned for the welfare of others
Meager—unsatisfactory in quantity, substance, or size
Obdurate—not easily persuaded or influenced
Unequivocal—allowing for no doubt or misinterpretation

Step 1: Read the sentence, looking for clues.

4. To an inexperienced trainer the dog appeared to be _____, whereas she could actually be quite _____.

In this sentence, are you able to make a prediction for the blanks? If you can't make a precise prediction for each blank, make sure you can identify the relationship between the blanks. Are these blanks similar, in direct contrast to one another, or do they share a combined meaning?

Step 2: Make a prediction.

What is the relationship between the blanks? _____
_____contrasting_____

Step 3: Select the answer that best matches your prediction.

(A) beautiful . . timid
(B) wild . . fearful
(C) docile . . aggressive
(D) hostile . . dangerous
(E) sleeping . . lethargic

While this sentence doesn't seem very difficult and doesn't contain many tough vocabulary words in the question stem or answer choices, it can have a surprising answer if you're thinking about the contrasting relationship between the blanks in only one way. The sentence doesn't provide any real definitional clues. The blanks could be predicted as "wild" and "tame" but there's no real way to know which blank should be which. We only know for certain that the relationship is a direct contrast because of the word *whereas*. (C) is the only answer choice that provides a direct contrast, even though some of the other answers may sound tempting. Since the questions are ordered by degree of difficulty, watch out for seemingly simple questions that have a specific relationship between the blanks.

Step 1: Read the sentence, looking for clues.

5. Even though we sometimes found it <u>difficult to understand</u> Beth's _____ political theories, none of us thought she was being _____ because we all knew that she had deep understanding of the current political climate.

Step 2: Make a prediction.

Blank 1: _arrange_   Blank 2: _unrealistic_

Step 3: Select the answer that best matches your prediction.

(A) learned .. amorphous

(B) insipid .. verbose

(C) loquacious .. terse

(D) erudite .. pretentious

(E) precocious .. ignorant

Structural clues: *Even though, none, because*
Definitional clues: *difficult to understand, she had a deep understanding of*
Predictions: complicated/particular/intelligent .. a know-it-all/smarty-pants

With these clues and a strong prediction, you can eliminate (E). By eliminating one answer, you know that you should take the guess. However, before taking a blind guess at the last four answers, look at roots, prefixes, and suffixes. There are a lot of those in this group of answer choices. Take a look at the definitions below to see how roots, prefixes, and suffixes can help you gather meaning for a word.

Amorphous—having no defined shape
    A = without/not   Morph = shape
Insipid—dull or bland
    In = in/not
Verbose—expressed in or using language that is too long-winded or complicated
    Verb = word
Loquacious—tending to talk a great deal
    Loq/Loc/Log = speech/word
Terse—brief and unfriendly, often conveying annoyance
Erudite—having or showing great knowledge gained from study and reading
Precocious—more developed, especially mentally, than is normal at a particular age
    Pre = before   Coc/Cogn = know
Make good use of your study time by learning the meanings of roots, prefixes, and suffixes.

● THE FINAL ACT
Self-Check Quiz

This quiz should take no longer than seven and a half minutes.

1. No one believed she could _____ such an act, after the tearful story she gave to the media professing her _____.

   (A) enable .. conscience

   (B) commit .. innocence

   (C) create .. deliverance

   (D) apply .. guilt

   (E) defend .. love

2. The professor _____, for what seemed an eternity, leaving us with no _____ notes to study for our exam.

   (A) carried on .. legible

   (B) cried out .. clear

   (C) spoke .. special

   (D) rambled on .. coherent

   (E) mumbled .. foggy

3. Many times the prophet was correct in his prescience, so when he
   _____ the year's upcoming _____, we always listened carefully.

   (A) acquired . . events

   (B) denied . . desires

   (C) averred . . tasks

   (D) predicted . . happenings

   (E) admired . . disasters

4. The screenwriter's critics scoffed at his claim of genius, pointing
   out the writer's _____ output of two scripts over the last 20 years,
   which was only _____ by the movies' clichéd themes.

   (A) meager . . underscored

   (B) prodigious . . trivialized

   (C) brilliant . . emphasized

   (D) declining . . measured

   (E) unremarkable . . terrorized

5. The usually _____ secretary, who always smiles at me when I come
   in, must have been having a bad day based on her _____ answer
   to my simple question.

   (A) tyrannical . . rude

   (B) mitigating . . concise

   (C) hassled . . sympathetic

   (D) affable . . terse

   (E) curt . . garrulous

6. John made a _____ error in judgment when he ran the red light
   and _____ another car.

   (A) lovely . . flew past

   (B) beautiful . . crashed into

   (C) moronic . . skirted by

   (D) complete . . met with

   (E) colossal . . collided with

7. She invested in technology stocks at a(n)_____ moment, just before the market _____.

  (A) great . . collapsed

  (B) precarious . . doubled

  (C) opportune . . exploded

  (D) indigenous . . shrank

  (E) illegal . . cracked

8. The new kid at school was _____; after she made fun of the popular and kind class president, the whole school _____ her.

  (A) elated . . hated

  (B) quieted . . loved

  (C) depressed . . helped

  (D) ostracized . . shunned

  (E) derided . . respected

9. The mayor's _____ remarks nearly _____ a riot.

  (A) incendiary . . stopped

  (B) inflammatory . . incited

  (C) timely . . caused

  (D) witty . . charged

  (E) compassionate . . instigated

10. The _____ had horded his money for so long, no one expected the _____ old man to give anyone anything.

  (A) malefactor . . magnanimous

  (B) curmudgeon . . inauspicious

  (C) charlatan . . sagacious

  (D) philanthropist . . greedy

  (E) miser . . penurious

● ANSWERS AND EXPLANATIONS

1. **B** *No one* believed she could _____ such an act, *after* the tearful story she gave to the media *professing* her _____.

Based on the clues, you are looking for a relationship that has combined meaning. If no one believes she could have "done" something, then she was likely "innocent" (B).

2. **D** The professor _____, *for what seemed an eternity*, leaving us with <u>no</u> _____ notes <u>to</u> *study* for our exam.

Your biggest clue in this sentence is the definitional phrase following the first blank. You then get a second structural clue as well as definitional information surrounding the second blank. Your predictions might be "talked...clear" and that could lead you to (D). (A) might seem tempting, but *legible* means to write something clearly, so if the professor was talking, we wouldn't refer to speech as *legible*.

3. **D** *Many* times the prophet was correct in his *prescience, so when* he _____ the year's *upcoming* _____, we *always* listened carefully.

If you know the meaning of *prophet* and *prescience*, this sentence is easier than it would be if you don't. Maybe you are familiar with the word *prophet*, but not *prescience*. In any case, think about what a prophet does and you can make a prediction for the first blank, "told the future." A good prediction for the second blank would be "events." However, in this question the first blank is enough to get you to the right answer since *acquired, denied, averred,* and *admired* don't match. If you don't know the meaning of *averred*, the second blank would help you to eliminate (C), leaving (D) as the correct answer.

4. **A** The screenwriter's *critics scoffed* at his *claim of genius*, pointing out the writer's _____ output of two scripts over the last 20 years, *which was only* _____ by the movies' *clichéd* themes.

Critics scoffing is *not* a good thing, so we know we're looking for something negative. Further clues indicate that the writer only wrote two scripts in 20 years, which doesn't seem like a lot, so our prediction could be "small..made worse."

Prodigious—great in amount
Meager—unsatisfactory in quantity

5. **D** The *usually* ____ secretary, *who always smiles* at me when I come in, must have been having a *bad* day based on her ____ answer to my simple question.

This sentence has very few structural clues and many more definitional clues. Since the secretary always *smiles*, we can conclude her *bad day* was indicated by a "negative" answer. Just use "smiling..negative" for your prediction. There's some tough vocabulary, but use roots, prefixes, suffixes, and word charge to help eliminate answers. And add these words to your vocabulary flashcards or list.

Tyrannical—rule with absolute power

Mitigating—capable of making something less harsh, severe, or violent

Concise—expressing necessary information in as few words as possible

Affable—good-natured, friendly

Terse—brief and unfriendly, often conveying annoyance

Curt—rude or abrupt

Garrulous—excessively or pointlessly talkative

6. **E** John made a ____ *error* in judgment *when* he ran the red light *and* ____ *another* car.

When people run *red lights*, bad things often happen. So the second blank is easier to predict than the first, "crashed into." You could get rid of (A), (C), and (D). An *error in judgment* is not often referred to in a positive way, which leaves you with (E).

7. **C** She invested in technology stocks at a(n) ____ moment, *just before* the market ____.

All we really know about these two blanks is that they will have a similar relationship, so eliminate any word pairs that don't have similar meaning.

Precarious—dangerously unstable

Opportune—occurring at just the right time

Indigenous—originating in/typical of a region or country

8. **D** The new kid at school was ____ ; *after* she made fun of the *popular and kind* class president, the *whole* school ____ her.

If a person who is new to a situation makes fun of a person who is well liked by the established group, the outcome is going to be negative. Based on these clues, you should look for a word pair with two negative words.

Elated—made somebody very happy and excited

Ostracize—banish or exclude somebody from society or a group

Shun—to avoid somebody or something intentionally

Deride—to ridicule or show contempt for someone/thing

9. B The mayor's _____ remarks *nearly* _____ a *riot*.

Although it is difficult to tell whether these blanks are positive or negative, we can tell that they have similar meaning. Either the *mayor's* "positive" *remarks nearly* "stopped" *a riot*, or his "angry" *remarks nearly* "started" *a riot*. So, you are looking for a word pair with similar meaning.

Incendiary—flammable; designed to cause civil unrest

Inflammatory—liable to arouse strong emotions, especially anger

Incite—to stir up feeling in or provoke action by somebody

Instigate—to cause trouble

10. E The _____ had *horded his money* for *so long*, *no one* expected the _____ old man to *give anyone anything*.

You get lots of clues in this sentence, with lots of tough vocabulary to deal with in the answer choices. Your predictions don't need to be fancy; "greedy man" and "greedy" will work. Then you would need to use roots, prefixes, and suffixes to determine the basic meaning of any of the words you don't know. Also, word charge could be very helpful since you know you're looking for two negative words.

Malefactor—evildoer

Magnanimous—generous

Curmudgeon—bad-tempered, disagreeable, or stubborn person

Inauspicious—suggesting that success is unlikely

Charlatan—someone who falsely claims a special skill or expertise

Sagacious—wise, intelligent, and having good judgment

Philanthropist—one who improves the welfare of humanity, especially through charity

Miser—a greedy person

Penurious—having little money; not generous with money

LESSON 12

Inference

DIFFICULTY: ★ ★ ★ ★

FREQUENCY: ★ ★

SURPRISE FACTOR: ★

● INTRODUCTION TO INFERENCE QUESTIONS

Have you ever been asked to draw a conclusion based on the way a person is behaving? For instance, if your friend tells you she has "something to talk to you about" while fidgeting and avoiding eye contact, you can conclude that she has bad news. On the other hand, if she runs up to you and gives you a hug while shouting, "I have something to talk to you about!" you can infer that the news is good. When you make a reasonable assumption based on information you have, you are making an inference. An inference is a logical conclusion drawn from reasoning and evidence.

Inference questions comprise one-fifth of the passage-based questions of the Critical Reading test on the SAT. Many students find this type of question to be the most challenging because these questions ask you to look beyond the specific details in a passage and *infer* what the author did not explicitly write. Inference questions seek an answer that is not directly stated on the page, so you must deduce what the author was "getting at" instead of pointing to a line in the passage. It is important to remember that the answers to Inference questions are *not* simply a matter of opinion. There *is* a right answer. The strategies in this chapter can help you get there.

Lucky for you, Inference questions on the SAT can come in a few easy-to-recognize forms! The question stems typically use words like *most likely means, suggests,* or *implies.* Once in a while test-makers even use the word *infer.* Some Inference questions ask you to deduce the author's thoughts or feelings. Other questions may explore the author's attitude toward another researcher's evidence. If you are reading a fiction passage, these questions could ask you to assess a character's relationship with another character, or a character's thoughts and feelings. Some Inference questions ask you to deduce something from a specific part of the passage, while others ask you to conclude something from the passage as a whole.

Inference questions may also ask you to consider two or more pieces of information from different parts of the passage and draw a conclusion based on the combined meaning from each set of information. These questions ask you to "connect-the-dots" between pieces of information in the passage. For example, if a passage contains a series of reasons supporting the author's point, an Inference question might ask you which is the most important supporting factor. Based on the content of the passage (which reason the author stresses, which reason is mentioned most often or discussed in the most detail), you can logically identify the primary supporting factor.

By learning what an Inference question looks like on the SAT, you will know what tools to use to attack these challenging questions.

● THE TRAP DOOR
Steering Clear of Answer Traps

While there are a few different traps throughout the Critical Reading section, there are certain traps that you will see more often in Inference questions. Of these, one particular type of trap causes students to trip and fall on Inference questions more often than any other trap.

Answers that are *out of scope* are the incorrect answers that students choose most frequently on SAT Inference questions. Be on the lookout for out-of-scope answers in the Inference answer choices. They appear frequently, and are *never* the right answer.

Don't forget the other answer traps, too—distortions, misused details, extremes, and opposites. They may not be as treacherous as the dreaded out-of-scope trap, but they can definitely affect your score. Another thing to keep in mind is that Inference questions don't ask you for specific detailed information, but rather ask you to deduce something *from* the details. Therefore, if you see a misused detail as an answer, it can *never* be the correct answer to an Inference question.

● **PERFORMANCE TECHNIQUES**
Key Formulas and Rules

There are rules to keep in mind when tackling the Inference questions. The first rule deals with how you read the passage on Test Day.

Actively Read!

As you read through the passages in the Critical Reading section, pay close attention to the author's attitude, thoughts, and feelings. Notate the author's thoughts by underlining that information. If you come across an attitude, thought, or feeling that is *not* the author's but belongs to someone else, mark that part of the passage by circling the information. Underlining means the author is saying it. Circling means someone else is saying it.

Also, remember that some Inference questions ask about the passage as a whole. Pause after reading through the passage and before you jump into the questions to put the main point of the passage into your own words.

Why Is More Important Than *What*

Any time you are faced with an Inference question that is specifically asking about thoughts, feelings, or relationships, pay close attention to *why*—why a certain sentence has been written or why a character behaves the way she does. Focusing on all of the details, instead of focusing on *why*, can be time-consuming and lead you away from the right answer.

Predict before You Peek

Once you've researched the passage for the information you need to answer the question, you then need to take another step and formulate a prediction in order to avoid making mistakes on this SAT question type. Many students resist making a prediction to the answer choice and are then easily tempted away from the correct answer. Out-of-scope, extreme, and distorted answers can look very tempting if you haven't tried to answer the question in your own words before looking at the answer choices provided by the test-makers.

It's Not a Matter of Opinion

The SAT is a standardized test with multiple-choice answers for the Critical Reading test. There is always one right answer and four wrong answers on Inference questions. You should never allow yourself to be tricked into thinking you can't figure out the right answer because it is a matter of opinion. The answer will take the next logical step in thought based on the information that is in the passage.

Eliminate Wrong Answer Choices

Any time you can eliminate a common wrong answer trap from the answer choices, do it! It's always best to increase your chances of getting the correct answer by eliminating the answers that are obviously wrong. If you are ever unable to make a prediction about the answer or are having a difficult time locating the right answer, start crossing off the wrong answers. By crossing off the wrong answer choices, you give your brain a bit of a break because you won't continue to reread answers that you know are wrong.

● DRESS REHEARSAL
Sample Questions and Detailed Explanations

Here are two sample passages with questions. Use the Kaplan Method for Reading Comprehension to work through all reading passages.

Kaplan Method for Reading Comprehension

Step 1: Read the passage, taking notes.

Step 2: Examine the question stem.

Step 3: Predict an answer and **select** the answer that best matches your prediction.

Questions 1 and 2 refer to the following passage.

Step 1: Read the passage, taking notes.

Remember to read through the passage quickly, focusing on why—why did the author write this?—as well as on the author's thoughts, feelings, and attitude. Take notes!

The librarian raised his brow as he found the evidence in my bag. I stood before him, a college student who refused to shave, sporting a black beret and dark glasses. I wanted to follow my parents' example; they had fought the Communists in Russia by running an underground
(5) museum. None of this mattered to my accuser. He simply removed the book from my bag and reminded me in his purple air that "one does not take books from the Bodleian Library at the University of Oxford—not even Her Majesty the Queen possesses borrowing privileges." I walked away, but not before proclaiming, "This library is an evil institution like
(10) the Soviet Union, and I am attempting to liberate information!"

Step 2: Examine the question stem.

What is this question asking you? Where can you find that information in the passage?

1. Based on the passage, the narrator feels that information

Step 3: Predict an answer

Now that you've found the information write your prediction in the blank below.

That it's free + people should b allowed to leave w/ books

and **select** the answer that best matches your prediction.

(A) should be guarded

(B) belongs to the public

> Do these answers match your prediction? If not, cross them off.

(C) is unavailable to the Queen

(D) does not cost anything

(E) is a precious gift

The correct answer is (B). The narrator says, "I am attempting to liberate information!" as he is trying to take a book from the library that is not available for checkout. It is reasonable to assume that he believes that the information contained in the book should be available to people to check out of the library. (B) is a good restatement of that idea, while (A) is the opposite. Since the librarian mentions the book is not even available to the Queen, but that fact doesn't answer the question, (C) is a misused detail. Even though *liberate* means to free, it doesn't have anything to do with the cost of information (D), and (E) is out of the scope of the passage. The narrator may or may not believe that information is a *precious gift*, but there's nothing in the passage to tell us that.

Repeat Step 2: Examine the question stem.

What is this question asking you? Where can you find that information in the passage?

2. The narrator's use of the term "purple air" suggests he thinks the librarian is

Step 3: Predict an answer

Now that you've found the information, write your prediction in the blank below

stuo snobish

and **select** the answer that best matches your prediction.

(A) dismayed by the student's impudence

(B) better than anyone else

(C) certain the student understands that books cannot leave the library

(D) of royal blood

(E) evil like the Soviet Union

The correct answer is (C). The narrator's description of the librarian is followed by a quote that tells us no one has borrowing privileges at the library, a policy we can assume the student knows about since he hid the book inside his bag (C). (A) is a distortion since the librarian seems more haughty than dismayed. In the passage, the narrator refers to the library as *an evil institution like the Soviet Union*, but not to the librarian (E). While (B) and (D) might each make sense out of the context of the passage, neither of them make any sense within the context of the passage, so both of these answers are out of scope.

Now let's take a look at a longer passage. Inference questions 3 through 5 refer to the following passage.

Repeat Step 1: Read the passage, taking notes.

As you read the passage, **take notes** on the author's purpose, thoughts, and feelings in each paragraph. These notes will help you focus on what's important for answering questions on the SAT.

Aside from her hardships, the other thing that Boori Ma, who swept the staircases of the old building in Calcutta, liked to chronicle was easier times. And so, by the time she had swept the stairs up to the second-floor landing, she had already drawn the whole building's
(5) attention to the menu of her third daughter's wedding. "She married a school principal. The rice was cooked in rosewater. The mayor was invited. Everybody washed their fingers in pewter bowls."

Here she paused, evened out her breath, and readjusted the broom under her arm. "Not that this was an extravagance for us. We
(10) had a big house, and a pond on our property, full of fish. A man came to pick our dates and guavas. Yes, there I tasted life. Here I eat my dinner from a rice pot." At this point in the recital, Boori Ma's ears started to burn; a pain chewed through her swollen knee. "Have I mentioned that I crossed the border with just two bracelets on my wrist? Yet once
(15) there was a day when my feet touched nothing but marble. Believe me; don't believe me; you can't even dream of such comforts."

Whether there was any truth to Boori Ma's litanies no one could be sure. For one thing, every day, the perimeters of her former estate seemed to double, as did the contents of her jewelry box. No one
(20) doubted that she had come to Calcutta as a refugee, but the residents of the building found it hard to reconcile Boori Ma's stories of her former wealth with the stories of how she had come to the city: on the back of a truck, between sacks of grain.

"What kind of landowner ended up sweeping stairs?" That was
(25) what Mr. Dalal on the third floor always wondered as he passed Boori
Ma on the way to and from the office. "She probably constructs tales
as a way of mourning the loss of her family," was the collective hypothesis of many of the women in the building.

So she garbled facts. She contradicted herself. She embellished
(30) almost everything. But her rants were so persuasive, her fretting so
vivid, that it was not so easy to dismiss her. And all agreed that she
was a superb entertainer, and she kept the crooked stairwell spotlessly clean.

Repeat Step 2: Examine the question stem.

3. The first paragraph suggests

Repeat Step 3: Predict an answer

she been through some tough time.
+ she talks a lot

and **select** the answer that best matches your prediction.

Did you remem-
ber to cross off the
answers that didn't
match your predic-
tion? Crossing off an-
swers relieves strain.
Don't overtax your
brain by asking it to
do more work than it
has to on Test Day.

(A) Boori Ma was a key member of Calcutta's
     society

(B) Boori Ma exaggerated all of her stories

(C) Boori Ma enjoyed an easy life

(D) Boori Ma's daughter was a schoolteacher

(E) Boori Ma liked to talk about the good
     and bad parts of her life

The correct choice is (E). Since this
question refers specifically to the first
paragraph, that should be the only
information considered for answer-
ing this question. The first paragraph says that aside from her
hardships Boori Ma also like to chronicle easier times. You can
take this to mean that she enjoyed sharing both the good and
the bad stories from her life (E). (B) may seem tempting, but
remember the question is only asking us to consider the information in the first paragraph, so (B) is out of the scope of the
first paragraph. Even though we later learn the Boori Ma exag-
gerates her stories, we don't know that in the first paragraph.
The passage mentions that the mayor of Calcutta was invited

to her daughter's wedding and that her daughter married a school principal, but neither of these facts is enough to support (A) or (D). (C) is an opposite.

Repeat Step 2: Examine the question stem.

4. The author would most likely agree that

Step 3: Predict an answer and **select** the answer that best matches your prediction. Sometimes prediction is not possible. If you see a question for which you can't make a prediction, just focus on the author's point of view, and eliminate answers that don't correspond with the main point of the passage.

(A) despite her contradictions, Boori Ma was well liked by the residents of the building

(B) Boori Ma's neighbors thought she was a malicious liar

(C) no one in Calcutta liked Boori Ma

(D) the political and ideological differences in Calcutta forced Boori Ma to leave the country as a refugee

(E) rice tastes best when cooked in rosewater

(A) is the correct answer. In the last paragraph, the author sums up the thoughts that other people have about Boori Ma and her stories. The residents agree that she is a *superb entertainer* and *not so easy to dismiss*, despite her obvious embellishments and contradictions (A). Nothing supports that the tenants of the building thought she was being hurtful with her lies (B) or that she was not liked by anyone (C), both of which are extreme answers. (D) and (E) are both out of the scope of the passage since we don't know exactly what made Boori Ma a refugee from Calcutta or whether or not the author has even tasted rice cooked in rosewater.

Repeat Step 2: Examine the question stem.

5. The passage suggests that the residents believe Boori Ma

Repeat Step 3: Predict an answer

dealing with the loss of her
family

and **select** the answer that best matches your prediction.

(A) would make an excellent public speaker

(B) works too hard

(C) was once a wealthy princess

(D) finds it difficult to deal with the loss of her family

(E) is the best cleaning woman they have ever had

The correct answer choice is (D). The passage states that the collective hypothesis of the women in the building was that Boori Ma tells stories *as a way of mourning the loss of her family* (D). Although she seems tired in the story from her work, the passage doesn't say anything about whether or not the residents believe she works too hard (B), and while they enjoy and are persuaded by her stories, there's nothing to support the belief that she would be a good public speaker (A). (C) is incorrect since there is no mention of Boori Ma being royalty. (E) may be a tempting answer, but is too extreme. The passage does say that she keeps the stairwell spotlessly clean, but doesn't indicate any thoughts about previous cleaning staff.

Did You Remember To

- Notate the passage as you read, looking for the author's purpose
- Skim through details
- Focus on why
- Read the question stem deliberately
- Make a prediction
- Eliminate wrong answers

● THE FINAL ACT
Self-Check Quiz

Questions 1 and 2 refer to the following passage.

Hollywood has been more than a little kind to him, a boy who knew fame before most children learn their own name. He was an instant hit, a beautiful baby who appeared on commercials for diapers and showed up on sitcoms as a newborn star. When he reached the age (5) of 12, his experience as a child actor earned him a coveted role on

Broadway and propelled him into Hollywood. By 25, after years of hard work, he was richer than his wildest dreams. He devoted the next two decades to public service and philanthropy, creating a charity to support arts education for underprivileged children—perhaps to find
(10) the next child star—and supporting antifamine efforts in Africa.

1. The passage suggests the actor in the story

(A) became famous almost immediately after birth

(B) was only a modest success

(C) found fame at 25 years of age

(D) lived in Africa

(E) was only interested in philanthropy

2. The actor in the passage most likely discovered

(A) he could do more with his fame than just act by creating a philanthropic organization

(B) he'd wanted to act on Broadway since he was a child

(C) making money was more important than dedicating his life to public service

(D) a love for teaching new artists

(E) the next child star

Questions 3 and 4 refer to the following passage.

Although not quite as famously endemic of the Everglades as the American crocodile, the far more endearing manatee is perhaps more symbolic of the unique wildlife found in this vast tropical swamp. In particular, the manatees found in the Florida Everglades, though
(5) occasionally observed in unprotected waterways in the northern regions of the state, are rarely found anywhere else in the country. This manatee concentration in southern Florida is not surprising, given the fact that swimming in water even a single degree colder than 68° Fahrenheit can be fatal to these bulbous, slow, and exceed-
(10) ingly fragile creatures.

3. Manatees are most likely considered to be

(A) endangered animals

(B) are never seen by humans

(C) food for other animals

(D) less widely known than crocodiles

(E) friendly creatures

4. Based on the passage, one could infer that manatees could not live

(A) with American crocodiles

(B) in cold Alaskan waters

(C) anywhere outside of southern Florida

(D) without large quantities of fresh plant life for food

(E) unless protected by human beings

Questions 5 through 10 refer to the following passage.

The Bet
By Anton P. Chekhov

It was a dark autumn night. The old banker was pacing from corner to corner of his study, recalling to his mind the party he gave in the autumn fifteen years before. There were many clever people at the party and much interesting conversation. They talked among other
(5) things of capital punishment....Some of them thought that capital punishment should be replaced universally by life-imprisonment.

"I don't agree with you," said the host. "I myself have experienced neither capital punishment nor life-imprisonment, but...in my opinion capital punishment is more moral and more humane than
(10) imprisonment. Execution kills instantly, life-imprisonment kills by degrees. Who is the more humane executioner, one who kills you in a few seconds or one who draws the life out of you incessantly, for years?"

Among the company was a lawyer, a young man of about twenty-
(15) five. On being asked his opinion, he said, "Capital punishment and life-imprisonment are equally immoral; but if I were offered the choice between them, I would certainly choose the second. It's better to live somehow than not to live at all."

There ensued a lively discussion. The banker who was then
(20) younger and more nervous suddenly lost his temper, banged his fist on the table, and turning to the young lawyer, cried out, "It's a lie. I bet you two millions you wouldn't stick in a cell even for five years."

"If you mean it seriously," replied the lawyer, "then I bet I'll stay not five but fifteen."

(25)   "Fifteen! Done!" cried the banker. "Gentlemen, I stake two millions..."

So this wild, ridiculous bet came to pass. The banker, who at that time had too many millions to count, spoiled and capricious, was beside himself with rapture. During supper he said to the lawyer
(30) jokingly, "Come to your senses, young roan, before it's too late. Two millions are nothing to me, but you stand to lose three or four of the best years of your life. I say three or four, because you'll never stick it out any longer. Don't forget either, you unhappy man, that voluntary is much heavier than enforced imprisonment. The idea that you have
(35) the right to free yourself at any moment will poison the whole of your life in the cell. I pity you."

And now the banker, pacing from corner to corner, recalled all this and asked himself, "Why did I make this bet? What's the good? The lawyer loses fifteen years of his life and I throw away two millions. Will
(40) it convince people that capital punishment is worse or better than imprisonment for life? No, no! all stuff and rubbish. On my part, it was the caprice of a well-fed man; on the lawyer's pure greed of gold."...

Fifteen years before he had too many millions to count, but now he was afraid to ask himself which he had more of, money or debts.
(45) Gambling on the Stock-Exchange, risky speculation, and the reckless-ness of which he could not rid himself even in old age, had gradually brought his business to decay; and the fearless, self-confident, proud man of business had become an ordinary banker, trembling at every rise and fall in the market.

(50)   "That cursed bet," murmured the old man clutching his head in despair…."Why didn't the man die? He's only forty years old. He will take away my last farthing, marry, enjoy life, gamble on the Exchange, and I will look on like an envious beggar and hear the same words from him every day: 'I'm obliged to you for the happiness of my life.
(55) Let me help you.' No, it's too much! The only escape from bankruptcy and disgrace—is that the man should die."

5. The banker's attitude toward the lawyer during the party could
    best be described as

    (A) dangerous

    (B) condescending

    (C) infuriating

(D) enthusiastic

(E) cold

6. The author regards the banker as

 (A) an impulsive and wild gambler

 (B) an empathetic figure in this tragic tale

 (C) thoughtful and courageous risk taker

 (D) a commentator reflecting on an educational experience

 (E) an adult reminiscing fondly about his youth

7. The author implies that the primary reason the banker takes the bet is to

 (A) make a serious point about the nature of capital punishment

 (B) earn a better reputation with his party guests

 (C) enliven the atmosphere at the party

 (D) prove he is right and the lawyer is wrong without considering the consequences

 (E) promote capital punishment as a solution to over-crowded prisons

8. The author suggests the bet is

 (A) unable to determine whether capital punishment is right or wrong

 (B) a preposterous idea based on the complete recklessness of two young and egotistical professionals

 (C) made in haste but given careful consideration by both gentlemen

 (D) encouraged by the other guests at the party

 (E) is almost called off by the lawyer during dinner

9. The statement in lines 33–36 ("Don't forget either, you unhappy man") is best interpreted as conveying

 (A) doubt in the ability to hold one's self accountable for wrongdoings

 (B) a recognition of the banker's doubts in the bet he has made

 (C) the difficulty of enduring being imprisoned by one's own choice rather than by being forcibly imprisoned

(D) bets do not prove the validity of capital punishment

(E) frustration at the impossibility of knowing what might have been

10. In the last paragraph of the passage, the banker most likely believes

(A) the lawyer is a more ethical man than he is

(B) bets of this nature should never be made

(C) he is poor

(D) the lawyer is not interested in his money

(E) the only remedy to his dilemma is to kill the lawyer

● ANSWERS AND EXPLANATIONS

1. **A** The passage states the actor knew fame before most children know their own names, and that he appeared in diaper commercials, so (A) fits this description of the actor's fame best. (B) is the opposite of what we learn from the passage, and although the actor's fame is talked about at the age of 25, the passage infers that his fame began before that (C). (D) is out of the scope of the passage since it never tells us where he lived, and (E) is an extreme answer.

2. **A** Since the passage tells us that the actor began charity work after becoming rich and famous, we can conclude that he made a discovery about the power of fame and wealth and using those things for a good purpose (A). (C) is exactly the opposite of this. (B), (D), and (E) are all details mentioned in the passage, but they don't answer the question at hand.

3. **D** The passage states that manatees are *not quite as famously endemic of the Everglades as the American crocodile* which leads us to believe they are less known than the crocodile (D). Although manatees might be endangered species, might be prey for other animals, and might be friendly, the passage doesn't ever say anything about any of these qualities (A), (C), and (E). (B) uses the classic extreme word *never* which makes a claim unsupported by the passage.

4. **B** The passage states that manatees die if water temperatures drop below 68 degrees, so it is safe to assume that cold waters as far north as Alaska are not a suitable environment for the manatee (B). Although crocodiles are mentioned in the passage, we don't know if these creatures live in harmony or in the same environments so (A) is out of scope. The dietary needs of these animals (D) are not discussed nor is their ability to live without human protection (E) so these are also out of scope. (C) is an extreme answer since the passage says that manatees are *rarely* seen outside of southern Florida.

5. **B** This is one of those Inference questions that asks you to connect the dots. The banker bangs his fists on the table and *cries out* at the lawyer, later joking with him over dinner and calling him a *young roan*, inferring that the banker believes the lawyer is too young to understand what he's gotten himself into (B). (A) and (C) both refer to the banker's attitude later in the story when the lawyer is about to be freed and win the bet. (D) is the way the banker feels about the bet, but not how he feels toward the lawyer, a distortion, while (E) is the opposite since the banker is excited by the prospect of the bet with the lawyer.

6. **A** The author uses many words to describe the banker: *younger, nervous, spoiled, capricious*. He also says that the banker engaged in risky speculation and recklessness even as an older man (A). (B) and (E) are quite the opposite of how the banker is portrayed by the author. Even though the banker is learning some very difficult lessons, he is not the commentator in the story, so (D) is a distortion. The author's description of the banker takes place in the past, but the banker is not remembering the past *fondly* (E).

7. **D** The author's emphasis throughout the beginning of the passage is on the banker's wildly impulsive nature and his passionate belief in his own opinions (D). The bet is not about capital punishment, but more so about the banker's belief in himself and his own ideas (A) and (E). And while the party certainly becomes more frenzied around the discussion and bet, the banker doesn't make the bet simply to make the party

more lively or to look good in front of his guests (C) and (B). All of the wrong answers here are out of the scope of the passage.

8. **A** The author's main point in the passage is that this bet doesn't prove anything about the morality of capital punishment, but instead suggests that the bet proves something about the nature of the banker and the lawyer (A). (B) is a tempting answer, but uses language that creates an extreme answer that cannot be supported by the passage. (C) is the opposite of what the passage says, and (E) is a distortion since it is the banker who asks the lawyer to reconsider the bet over dinner. (D) is out of the scope of the passage since the other party guests' feelings are not mentioned.

9. **C** (C) is a good restatement of the quote from the passage. (A), (B), and (D) don't have any thing to do with the question at hand. (E) sounds tempting but is too broad and is therefore out of the scope of the passage.

10. **E** In the last paragraph the banker says, "The only escape from bankruptcy and disgrace—is that the man should die." We can assume that since he uses the word *only* he believes the lawyer's death is the way out of his problem (E). At this point in the story the banker has made no revelations about his own rash nature so (A) and (B) are incorrect. (C) might seem tempting since the banker is lamenting potential loss of his money, but he still has at least two million to pay the lawyer with. (D) is the opposite of what the banker believes.

Vocabulary in Context

DIFFICULTY: ★ ★

FREQUENCY: ★

SURPRISE FACTOR: ★ ★ ★ ★

● INTRODUCTION TO VOCABULARY-IN-CONTEXT QUESTIONS

Although these questions appear to be "easy," they are known for catching students off guard. They don't appear on the test as frequently as the other question types, but Vocabulary-in-Context questions can help you quickly gain points.

Vocabulary-in-Context questions are just that—getting the meaning of a word based on the way it is used in the sentence. Studying vocabulary words is not likely to help you with these questions (even though you should be strategically studying vocabulary words to help with Sentence Completion questions). However, thinking about answering Vocabulary-in-Context questions in a way similar to answering Sentence Completions will be helpful.

You will only see two different kinds of Vocabulary-in-Context questions. The first kind of question tests a vocabulary word that you have probably seen before but that is being used in a way different from its most common meaning. The second is a more difficult vocabulary word that you must figure out based on the context of the passage.

Let's take a closer look at some strategies for dealing with Vocabulary-in-Context questions!

● THE TRAP DOOR
Steering Clear of Answer Traps

The traps for Vocabulary-in-Context questions are typically the same as for the others. If you have any questions about the traps, refer to the introduction to Critical Reading.

● PERFORMANCE TECHNIQUES
Key Formulas and Rules

When you encounter a Vocabulary-in-Context question in the Critical Reading section, be sure to look for clue words, both structural and definitional, in the sentence that contains the vocabulary word. Once in a while, you will need to look at the sentence before or after to gain more context clues for the vocabulary word. Underline structural clues and circle definitional clues, just like you would for a Sentence Completion question. Then, take the word from the question stem out of the sentence and create a blank.

If you saw this question on the SAT,

1. The word *alighted* (line 23) most nearly means

and the sentence from the passage read:

The fragile creature did not know of the impending danger that awaited her arrival, so I watched as the bird alighted onto the cat's water bowl, which had been placed outside when the weather grew hot.

Then, you would replace *alighted* with a blank or just draw a line through it.

…the bird _____ onto the.…

Now, predict a word for the blank with a word that makes sense to you, and then match your prediction to the answer choices—a quick way to pick up some easy points.

Tougher Vocabulary

If you see a tough vocabulary word in the question stem, don't sweat it. All you need to do is remember the following steps:

Step 1: Read the sentence, looking for structural and definitional clues.

Step 2: Draw a line through the tested word and create a blank.

Step 3: Predict an answer and **select** the answer that best matches your prediction.

We'll use the following sentence for an example.

Although not quite as famously endemic to the Everglades as the American crocodile, the far more endearing manatee is perhaps more symbolic of the unique wildlife found in this vast tropical swamp.

1. In line 1, the word *endemic* most nearly means

Step 1: Read the sentence, looking for structural and definitional clues.

Step 2: Draw a line through *endemic* and create a blank.

Although not quite as famously _____ to the Everglades as the American crocodile, the far more endearing manatee is perhaps more symbolic of the unique wildlife found in this vast tropical swamp.

Step 3: Predict an answer

Next, you would fill in the blank with a word that makes sense to you before looking at the answers

known

and **select** the answer that best matches your prediction.

   (A) popular

   (B) characteristic

   (C) well-liked

   (D) dangerous

   (E) relative

The correct answer here is (B). It's important to remember that if you have two words that mean the same thing (A and C), then neither of them can be the correct answer. There's only one best answer choice.

Always read your choice back into the sentence to make sure it makes sense. If it sounds wrong, it probably is wrong!

Common Vocabulary Words

If you're dealing with a more common word, like *pluck*, the most common definition is NOT going to be the right answer. Without even having a sentence, which of these answers could you eliminate if *pluck* was the word tested?

(A) pull

(B) tug

(C) courage

(D) organ meats

(E) excuse

Usually, this word means to pull or tug at something, like *pluck a guitar string*. On the SAT, that is not going to be the right answer. Always eliminate the most used definition to a common word.

Now take a look at the sentence that contains *pluck*.

The young wizard's pluck helped him vanquish the evil villain, in spite of everyone else's fears.

Since you've already eliminated (A) and (B), you only have three answers left to work with. If you plug all of the other answer choices back into the sentence, *courage* (C) is the only answer that makes any sense.

● DRESS REHEARSAL
Sample Questions and Detailed Explanations

Here is a sample passage with questions. You have already read this passage in the chapter on Inference questions. On Test Day, you will see a combination of different question types associated with each chapter. For our dress rehearsal, we'll use a passage you have already read and are familiar with to give you an opportunity to test your chops with the strategy for Vocabulary-in-Context questions.

Questions 1 and 2 refer to the following passage.

The librarian raised his brow as he found the evidence in my bag. I stood before him, a college student who refused to shave, sporting a

black beret and dark glasses. I wanted to follow my parents' example;
they had fought the Communists in Russia by running an underground
(5) museum. None of this mattered to my accuser. He simply removed the
book from my bag and reminded me in his purple air that "one does
not take books from the Bodleian Library at the University of Oxford—
not even Her Majesty the Queen possesses borrowing privileges." I
walked away, but not before proclaiming, "This library is an evil institu-
(10) tion like the Soviet Union, and I am attempting to liberate
information!"

Now that you've refamiliarized yourself with the passage,
let's look at the first Vocabulary-in-Context question.

1. In line 4, the word *underground* most nearly means

Step 1: Read the sentence, looking for structural and definitional clues.

Go back to the passage and locate the sentence. Find the
clue words in the sentence. You might have to read around
the sentence (look at the sentences before and/or after) in
order to gather context.

Step 2: Draw a line through the tested word and create a
blank.

Step 3: Predict an answer

_____ unknown _____

_____

and **select** the answer that best matches your prediction.

(A) buried

(B) secret

(C) collective

(D) authentic

(E) crude

The correct answer is (B). Since the narrator wanted to follow his parents' example and was trying to make information
available to other people, we can conclude that his parents'
museum was something that they had to hide from the Com-
munist rulers. If they had made the museum public, they
would have been shut down. The answer won't be (A) since

this is the most common definition for *underground*. (C), (D), and (E) don't make sense within the context of the passage.

2. In line 8, the word *privileges* most nearly means

Repeat Step 1: Read the sentence, looking for structural and definitional clues.

Go back to the passage and locate the sentence. Find the clue words in the sentence. You might have to read around the sentence (look at the sentences before and/or after) in order to gather context.

Repeat Step 2: Draw a line through the tested word and create a blank.

Repeat Step 3: Predict an answer

favors

and **select** the answer that best matches your prediction.

(A) special treatment

(B) penance

(C) rights

(D) paradox

(E) circumlocution

This sentence seems pretty clear since many of us have a library card and know what it means to be able to borrow books from the library. (A) is our typical wrong answer trap since privilege can mean special treatment. Even if you don't know any of the other words, you know that **(C), rights, is the best answer choice** because it matches your prediction so well.

Penance—repayment for wrongs

Paradox—a statement or situation that seems to be absurd or contradictory but is or may be true

Circumlocution—the use of more words than necessary to express something, in order to avoid saying it directly

● **THE FINAL ACT**
Self-Check Quiz

Questions 1-4 refer to the following passage.

Many art lovers have never heard of Dieter Roth. Of all the Swiss artists of the past century, he is probably the least well-known. He attended school in Switzerland, where he cultivated a love of poetry and art and became known for his graphic work in prints and art books. He made
(5) his living designing books, textiles, jewelry, and plywood furniture. In 1953, Roth became involved with a group of artists and writers who published a journal called *Spirale*. He designed the first cover of the magazine in 1953.

In 1960, Roth encountered Swiss artist Jean Tinguely's kinetic
(10) sculptures, some of which were built to self-destruct or move of their own volition. Tinguely's belief that art and life were part of the same process had a profound effect on Roth. By 1966, Roth was using odd materials, such as bananas and sausages, in his printmaking instead of metal. The main theme in his works focused on the passage of time,
(15) as was illustrated with depictions of visible decay, chance, and mind-less accumulation. Dieter Roth is now regarded as an anti-art satirist because of his use of unconventional materials in his artwork.

1. In line 3, the word *cultivated* most nearly means

    (A) grew

    (B) planted

    (C) improved

    (D) developed

    (E) despised

2. In line 9, the word *kinetic* most nearly means

    (A) active

    (B) experimental

    (C) odd

    (D) creative

    (E) immobile

3. In line 12, the word *profound* most nearly means

   (A) enormous

   (B) long-lasting

   (C) plunging

   (D) perceptive

   (E) peculiar

4. In line 15, the word *depictions* most nearly means

   (A) representations

   (B) caricatures

   (C) models

   (D) entities

   (E) piles

Questions 5–10 refer to the following passage.

Australia's first European settlers took a long time to adjust to the continent's supreme emptiness and enormous size. Several of the earliest explorers were so convinced that they would encounter mighty river systems, or even an inland sea, that they took boats with them.
(5)   Thomas Mitchell, a soldier who explored vast tracts of southeastern Australia in the 1830s, dragged two wooden skiffs over three thousand miles of arid land without once getting them wet. "Although the boats and their carriage had been a great hindrance to us," he wrote with a touch of understatement after his third expedition, "I was very
(10)   unwilling to abandon such useful appendages to an exploring party."
     From this and other accounts of early expeditions, it is clear that the first explorers were often ludicrously out of their depths. In 1802, Lieutenant Francis Barrallier described a temperature of 82 degrees Fahrenheit as "suffocating." His men tried for days without success to
(15)   hunt kangaroos before it occurred to them that they might stalk the creatures more effectively if they first removed their bright red coats. In seven weeks they covered just 130 miles, an average of about 1.5 miles a day.

5. In line 2, the word *supreme* most nearly means

 (A) best

 (B) first

 (C) extreme

 (D) untouchable

 (E) top

6. In line 5, the word *tracts* most nearly means

 (A) anthems

 (B) pamphlets

 (C) lands

 (D) organs

 (E) long periods of time

7. In line 6, the word *skiffs* most nearly means

 (A) boats

 (B) oars

 (C) sails

 (D) swim suits

 (E) carriages

8. In line 10, the word *appendages* most nearly means

 (A) limbs

 (B) baggage

 (C) adjuncts

 (D) climates

 (E) compasses

9. In line 12, the word *ludicrously* most nearly means

 (A) carefully

 (B) impractically

 (C) suitably

 (D) nonchalantly

 (E) absurdly

10. In line 14, the word *suffocating* most nearly means

    (A) dying

    (B) deprived of air

    (C) extremely uncomfortable

    (D) restrictive

    (E) confined

● ANSWERS AND EXPLANATIONS

1. **D** Usually when we see the word *cultivate* it has to do with planting things and doing what is necessary to see those things grow. Remember that common definitions are often not the right answer, so you can eliminate (A) and (B). (C), *improved*, does not make sense within the context of the sentence. If you read it back into the sentence, it sounds strange. *Despised* is an opposite (E). If you work at a talent to make it better, you develop that talent (D), which makes the most sense within the context of the sentence.

2. **A** You get your biggest context clues for this question after the comma in this sentence, *some of which were built to self-destruct or move of their own volition* (A). (B), (C), and (D) are all misused details, since Roth's artwork could be described that way. However, in the context of this particular sentence, they don't work. *Immobile* is quite the opposite of what you're looking for (E).

3. **B** (A), (C), (D), and (E) are all possible straight definitions for *profound*. In the context of the sentence, though, you're looking for a word that means *lasting* (B).

4. **A** You're looking for a word that means a "picture" or a "description" (A). All of the other words in the answer choices mean something different. A *caricature* (B) is an exaggeration of someone or something, and *entities* (D) are single objects, which won't work in this context. *Piles* (E) is opposite, while *models* (C), which are copies, doesn't capture the meaning of *depictions* in this sentence.

5. **C**   All of the answer choices are appropriate definitions for *supreme*. However, (C) is the only answer choice that works within the context of this sentence.

6. **C**   The word *tracts* has many different definitions. In this sentence you get the clue *explored vast _____ of southeast Australia*, which leads you to believe that this person was exploring different lands (C). *Anthems* (A), *pamphlets* (B), and *organs* (D) don't fit. (E) *Long periods of time* would not be explored in southeast Australia in this context, either.

7. **A**   The biggest clue for this question comes in the sentence that follows. The quote from Thomas Mitchell uses the words *boats* and *carriages*. With further examination of the sentence in which the vocabulary word is contained, you can see that they never got the skiffs wet. Therefore, *boats* make more sense than *carriages*.

8. **B**   The appendages that are being discussed in this sentence refer to the boats in the earlier part of the quote. The boats had to be carried by the exploration party—very heavy baggage! So (B), *baggage*, is the best answer choice. Although appendages often refer to limbs, that's not how the word is used in this context (A). The other three answers (C), (D), and (E) have nothing to do with the question. It's important to remember that even if you don't know one of the words, if you have a strong prediction and find a match for that prediction, you can find the correct answer choice.

9. **E**   If you take the word *ludicrously* out of the sentence and make a prediction for this blank, you would come up with something like *ridiculously*. The best match for that is (E) *absurdly*. Even if you had a hard time making a prediction, read the other words back into the sentence and none of the others create a logical sentence the way *absurdly* does.

10. **C**   *Suffocating* normally means depriving something of air, which is one of the answer choices. But you already know not to choose (B) because a common vocabulary word won't have the most common answer as the correct choice. *Dying* is too extreme (A), while *restrictive* and *confined* have similar meanings (D) and (E). The best choice is (C), which captures the essence of the oppressive heat.

Global Questions

DIFFICULTY: ★ ★ ★

FREQUENCY: ★ ★

SURPRISE FACTOR: ★

● INTRODUCTION TO GLOBAL QUESTIONS

Global questions should never be a surprise on the SAT. They always ask you the same thing, "What is the author's point of view or purpose?" Global questions are asking you to take a look at the big picture, often using words like *the primary purpose of the passage*, *the author regards*, or *the main point of the passage*.

If you are taking notes while you read the passage regarding the purpose of each paragraph and the author's point of view, then you should have the answer to most Global questions you'll see on the SAT before you even begin reading the questions. By actively reading and paying attention to the main point of the passage, you can predict the answers to those questions and jot them down. That way you'll have already predicted the answer to the Global questions before you ever read them.

While most Global questions are asking you to recognize the big picture, you could see other Global questions that are asking you to generalize from specifics within the passage. If you see this type of Global question, though, you'll still want to keep that big picture in mind while you think about how specific points from the passage relate to the main idea.

Global questions often seem difficult to those taking the SAT because they get too bogged down in the details of the passage. As you read, be sure you are looking for the big picture. Many details can be skimmed, so that you can spend more time thinking about the purpose of the writer. You'll see them often enough on the test that you should always write down or take a mental note of the main point in each long passage that you read. When the author's point of view is stated outright in the passage, be sure to circle it so you can easily research the answers to Global questions.

● THE TRAP DOOR
Steering Clear of Answer Traps

The traps for Global questions are typically the same as the others. If you have any questions about the traps, refer to the introduction to Critical Reading. There is one trap, however, that looks quite a bit different on this question type than it does on the rest of the reading comprehension questions.

Out-of-Scope Answers

Typically this answer choice would simply go beyond what is stated in the passage. In Global questions it can appear differently. Out-of-scope answers will go in one of two directions: they will either be too broad or too narrow to answer the question correctly. The answer to a Global question must look at the big picture. If a question asks about the passage as a whole, the correct answer *cannot* only cover the first paragraph, nor can it cover more than what is discussed in the passage. So, out-of-scope answer traps in Global questions will either be too broad or too narrow.

Distortions

Distortions appear frequently as wrong answers for Global questions, too. Remember, if an answer is only half right, that answer is all wrong.

Extremes

The use of extreme language should act as a caution sign to you on the SAT. With Global questions, keep in mind that extreme language used in an answer choice signals a wrong answer. The only time an answer containing extreme language can be correct is when the extremity can be supported by specific information from the passage, which includes the author's attitude.

● PERFORMANCE TECHNIQUES
Key Formulas and Rules

Many Global questions can be answered before you ever start reading the questions. As you are actively reading, pay particular attention to the author's purpose and attitude. Once you've finished reading the passage, having taken notes, quickly write down the main point. This should always be the last thing you do on a long passage before you hit the questions. Then, when you see a Global question, you can simply refer back to the main point note you wrote down in order to have a predicted answer for the question.

If you have trouble honing in on the author's purpose for writing a passage, look to the introduction and conclusion. When you learned how to write a strong essay or paper for school, you may have heard you should tell your reader what you are going to say in the introduction; next, tell the reader what you want to say in the body of your paper; then, tell the reader what you just said in your conclusion. Most well-written material gives you some clues as to the author's purpose in the introduction and often in the conclusion as well, so focus on the introduction. If you don't find the information you need there, check the conclusion. You will likely find plenty of useful information regarding Global questions in those two areas.

When you're looking at Global questions that ask for the main *purpose* of the passage, the first word of each answer choice usually offers you a tremendous clue. For example, if you read a passage that simply *explains* the restoration process that was used to clean the Sistine Chapel's ceiling, you know you must be looking for an answer that encompasses an *explanation*. Many times that first word in each of the answer choices will allow you to eliminate some of the answers.

So, if you saw the following answer choices for a question concerning the main point of this passage about the restoration of the Sistine Chapel, which ones could you eliminate just based on the first word?

(A) refute

(B) explore

(C) argue

(D) provide

(E) relate

Were you able to eliminate at least two answers? Since there's no argument taking place in this example, we could eliminate (A) and (C). Now take a look at the rest of the answers in their entirety and see if there are any others that you could eliminate.

(A) refute a commonly held belief

(B) explore the effects of a process

(C) argue for a course of action

(D) provide a new perspective on an ancient issue

(E) relate the history of an invention

You can see that (A) and (C) still clearly make no sense in the context of this example. But now we can also eliminate (D) and (E) since an explanation of the process used to restore the Sistine Chapel does not *provide a new perspective on an ancient issue* nor would it *relate the history of an invention*. When you see Global questions about purpose, pay special attention to those first words in the answer choices. They can help you quickly eliminate wrong answers. If you've made a strong prediction for the main purpose, you can recognize whether or not those first words match the author's purpose.

In addition to these helpful strategies, let's review the Kaplan Method for Reading Comprehension questions.

The Kaplan Method for Reading Comprehension

Step 1: Read the passage, taking notes.

Step 2: Examine the question stem.

Step 3: Predict an answer and **select** the answer that best matches your prediction.

Remember to stay focused on the *why*. *Why* is more important than *what*, especially on Global questions. Don't get bogged down in the details!

● **DRESS REHEARSAL**
Sample Questions and Detailed Explanations

Now that you've got several strategies for dealing with Global questions, as well as the Kaplan Method for Reading Comprehension, take a look at these short passages along with the accompanying questions.

Questions 1 and 2 refer to the following passage:

Step 1: Read the passage, taking notes.

The local public theater has brought our townsfolk great theater for over 30 years, but it is beginning to harm the town's children. Over the course of its history, it has (5) become an increasingly sophisticated institution, requiring greater and greater time commitments from volunteer actors. This year, children and adult participants alike were required to attend rehearsals four days a week for two hours each. Teachers are complaining of missed assignments (10) and exhausted students. The theater's leaders must reconsider the taxing requirements they have imposed on child volunteers, virtually all of whom will never become star actors.

> Your notes should focus on the big picture!

[handwritten margin note: Theater is harming the children now.]

Step 2: Examine the question stem.

The primary purpose of the passage is to

Step 3: Predict an answer

[handwritten: show that "has the theater" frighten the children ed.]

and **select** the answer that best matches your prediction.

(A) illustrate common misperceptions about local public theater

(B) warn community theaters about star actors

(C) argue against the formation of a local public theater

(D) analyze the effects of long rehearsals on adults and children

(E) advise leaders to cut back rehearsal time to avoid a potentially worsening problem

Here is an example of the type of Global question, a big picture purpose question, discussed in Performance Techniques in this chapter. Just by looking at the first word of each choice, were you able to eliminate any of the answers? *Warn* (B) and *advise* (E) are words that should most closely match your prediction. You may have been able to eliminate as many as three answer choices (A), (C), and (D) just by looking at that first word. The last sentence of this short passage tells us that the author wishes the local theater would reconsider the time requirements of student actors. The main purpose of the passage is to urge the theater leaders to lessen requirements on the student actors since they are missing assignments in school and becoming exhausted—a potentially dangerous problem, **making (E) the best answer.**

Repeat Step 2: Examine the question stem.

> The author's attitude toward the "taxing requirement" placed on "child volunteers" appears to be one of

Repeat Step 3: Predict an answer

_____

_____

and **select** the answer that best matches your prediction.

(A) skeptical acceptance

(B) partial refutation

(C) aloof disapproval

(D) veiled apathy

(E) unapologetically vindictive

The author's attitude often comes into play in Global questions. In this question you are asked about the author's attitude on a specific matter. Even if you're asked about the author's feelings about a specific portion of the passage, you still need to think about the passage as a whole in order to answer this question. Consider the purpose of the passage and the author's thoughts and feelings throughout. In this short passage, the author does say that teachers are complaining about the children's grades suffering and asks that the theater's leaders reconsider the time commitment placed on the kids. The author does not like the current approach and wants it changed. (C) is the answer that best matches this prediction. (A) does not work since the author does not approve of the time commitment and doesn't refute what is happening in part (B), but instead presents her own ideas about the situation and its need to be solved. (D) is the opposite of the author's attitude, and (E) is too extreme. So, **(C) is definitely the best choice.**

Questions 3 and 4 refer to the following passage.

Step 1: Read the passage, taking notes.

The introduction to *Colonial Adventurers in Little Ships*
By Ralph D. Paine

The story of American ships and sailors is an epic of blue water which seems singularly remote, almost unreal, to the later generations. A people with a native genius for seafaring won and held a brilliant supremacy through two centuries and then forsook this heritage of (5) theirs. The period of achievement was no more extraordinary than was its swift declension. A maritime race whose topsails flecked every ocean, whose captains courageous from father to son had fought with pike and cannonade to defend the freedom of the seas, turned inland to seek a different destiny and took no more thought for the (10) tall ships and rich cargoes which had earned so much renown for its flag.

Vanished fleets and brave memories—a chronicle of America which had written its closing chapters before the Civil War! There will be other Yankee merchantmen in times to come, but never days like (15) those when skippers sailed on seas uncharted in quest of ports mysterious and unknown...

Step 2: Examine the question stem.

3. The author's tone in this passage might best be described as

Step 3: Predict an answer

_____ passionate about ships _____

_____

and **select** the answer that best matches your prediction.

(A) impartial

Remember to cross off any answers that don't match your prediction.

(B) humorous

(C) reserved

(D) critical

(E) nostalgic (wishful or past)

The correct choice is (E). The author of this passage talks about ships from a time that has past. He also remarks about those *vanished fleets and brave memories,* leading us to believe that he is reminiscing about a time and subject for which he has fond feelings. Your prediction would be a positive word. It could not be *impartial* (A) since the author has strong feelings for the ships and the era that contained them. Nor would it be (C) *reserved* or (D) *critical,* since your prediction is a positive word. *Humorous* (B) cannot work either because the author doesn't treat the subject matter lightly. *Nostalgic* (E) works well here since the author longs for people to remember this era fondly and asks them not to forget the importance of the ships and shipping industry.

Repeat Step 2: Examine the question stem.

4. This passage is best described as

Repeat Step 3: Predict an answer

_____

_____

and **select** the answer that best matches your prediction.

(A) a scholarly analysis of seafaring traditions

(B) a fond remembrance of a time and tradition since forgotten

(C) a scathing condemnation of an outdated concept

(D) a general overview of maritime life

(E) a theoretical statement about the value of a way of thinking

The correct choice here is (B). Since you've already answered a question about the author's tone, describing the passage becomes a little bit easier than if you hadn't had to answer that question. You could even use words from the question you just answered to make your prediction for this question. The passage is a nostalgic look at the mariner's life and ships from the past. As you examine the answer choices you can see that (C) is an opposite answer. (A), (D), and (E) are out of the scope of the passage. This leaves only (B), which is a good match to your prediction!

● **THE FINAL ACT**
Self-Check Quiz

Questions 1 and 2 refer to the following passage.

An excerpt from *Theodore Roosevelt*
By Edmund Lester Pearson

...Theodore Roosevelt was born October 27, 1858, in New York City, at 28 East Twentieth Street. The first Roosevelt of his family to come to this country was Klaes Martensen van Roosevelt who came from Holland to what is now New York about 1644. He was a "settler," and

(5) that, says Theodore Roosevelt, remembering the silly claims many people like to make about their long-dead ancestors, is a fine name for an immigrant, who came over in the steerage of a sailing ship in the seventeenth century instead of the steerage of a steamer in the nineteenth century. From that time, for the next seven generations,

(10) from father to son, every one of the family was born on Manhattan Island. As New Yorkers say, they were "straight New York."

Immigrant or settler, or whatever Klaes van Roosevelt may have been, his children and grandchildren had in them more than ordinary ability. They were not content to stand still, but made themselves use-

(15) ful and prosperous, so that the name was known and honored in the city and State even before the birth of the son who was to make it illustrious throughout the world...

1. The primary purpose of the passage is to

  (A) perpetuate the rumors that New Yorkers made about Theodore Roosevelt

  (B) explain how Klaes Martensen van Roosevelt came to America

  (C) dispel the silly claims of many people

  (D) introduce a tribute to Theodore Roosevelt

  (E) limit the scope of Theodore Roosevelt's accomplishments

2. Based on the passage, the author would regard Theodore Roosevelt as a

    (A) renowned figure

    (B) useful militant

    (C) ordinary man

    (D) prosperous worker

    (E) illusive legend

Questions 3 and 4 refer to the following passage.

I knew it would come. That precious moment when, stepping out of the airport doors into the atmosphere of a foreign country for the first time, I could breathe in my total displacement and relish the freshness of it all. I had never known this place, and for that moment only (5) would it be truly new. So there was great anticipation as I pushed eagerly against the last door and felt, suddenly checked by familiarity, the same chilling damp I thought I had left back at home, halfway around the globe. I just stood there, watching the buses cough out the same exhaust and the rain fall just as it always had.

3. In the passage as a whole, the author's attitude toward traveling to a foreign country might best be described as

    (A) nervous and then elated

    (B) anxious and then disappointed

    (C) disruptive and then familiar

    (D) angry and then wary

    (E) crazed and then depressed

4. The major focus of the passage is on the

    (A) plane ride to a foreign country

    (B) weather in the place the author was visiting

    (C) pollution the author was leaving behind

    (D) author's thoughts leading up to experiencing the newness of a foreign country

    (E) author's feelings about traveling to and arriving in a foreign country

Questions 5 and 6 refer to the following passage.

The young dancer was known as a star in her small town. She was the proverbial large fish in a small pond. When any recital was tak- ing place, the highlight of the show was always the solo done by the young girl. As her high school years ended, she decided to further her
(5) dance study at one of the prestigious dance academies on the east coast. Some people said that while she was good, she was not that good. However, a former professional dancer assured them that the standards at those schools were very high. "They will look carefully at her audition tape and her application and will not admit her to the
(10) school if she cannot demonstrate that she has the potential to suc- ceed in the troupe." The young girl knew she that she would have to work very hard on her audition tape in order to be accepted at one of the schools of her choice.

5. The main purpose of the passage is to

(A) argue for dance to be taught in public schools

(B) recount a young girl's ambitions

(C) offer advice from a professional dancer

(D) equate a young dancer's gifts with a professional dancer's experience

(E) remember a girl who left her small town and moved to the big city

6. The author's tone is best described as

(A) ruthless

(B) hopeful

(C) jealous

(D) ecstatic

(E) humorous

Questions 7 and 8 refer to the following passage.

What plagues both political parties in the United States today is their need to win over the voting public at any cost. Since the average American voter has only an acquaintance with the crucial issues of the day and an even narrower grasp of the ways in which policy can
(5) address them, politicians are forced to mount often-vicious attacks

on their competitors to capture the interest of the electorate. Rather than elect the best candidates for the task at hand, the American voter, election after election, chooses what appears to be the lesser of multiple evils, electing, in effect, the best worst candidate for the
(10) job.

7. The second sentence of the passage implies that the main problem with American voters is that they

(A) never have any good candidates to choose from

(B) need to win at any cost

(C) do not believe in political process

(D) are duped by politician's negative policies

(E) have a limited understanding of important political issues

8. The author's primary purpose in writing this passage was most likely to

(A) describe the electoral process in America

(B) cite specific problems undermining American voters.

(C) depict the lesser of two evils between the political parties in the United States

(D) determine the outcome of future presidential elections

(E) assuage American's fears about voting in major political elections

Questions 9 and 10 refer to the following passage.

Teaching across the curriculum is a current trend in education. In the past, classroom subjects were taught individually. Now, students are often taught material in a particular discipline within the context of another classroom subject. This particular strategy utilizes the con-
(5) cept that true learning involves making connections and invoking positive transfer. Positive transfer involves having a student remember prior knowledge and then attaching the new concepts being taught to the previously learned concepts. Many current pedagogical organizations believe that teaching across the curriculum is a posi-
(10) tive trend. It will help students with various learning styles apply new knowledge and concepts rather than simply having to learn things by rote.

9. The author's primary purpose in writing this passage was most likely to

(A) convince others of the strength of teaching across the curriculum

(B) ask others to consider the benefits of teaching one subject at a time

(C) create a new approach to classroom learning

(D) argue against the current ideals of pedagogical organizations

(E) increase awareness of all the new trends in public education

10. The main contrast in the passage is between

(A) positive transfer and new knowledge

(B) true learning and pedagogical organizations

(C) students and teachers

(D) teaching one subject at a time and teaching across the curriculum

(E) application of knowledge and conceptualizing problems

● ANSWERS AND EXPLANATIONS

1. **D** (A) and (B) are out of the scope of the passage. The passage does not address any rumors about Theodore Roosevelt (A), and (B) is too narrow an answer since Klaes's move is only discussed in one sentence. (C) is a distortion and (E) is the opposite.

2. **A** The author is very complimentary of Theodore Roosevelt saying that he was known to be *illustrious throughout the world*. (A) is the best match for your prediction. (C) is the opposite, while (B), (D), and (E) are all distortions.

3. **B** In this passage, the author says that she was filled with *great anticipation*, but then *checked by familiarity*. Instead of *relishing the freshness* of the experience, this new country felt dull and commonplace to her. (B) is a great match for your prediction.

4. **E** (A), (B), (C), and (D) are all out of the scope of the question. Each of these answers is too narrow, focusing only on

pieces of the passage rather than the passage as a whole. You can eliminate answers that don't address the big picture in Global questions. (E) does just that, encompassing the whole passage.

5. **B** Remember to look at those first verbs in each answer choice. (A) has nothing to do with the passage. (C) is a distortion of a detail. There's no comparison being made in the passage between the young dancer and the professional (D). And (E) is out of the scope of the passage since we never find out in this passage whether or not the young lady is accepted to a dance school or not. (B) is the best match for your prediction.

6. **B** The author's tone should be considered throughout reading the passage. It is positive so you can eliminate (A) and (C). It's light, but not particularly funny (E), and (D) is an extreme answer. Hopeful makes the most sense, since you can feel the author is rooting for the girl to get to school.

7. **E** (A), (B), and (D) are all extreme answers. (C) is out of the scope of the passage since the passage never discusses whether or not American voters believe in the political process. Even if this statement were true, it's not contained in this passage so it cannot be the right answer. (E) is the remaining choice and should also be a good fit with your prediction.

8. **B** (A) and (C) are both too narrow to encompass the whole purpose of the passage, while (D) and (E) are not talked about in this passage. (B) is the answer that should match your prediction.

9. **A** The author of this passage sees teaching across the curriculum as a *positive* trend (A). (B) is exactly the opposite of this statement. The author isn't creating anything new in this passage (C) or arguing against anything in the passage (D). (E) is too extreme and out of the scope of the passage since there is only one trend in education discussed.

10. **D** The main contrast within the passage is between teaching across the curriculum or simply teaching one subject at a time (D). (A) and (B) contain misused details; (C) is out of the scope of the passage; (E) is a distortion.

LESSON 15

Detail Questions

DIFFICULTY: ★

FREQUENCY: ★ ★ ★

SURPRISE FACTOR: ★ ★

● INTRODUCTION TO DETAIL QUESTIONS

Many people who have taken the SAT find the Detail questions to be the easiest questions. Since they deal with specific points that you pull directly from the passage, these questions are understandably less intimidating than many others. The terrific news is that Detail questions make up a large percentage of the questions in the Reading Comprehension section of the Critical Reading test. Although most Detail questions seem relatively easy, a few others are surprisingly difficult, and we will pay particular attention to the most surprising questions and how to deal with them.

All Detail questions ask you to draw upon specific points in the passage. You can often spot Detail questions because they refer to specific lines or sentences. In order to answer Detail questions effectively, you must find specific support in the passage to support your answer. Especially with Detail questions, you can often put your finger on the words in the passage that mark the right choice as *right*.

Detail questions can also be seen as *not* and *except* questions. Read these questions carefully so you don't start looking for the answer that is *in* the passage; instead, *eliminate* the answers that you locate in the text and choose the answer that does *not* appear or is *not* supported by the passage. You might also see Roman numeral questions that appear as Detail questions. The important thing to remember is that no matter how the Detail questions appear on the SAT, don't be thrown by a question just because it looks different from the others. Always read the question actively and decipher the question stem if it is long or wordy. Keep the Kaplan Method for Reading Comprehension in mind, which you have been using in all of your dress rehearsals throughout the chapters on passage-based questions.

● THE TRAP DOOR
Steering Clear of Answer Traps

You've seen the different types of wrong-answer traps in the introduction to Critical Reading, so let's look at the most commonly used traps for Detail questions.

Misused Detail

The misused detail will be seen in almost every Detail question you encounter on the SAT. You must be careful when reading these answers because the answer comes from something that was stated directly in the passage, but has nothing to do with the question being asked. They are very tempting because they will sound and look like something that was directly stated in the passage.

When you're looking at a Detail question, make sure you understand *exactly* what the question is asking before you research the answer and make your prediction.

Distortions

Distortions are also seen quite often in the answer choices of Detail questions, since they take something directly from the passage and then change or distort part of the answer making it wrong. Remember, an answer that is only half right is *all* wrong.

Opposites

Opposite answers often appear in the answer choices. They typically are the easiest to recognize since opposite answers are just plain wrong. Keep straight what is being asked so that you can make sure to avoid an opposite answer choice. The word *not* can completely change the meaning of a question stem or answer choice, so read carefully.

Extreme Answers

You will see extreme answers that often look like an appropriate answer for a Detail question. However, these answers will contain words like *always, never, everybody,* or *no one,* which skews the choice and makes it wrong. The only time an extreme answer is correct on a Detail question is if you can find specific support for that answer in the passage. If you were to see an answer that read, "Everyone on the platform was waiting silently in anticipation," the only way it could be correct is if you found something in the passage to support it. For instance, if the passage contained a line that read, "All of the people on the platform held a singular breath, awaiting the arrival of the plane," then you could choose an extreme answer because the passage says "all of the people."

No matter what traps you encounter on Test Day, remember to predict an answer and select the choice that best matches your prediction. It will save you time and energy on the SAT, giving you more opportunities to increase your score.

● PERFORMANCE TECHNIQUES
Key Formulas and Rules

Because Detail questions appear to be the easiest, they are often the questions on which students make careless mistakes. Much like the simplest arithmetic questions on the math test, Detail questions get missed because students don't take the time to answer the question using the Kaplan methods and strategies. They will head straight to the answer choices before making a prediction and easily get convinced into choosing a tempting wrong answer choice. Remember, there is only one right answer, and it is in the passage.

As you take notes when reading through the passage, think headlines. You don't want to spend a lot of time or energy rewriting the paragraph. Just give yourself two or three words that will help you remember what the paragraph's purpose was, and it doesn't need to be fancy. "Movie bad" is just as effective a note as "the movie was less than inspiring." Your notes are only there to help you research your prediction quickly and efficiently.

Detail questions can appear more difficult on the SAT when they have lots of extra words and information added to the question stem. Be sure you are following the Kaplan Method for Reading Comprehension

Step 1: Read the passage, taking notes.

Step 2: Examine the question stem.

Step 3: Predict an answer, and **select** the answer that best matches your prediction.

The second step, examining the question stem, requires you to read the question stem carefully. By rewording or paraphrasing a wordy stem, you can gain understanding of what the question is asking you. This will help you figure out where to go in order to research the passage or your notes to find the answer.

The last step of the method is equally important and often skipped by many students on Detail questions. Don't rely on your brain to remember all the details from the passages you read on the SAT. If you're following the first step of the Kaplan Method for Reading Comprehension appropriately, you should be focusing on the big picture and skimming through the details anyway. Even if you have a stupendous memory, your brain is still capable of making mistakes, so don't rely on just your memory when you have a way to track down the correct answer on Detail questions every time. Always research those answers to Detail questions and put your finger on the information in the passage. That way you ensure making a correct prediction, which will lead you directly to the right answer.

● DRESS REHEARSAL
Sample Questions and Detailed Explanations

Practice the Kaplan Method for Reading Comprehension with each of the passages and Detail questions that proceed.

You may have seen these passages in the vocabulary-in-context chapter, but now you'll be asked Detail questions from these passages.

Questions 1 and 2 refer to the following passage.

Step 1: Read the passage, taking notes.

Many art lovers have never heard of Dieter Roth. Of all the Swiss artists of the past century, he is probably the least well-known. He attended school in Switzerland, where he cultivated a love of poetry and art and became known for his graphic work in prints and art books. He made
(5) his living designing books, textiles, jewelry, and plywood furniture. In 1953, Roth became involved with a group of artists and writers who published a journal called "Spirale." He designed the first cover of the magazine in 1953.

In 1960, Roth encountered Swiss artist Jean Tinguely's kinetic
(10) sculptures, some of which were built to self-destruct or move of their own volition. Tinguely's belief that art and life were part of the same process had a profound effect on Roth. By 1966, Roth was using odd materials, such as bananas and sausages, in his printmaking instead of metal. The main theme in his works focused on the passage of time,
(15) as was illustrated with depictions of visible decay, chance, and mind-less accumulation. Dieter Roth is now regarded as an anti-art satirist because of his use of unconventional materials in his artwork.

1. According to the passage, Dieter Roth

Step 2: Examine the question stem.

Step 3: Predict an answer

changed art
_____

and **select** the answer that best matches your prediction.

(A) is unknown to all art lovers

(B) is a world-renowned anti-art satirist

(C) is one of the least well-known Swiss artists of the 20th century

(D) is a patron of the arts

(E) made his living outside of the arts

Even though you might find it a little difficult to make a succinct prediction for this question, think about what the passage says in reference to Dieter Roth. Lines 4–5 tell us that Roth "made his living designing books, textiles, jewelry, and plywood furniture." This information supports (E). All of the other answer choices cannot be found in the passage; they are misused details or extreme answers.

2. According to the passage, Dieter Roth used all of the following in his works EXCEPT

Repeat Step 2: Examine the question stem.

Repeat Step 3: Predict an answer

_____

_____

and **select** the answer that best matches your prediction.

  (A) plywood furniture

  (B) chance

  (C) visible decay

  (D) mindless accumulation

  (E) bananas and sausages

On a question like this one that includes NOT or EXCEPT in the stem, you may not be able to make a prediction. Go to the answers immediately and start eliminating. (A) is not found in the passage. However, (B), (C), and (D) can be found in line 15, while (E) can be found in line 13.

Questions 3 and 4 refer to the following passage.

Australia's first European settlers took a long time to adjust to the continent's supreme emptiness and enormous size. Several of the earliest explorers were so convinced that they would encounter mighty river systems, or even an inland sea, that they took boats with them.

(5) Thomas Mitchell, a soldier who explored vast tracts of southeastern Australia in the 1830s, dragged two wooden skiffs over three thousand miles of arid land without once getting them wet. "Although the boats and their carriage had been a great hindrance to us," he wrote with a touch of understatement after his third expedition, "I was very

(10) unwilling to abandon such useful appendages to an exploring party."

From this and other accounts of early expeditions, it is clear that the first explorers were often ludicrously out of their depths. In 1802, Lieutenant Francis Barrallier described a temperature of 82 degrees Fahrenheit as "suffocating." His men tried for days without success to (15) hunt kangaroos before it occurred to them that they might stalk the creatures more effectively if they first removed their bright red coats. In seven weeks they covered just 130 miles, an average of about 1.5 miles a day.

3. The boats, mentioned in lines 4–10, were not left behind by Thomas Mitchell because he

Step 2: Examine the question stem.

Step 3: Predict an answer

_____ they were valueable _____
_____

and **select** the answer that best matches your prediction.

   (A) stubbornly believed they might prove to be useful on his expedition

   (B) thought the soldiers could be carried in the boats when they became tired

   (C) received information about river systems in Australia

   (D) knew the boats would not be used

   (E) planned for a water vacation

Look carefully at what this question is asking. "Why did Thomas Mitchell NOT leave the boats behind?" is a good way to rephrase this question. If you look at lines 9–10, you can see that Mitchell was unwilling to give up the boats because he thought they would prove useful. (A) matches your prediction very well! (B), (C), and (E) are out of scope, and (D) is an opposite.

4. The passage indicates that the red coats described in line 16 were significant because they

Repeat Step 2: Examine the question stem.

Repeat Step 3: Predict an answer

_____ scared the k's away _____
_____

and **select** the answer that best matches your prediction.

(A) retained body heat in the suffocating temperatures

(B) made it nearly impossible to succeed at hunting kangaroos

(C) helped them travel over long distances

(D) could spot one another at great distances

(E) lured the kangaroos into the hunting traps

The red coats are mentioned in the passage in association with the hunting of kangaroos. The passage says the explorers were unable to effectively hunt for the kangaroos until they removed their red coats (B). (A) and (D) are out of the scope of the passage; (C) and (E) are opposites.

● THE FINAL ACT
Self-Check Quiz

Questions 1–4 refer to the following passage.

On my recent trip to the Mojave Desert there was one thing that completely amazed me. At night, millions of stars were clearly visible in a way they never are at home. When glaring city lights shine into the sky, they obstruct our view of the galaxy. Scientists have given this
(5) phenomenon a name: light pollution.

I am concerned about light pollution because I love stargazing and believe it is an important intellectual and historical pastime. Looking at the night sky helps us remember that we all inhabit the same planet in space. I have enjoyed many evenings studying the constel-
(10) lations and talking with my friends about ancient Greek myths. I hope people will work to lessen the effects of light pollution because it is a growing concern.

There are many simple solutions for reducing light pollution. For example, individuals can simply turn off lights when they aren't
(15) using them. In some cities, local ordinances require people to install lights that are directed down toward the ground rather than pointed upward into the night sky. Lights around malls and used car lots don't need to light up the whole sky just to advertise their products. We can approach our political leaders to enact legislation to restrict the num-
(20) ber of lights or wattage usage in those places. Anyone who views the brilliant night sky in a remote rural area will understand the importance of reducing light pollution.

1. The first paragraph indicates that light pollution is
   (A) an increasingly dangerous problem in urban areas
   (B) a phenomenon that occurs when city lights obstruct our ability to see stars at night
   (C) an annoying situation for people who visit the desert
   (D) an indication of progress in cities
   (E) a challenge that everyone faces in both urban and rural areas

2. The author states that stargazing is significant for all of the following reasons EXCEPT that it
   (A) is an enjoyable hobby
   (B) forces us to talk about ancient Greece
   (C) is an important intellectual pursuit
   (D) reminds us that humans live on the same planet
   (E) is an historical pastime

3. The author mentions which of the following as a way to reduce light pollution?
   (A) Support organizations that protect us from light pollution.
   (B) Encourage all people to stop using lights at night.
   (C) Use lower wattage lamps in car head lights.
   (D) Direct lights towards the ground instead of into the sky.
   (E) Teach children to properly use lights.

4. The passage indicates that local laws have
   (A) helped to reduce light pollution in some communities
   (B) required a lot of time and work in order to be enacted
   (C) stopped the emission of light pollution in urban areas
   (D) managed to increase public awareness on this devastating issue
   (E) required malls and used car lots to decrease the lights used at night

Questions 5–10 refer to the following passage.

Mention a rock garden to most people, and in response, they may ask you how to grow rocks, and why you would want to do so. Actually, a rock garden (also known as an alpine garden) contains not only rocks but also

flowers that grow in mountainous regions. The flowers are planted in
(5) a bed of rocks, hence the name. Rock gardens are believed to have
originated in China and Japan; they were introduced to the West in
the 17th century. The popularity of rock gardens has increased dra-
matically since then, and today there are numerous international rock
garden societies with many thousands of members.

(10)   One aspect of the appeal of rock gardens is that they provide
gardeners the opportunity to cultivate beautiful plants in growing conditions that are less than ideal. If the land is hilly, stony, or awkwardly
arranged, for example, a gardener would be unable to raise many traditional garden plants, since they could not survive such conditions.
(15) In contrast, alpine plants such as gentians, edelweiss, stonecrops, and
saxifrages, as well as rockrose, columbine, phlox, and bluebell, not
only survive but also thrive in these conditions because their native
soils have characteristics similar to those of mountainous regions.

In order to plant a rock garden, a gardener must start with the
(20) rocks, ensuring that they are arranged in a manner that is both beautiful and conducive to plant growth. If the ground is already rocky, the
gardener need only rearrange the rocks into a growing area. In order
to avoid uninspired placements that work against the beauty of the
garden, the gardener should draw up plans of his rock garden before
(25) he begins the work. In addition, the rocks must be planted deeply
into the soil—in some cases, half or more of a rock will be buried—so
that they are stable and cannot be dislodged easily, which would
upset the plants.

Gardeners whose plot lacks a sufficient number or the proper
(30) kinds of rocks can buy them from local nurseries. Rocks native to a
gardener's region work best and are usually readily available and
inexpensive. Limestone is a good choice because water and air are
admitted into its pores. Some sturdy alpine plants even have roots
strong enough to push through limestone's porous surface and
(35) become firmly established in the rock. Limestone is also characterized
by nooks and crannies that provide opportunities for the gardener to
plant moss and lichens. The gardener should look, too, for rocks that
have interesting and aesthetically pleasing shapes and colors, since
it is the juxtaposition of the rocks and plants, not the beauty of the
(40) plants alone, that makes a rock garden succeed. In this respect, rock
gardens differ from traditional gardens, which focus on plants and do
not take the beauty of the medium in which flowers are planted into
consideration.

Once the rocks have been selected and put in place, a gardener
(45) can plant the flowers. H. Lincoln Foster, a famous American rock gardener, said that the reason rock gardeners go through the trouble and heavy lifting required to create a rock bed is that the plants that thrive in rock gardens "are among…the easiest and most abundantly flowering garden plants." However, rock gardens do require special care.
(50) Because plants in a rock garden are more exposed to the elements than are those in a flat bed, they need more protection. Nonetheless, rock garden devotees consider the time it requires to care for and maintain their gardens well spent, since the flowers and the rocks together provide such beauty and delight.

5. According to the passage, most people who hear about rock gardens _how → why_

   (A) make assumptions about what you would find in a rock garden

   (B) do not understand how a person could grow rocks

   (C) ask why someone would want a rock garden

   (D) associate them with China and Japan

   (E) join an international rock garden society

6. The second paragraph (lines 10–18) indicates that rock gardens

   (A) were introduced in the 17th century

   (B) provide healthy growing conditions for plants that thrive in mountainous regions

   (C) are barely capable of supporting phlox and columbine

   (D) appeal to traditional gardeners with their ability to raise many types of plants

   (E) coax plants to survive in conditions that are usually toxic

7. The author states that in order to start a rock garden one must have

   (A) plants

   (B) blueprints

   (C) a hill

   (D) gardening tools

   (E) rocks

8. According to the passage, some plants are so strong they are capable of

   (A) finding water in loose soil

   (B) forcing their limbs into buildings

   (C) dislodging large rocks

   (D) pushing their roots through porous rocks

   (E) lifting rocks out of their place in the soil

9. The two major contrasting elements contained in rock gardens, which lead to their success, are

   (A) flowers and plants

   (B) arrangement of the rocks and the gardener

   (C) interesting rocks and beautiful plants

   (D) the medium and the garden

   (E) shapely plants and limestone

10. People who maintain rock gardens say (lines 51–54) that these gardens are

   (A) worth the effort and time that it takes to care for them

   (B) the most special among American gardens

   (C) the easiest to care for and most abundantly flowering of all gardens

   (D) exposed to elements only if they are in a flat bed

   (E) the invention of H. Lincoln Foster

● **ANSWERS AND EXPLANATIONS**

1. **B** The last two sentences of the first paragraph give us the answer for this question (lines 3–5). (A) and (E) are distortions while (C) and (D) are out of scope.

2. **B** The second paragraph contains the author's reasons of importance for stargazing. All of the answers are mentioned in that paragraph, but one (B). Even though the author says he enjoys talking with friends about Greek myths, the answer choice has been given as an extreme answer. The passage never suggests that anyone is forced into this discussion while stargazing.

3. **D**   The answer for this question can be found in lines 15–17. (A), (C), and (E) are all out of scope. (B) is an extreme answer.

4. **A**   The first sentence of paragraph three indicates that there are many solutions for reducing light pollution, which is followed by a list of those things. (A) is contained in lines 15–17; (B) is out of scope; (C) is an opposite; (D) is an extreme answer; and (E) is a distortion.

5. **C**   The author states that many people when they hear about rock gardens *ask you how to grow rocks, and why you would want to do so.* This question could be a little tricky if you take this statement literally, but that is not the author's intent. This line from the passage tells us that the author thinks most people ask why anyone would want a rock garden (C). (B) might seem tempting, but no one would really wonder how you can grow rocks. (A), (D), and (E) are all misused details.

6. **B**   (B) is the only correct answer here because (A), (C), (D), and (E) are all opposites. They're wrong because there is something in the passage that contradicts each of them.

7. **E**   The first sentence of the third paragraph tells us that we must have rocks to start a rock garden (E). (A), (B), and (C) are misused details. (D) is out of the scope of the passage.

8. **D**   The information to answer this question can be found in lines 33–35. (A) is a misused detail, while (B), (C), and (E) are out of the scope of the passage.

9. **C**   ...*[I]t is the juxtaposition of the rocks and plants, not the beauty of the plants alone, that makes a rock garden succeed....*(lines 39–40) give the support for the answer to this question. The rest of the answers are both misused and distorted details.

10. **A**   ...*[R]ock garden devotees consider the time it requires to care for and maintain their gardens well spent....*This fits with (A). (B) and (C) are extreme answers. (D) and (E) are both distortions.

Function Questions

DIFFICULTY: ★ ★

FREQUENCY: ★ ★ ★

SURPRISE FACTOR: ★

● INTRODUCTION TO FUNCTION QUESTIONS

Function questions appear almost as frequently on the SAT as Detail questions. However, Function questions ask you about *purpose* or *usage* of specific parts of the passage. They might ask about the function of a word, sentence, paragraph, quotation, detail, or even punctuation marks. Function questions often require you to understand the passage as a whole even if the test-makers are asking about a very specific portion of the passage.

Function questions are easy to spot because they use distinctive phrasing in the question stems. You know you're looking at one of these questions if you see any of these phrases in the question stem: *serves primarily to, is meant to, in order to, functions primarily to, use of,* or *is used to.* The Function questions focus on the *why,* so taking notes concerning the purpose of each paragraph, as well as the purpose of the passage, should be very helpful in answering Function questions.

You wouldn't want to have to reread an entire paragraph or the whole passage again to figure out the answer to a Function question. Taking notes as you read and skim through the passage can save time and energy. If you are paying attention to purpose while reading the passage, the Function questions will be easier to answer. Without understanding the *why,* these questions can seem much more difficult than they really are. Once you understand the *why*, Function questions become very straightforward and easier to answer.

Remember that *why* is more important than *what* because details can always be researched after reading the question stem.

● THE TRAP DOOR
Steering Clear of Answer Traps

For Function questions the wrong-answer traps remain the same as for the other question types. Refer to the introduction to Critical Reading for the answer traps that appear in all Reading Comprehension questions on the SAT. You will likely see more out-of-scope answer traps and distortions in the answer choices for Function questions.

● PERFORMANCE TECHNIQUES
Key Formulas and Rules

First, let's review step one of the Kaplan Method for Reading Comprehension: *read the passage, taking notes*. You don't want to spend a long time reading through passages. Aim to spend no longer than two minutes on single long passages and about 20 to 30 seconds on single short passages. As you read, ask yourself the following questions:

- Why did the author write this passage?
- What's the purpose of this paragraph?
- Why include this example?

By asking yourself these questions while you read, you can zero in on purpose, which is what you need to know to answer the Function questions. Again, it is important to keep in mind that *why* is more important than *what*. When you come to details in the passage don't spend time reading or trying to memorize them. Skim through them, then simply note the purpose of the paragraph, and you will give yourself a set of clear signals that will help you locate answers quickly and easily.

The second step of the Kaplan Method for Reading Comprehension is to *examine the question stem*. Once you clearly understand what the question is asking you, then move on to the third step: *predict an answer, and select the answer that best matches your prediction.* Head back to the passage and look at your notes. The notes that you take on the purpose of each paragraph can often give you the answer to a Function question. If your notes don't give you an outright answer, they will generally help to inform your prediction. If you have trouble remembering your prediction once you start reading the answer choices, write it down. That way you'll have it there in the test booklet to compare to the answer choices, allowing you to eliminate the answers that don't match your prediction.

One way that the test-makers can make Function questions more challenging is to give answer choices that are very general even when the question seems to ask for something specific. Be prepared to generalize your answer if you take a look at the answer choices and none of them seem to match your prediction.

There are very few times that you cannot make a prediction to answer a question. If this happens, though, think about the traps and eliminate answers that you know are wrong. If you can eliminate one or more answers, then make a strategic guess. The odds are more and more in your favor if you eliminate answer choices that could not possibly be correct.

● **DRESS REHEARSAL**
   Sample Questions and Detailed Explanations

Take one more look at the Kaplan Method, and then begin.

Step 1: Read the passage, taking notes.

Step 2: Examine the question stem.

Step 3: Predict an answer and **select** the answer that best matches your prediction.

Questions 1–5 refer to the following passage.

Step 1: Read the passage, taking notes.

During the first half of the 19th century, the political and social currents in Europe in the aftermath of the French Revolution brought with them significant developments in the world of music.

(5) Patronage of the arts was no longer considered the exclusive province of the aristocracy. The increasingly prosperous middle class swelled the ranks of audiences at public concerts and music festivals. New opera houses were built to accommodate the demand, and these in turn enabled musicians to reach a larger public. Furthermore, the elevated status of the middle class increased the participation of (10) women in the musical field, which had traditionally been associated with men. Bourgeois families encouraged their daughters to take advantage of the new-found leisure time by studying voice or piano, since this would improve their marriage possibilities and thus be an asset in the family's climb to social acceptance. Singing in particular (15) became a focus of the woman's education, stemming from the traditional notion that a mother's singing was beneficial in nurturing a child. So many women became involved in amateur musical activities, in fact, that all the businesses that served music—piano-building, music publishing and music journalism—burgeoned. *Middle-class*

What is the purpose of the first paragraph? *Women in Music*

(20) Society was only beginning to enlarge its concept of appropriate musical education and activities for women, however. Female musical professionals were still very uncommon. Even the most competent could be forbidden by husbands and fathers to appear in public, to publish music under their own names, or to accept fees for their (25) teaching if the men feared that these activities would have a negative impact on the family's social status. The advice and support of a man was still a necessity in the musical career of a woman, no matter how talented she was.

What is the purpose of the second paragraph? *But W's still couldn't ring without man approval*

The prevailing negative opinions that continued to constrain women (30) musicians, especially composers, during this century can be traced back to the previous one. Many prominent 18th-century writers believed that women did not possess the intellectual and emotional capacity to learn or to create as artists. The influential social and educational philosopher Jean-Jacques Rousseau, for example, asserted (35) that "women, in general, possess no artistic sensibility…nor genius." Furthermore, it was held to be unnecessary and even dangerous for

women to acquire extensive musical knowledge, as such knowledge could only detract from the business of being a wife and mother.
(40) Johann Campe's opinion of female composers was representative of this view: "Among a hundred praiseworthy female composers hardly one can be found who fulfills simultaneously all the duties of a reasonable and good wife, an attentive and efficient housekeeper, and a concerned mother."

What is the purpose of the third paragraph? Distract Hrm baing mother ly

Most 19th-century men and women seemed to agree with these sen-
(45) timents. Women who performed publicly or attempted creative work therefore suffered not only societal censure but internal conflicts about the propriety and sensibility of their own aspirations. Even the great Clara Schumann, who was exceptional in that she was encouraged both by her husband and by the musical public to compose,
(50) entertained doubts about her creative ability. In 1839 she wrote, "I once believed that I possessed creative talent, but I have given up this idea; a woman must not desire to compose." Standard views on proper feminine behavior were so firmly entrenched that this mother of eight could not recognize the significance of her own accomplishments.

What is the purpose of the fourth paragraph? women aport believing this crap.

(55) Schumann was in fact a trail-blazer—one of the very first female composers to construct a large-scale orchestral work. In the early 19th century, the "art song" was considered to be the "safe," appropriate genre for women composers. The art song was a type of chamber music and as such fit comfortably into a domestic environment—the
(60) woman's domain. Women composers also gravitated to the art song as a medium for musical expression because its composition did not require the intensive training (often denied to women musicians) that the more intricate sonata or symphony did. Schumann defied convention, however, when she composed the "masculine" orchestral
(65) piece *Piano Concerto in A Minor*. Although not among those considered her finest, the work demonstrated to the women musicians who followed Schumann that female musical creativity could slip loose from the bonds of society.

What is the purpose of the fifth paragraph? *Women can produce great music*

What is the author's main purpose for writing this passage? *Women can be great musicians + K21*

Step 2: Examine the question stem.

1.   The discussion of the patronage of the arts in lines 4–6 is meant to

Step 3: Predict an answer *show how it's progressed*

and **select** the answer that best matches your prediction.

(A) give an example of a tumultuous time that brought about enormous artistic development

(B) illustrate the potential for women to become great musicians

(C) question the ability of women to become composers of symphonies and orchestral arrangements

(D) emphasize the significance of music's growing audience, especially among the middle class

(E) illustrate the social acceptance of raising children who have artistic hobbies

The correct choice is (D). Your notes should indicate what the first paragraph's purpose is. In this paragraph the author confirms that music is becoming more popular among the middle class after the French Revolution because people suddenly have more time and money to devote to the arts. The mention of the patronage of the arts emphasizes the author's point (D). (A) is out of scope. (B), (C) and (E) are misused details.

Repeat Step 2: Examine the question stem.

2.   The author discusses female musicians publishing music under their own names in lines 22–24 in order to

Step 3: Predict an answer

show how they weren't allowed to do it

and **select** the answer that best matches your prediction.

(A) demonstrate that women still need the approval of men in order to have a career in music

(B) emphasize the capabilities of women in teaching and performing music

(C) help evoke the attitude of the musical community in the early 1800s

(D) question the viability of orchestral and symphonic compositions created by women

(E) highlight the composing abilities of Clara Schumann

Your note for the second paragraph should show that men were still in charge of what women could or could not do in music. It was the opinion of men that ruled in the musical careers of women. Therefore, (A) is the best match. While other paragraphs discuss the capabilities of women, specifically Clara Schumann, this paragraph does not, (B), (D), and (E). (C) is too broad of an answer and out of the scope of this paragraph.

Repeat Step 2: Examine the question stem.

3. The author quotes Jean-Jacques Rousseau in line 35 and Johann Campe in lines 40–43 in order to

Step 3: Predict an answer

say women are domestic & busy

and **select** the answer that best matches your prediction.

(A) present a thesis that will be supported

(B) provide evidence for a previous statement

(C) cite a well-known example of a phenomenon

(D) counter an argument that follows

(E) question a common assumption

The quotes in the third paragraph further support the notion that most people at this time did not believe women capable of having worthy musical careers—(B) is the best match for this prediction. Even though the answers are more general than your prediction might be, it is still possible to eliminate the other answers even if you have trouble finding the match to your prediction. It is unlikely that the thesis of any paper would be a quotation (A), and there is no phenomenon (C), argument (D), or questionable assumption (E) mentioned.

Repeat Step 2: Examine the question stem.

4. The author cites Clara Schumann as an exceptional musician (lines 47–50) in order to

Step 3: Predict an answer

———————————————————————

———————————————————————

and **select** the answer that best matches your prediction.

(A) emphasize the support that Schumann received from her teachers in her studies of music

(B) provide an example of the style of playing that was most prevalent in 1839

(C) illustrate how society's entrenched, negative view on women musicians created emotional conflict within themselves

(D) praise her exceptional talents as a musician and composer who was highly regarded by the society of her time

(E) argue that women should have been given more opportunities to perform in public

In the fourth paragraph, we see how society's views on women in music are so pervasive that even an exceptional musician like Clara Schumann had doubts that she was worthy of playing and composing music (C). (A) is a distortion because the passage says that her husband supported her music, but it never mentions her teachers. (D) is another distortion, for while Schumann was exceptional she was not highly regarded by society. (B) is out of the scope of this paragraph, and (E) is an opposite.

Repeat Step 2: Examine the question stem.

5. The use of quotation marks around "safe" (line 57) serves primarily to emphasize

Step 3: Predict an answer

_____

_____

and **select** the answer that best matches your prediction.

(A) the cleverness of art songs

(B) the difficulty of categorizing the nature of art songs

(C) the comic nature of the discussion

(D) that the author does not fully endorse the use of this term

(E) that the appropriateness of having women write for this genre was shared by everyone in the society

In the last paragraph, the author is poking a little fun at the word "safe." The author does not agree with the notion that art songs were the only appropriate compositions for women (D). There is no mention of art songs being clever (A), only that they are short and suited to domesticity (B). The passage is not comic in nature (C). Finally, this point-of-view is not shared by everyone in society, making (E) an extreme answer.

● THE FINAL ACT
Self-Check Quiz

Questions 1–5 refer to the following passage.

The swimming sky of oceanic expanse in Van Gogh's *The Starry Night*, the human figure born of marble by the careful hands of Rodin, and the graceful, ethereal figure of Degas's ballerina all communicate both emotion and essence in a world where aesthetic reigns supreme. Art
(5) has forever been humankind's tool for expressing the ineffable, a form of communication when words fail or are wholly inadequate. Art challenges the artist by constructing a world in which opposing forces—impulse and control, emotion and thought, ideation and actuality—must cooperate to produce a piece of art. The artist must
(10) wrestle an almost untamable creative force for control in order to grant space to its expression. The process of facing and governing this force while conveying it to others makes artistic creation an especially valuable therapeutic tool for the emotionally disturbed.

The process of creation and the created product are equally
(15) valuable parts of therapeutic art. Creating art requires balancing

two aspects of personality that are, in the case of the emotionally disturbed person, especially irreconcilable. Like all artists, the emotionally
disturbed person must learn to control and harness the dangerous,
unpredictable forces of creation while remaining sufficiently unrestric-
(20) tive to allow its expression. Balancing these forces in a constructive way
while granting full play to both is an important ability to master, one
that art therapy teaches particularly well.

   The emotionally disturbed artist's goal is not the perfect expression
of an aesthetic ideal. Yet communicating the mind's content and hav-
(25) ing it recognized by others is intensely valuable to the disturbed artist's
healing. Taking ideas out of the isolation imposed by the mind and
reproducing them in a form that can be shared and understood by others releases those ideas from the mind and removes from them some of
their power. Using the brush where the pen and voice fail allows others,
(30) like the therapist, to recognize, understand, and begin to deconstruct
the mind's content.

   Artistic creation allows emotionally disturbed people to communicate ideas they are unable to express in words, and it provides therapists
with an otherwise unobtainable window into the mind. Examination of
(35) their artistic pieces reveals an inner world that the self of the disturbed
person cannot express another way. Art then becomes a new therapeutic medium through which to understand and address the complex
issues that threaten and haunt the disturbed person, and in which to
free them.

1. The first sentence of the passage serves primarily to

   (A) introduce a theory the author will later explain
   (B) state the author's central argument
   (C) refute the seriousness of art history
   (D) illustrate the limitations of art in its power to communicate
   (E) explain how art is capable of expressing ineffable human emotions

2. The author uses the phrase "impulse and control…actuality (lines 8–9), to reflect

   (A) how artists must wrestle with their personal demons before they can create masterpieces
   (B) the inability of art to express verbal language

    (C) that the world of art spans many historical eras

    (D) an inability to express human emotion in a constructive way

    (E) how the process of creating art can act as therapy for an individual

3. The purpose of the second paragraph is to

    (A) provide examples to support what art therapy teaches to an emotionally disturbed person

    (B) discuss the equality between creating art and art therapy

    (C) introduce the concept of art therapy being used to treat people who are emotionally disturbed

    (D) explain the meaning of art therapy and desires of art therapists throughout the world

    (E) refute the seriousness of art therapy

4. The author's purpose in mentioning the perfect expression of an aesthetic ideal (lines 23–24) is most likely to

    (A) indicate that it is important for patients to understand the beauty of their creative work

    (B) imply that patients feel conflicted by the nature of producing a final product instead of focusing on the creation

    (C) suggest that that the main focus of art therapy is on the process not on creating a masterpiece

    (D) explain why the brush is mightier than the pen

    (E) characterize art therapy as a remarkable remedy for healing emotionally disturbed clients

5. In the last paragraph of the passage, the author describes the process through which an emotionally disturbed person creates art primarily in order to

    (A) describe the characteristics of art therapy

    (B) introduce a possible method of curing patients

    (C) explain the reasons behind the a disturbed person's behavior

    (D) point to the benefits that art therapy has

    (E) outline the relationship between patients and therapists.

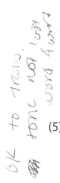

Questions 6 and 7 refer to the following passage.

Translating poetry from one language to another involves ingenuity and creativity, as well as technical skill. Some people think transla-tors should be as faithful as possible to the original author's wording, but I believe the spirit of the original should be preserved, even if this
(5) means using a bit of creative license when it comes to the actual words. Recently I read two different translations of "Tonight I Can Write" by Pablo Neruda. The first translation was quite literal, while the second took more liberty with Neruda's words but preserved the tone and flow of the original. I found the first translation dry and static, while
(10) the rhythm of the second translation was delightful.

6. The author mentions the two different translations (lines 7–10) in order to ex,

   (A) demonstrate the need for technical language skills in order to translate poetry

   (B) refute the idea that translators should always remain true to the author's original words

   (C) compare and contrast the use of technical skills and the author's wording in translations

   (D) trace the decline of translations to the original author

   (E) analyze the use of technical skill in translations in order to preserve rhythm and tone of the original piece

7. The author's primary purpose of the passage is to

   (A) show how the author has a preference for poetry in its origi-nal language

   (B) demonstrate a need for more proficient translators in poetry

   (C) depict the need for both technical skills and creativity in translating poetry into another language

   (D) showcase the author's ability to translate poetry

   (E) encourage young writers to begin translating poetry using only creativity as a guide

Questions 8–10 refer to the following passage.

Excerpt from *Democracy in America*
By Alexis de Tocqueville, translated by Henry Reeve

Some philosophers and historians have said, or have hinted, that the strictness of female morality was increased or diminished simply by the distance of a country from the equator. This solution of the difficulty was an easy one; and nothing was required but a globe and
(5) a pair of compasses to settle in an instant one of the most difficult problems in the condition of mankind. But I am not aware that this principle of the materialists is supported by facts.

The same nations have been chaste or dissolute at different periods of their history; the strictness or the laxity of their morals
(10) depended therefore on some variable cause, not only on the natural qualities of their country, which were invariable...

Although the travelers who have visited North America differ on a great number of points, they all agree in remarking that morals are far more strict there than elsewhere. It is evident that on this point
(15) the Americans are very superior to their progenitors the English. A superficial glance at the two nations will establish the fact.

In England, as in all other countries of Europe, public malice is constantly attacking the frailties of women. Philosophers and statesmen are heard to deplore that morals are not sufficiently strict, and the lit-
(20) erary productions of the country constantly lead one to suppose so.

In America, all books, novels not excepted, suppose women to be chaste, and no one thinks of relating affairs of gallantry. No doubt this great regularity of American morals originates partly in the country, in the race of the people, and in their religion: but all these causes,
(25) which operate elsewhere, do not suffice to account for it; recourse must be had to some special reason.

This reason appears to me to be the principle of equality and the institutions derived from it.

8. The author uses the first paragraph to

   (A) gently mock the materialists

   (B) agree with philosophers and historians

   (C) encourage a response from his detractors

   (D) dissuade the general public from holding high morals

   (E) praise America for its chaste women

9. In lines 17–20, the author mentions women in England in order to

(A) predict the moral integrity of the country

(B) counter the detractors of his argument

(C) emphasize the lack of morals in supposedly chaste parts of the world

(D) provide a direct contrast to the women in America

(E) describe a country that has experienced a sharp decline in morality

10. The author uses the last line of the passage to emphasize what point?

(A) The reasoning behind his argument is sound, while the main principle steering morality still remains vague and difficult to define.

(B) The underlying cause of morality will forever remain mysterious because no one can possibly understand all of its complexities.

(C) Europeans have less regard for moral standards than Americans do.

(D) Women have higher moral standards the closer they live to the equator.

(E) No one has any ideas about the true nature of morality in women.

● **ANSWERS AND EXPLANATIONS**

1. **E** The first paragraph begins with how art has opened our eyes to humanity's ability to express emotion that normally cannot be expressed (E). (A), (C), and (D) are opposites. (B) is distortion.

2. **E** The *opposing forces* that are listed in the first paragraph show how art can act as therapy (E). (A), (B), and (D) are misused details. (C) is out of the scope of the passage.

3. **A** The second paragraph focuses on what lessons art therapy holds for the emotionally disturbed individual (A). (B) and (C) are distortions. (D) is out of the scope of the passage. (E) is an opposite.

4. **C** The fourth paragraph focuses on the process of creating art and how that is the most important step in art therapy (C). (A) and (B) are out of scope. (D) and (E) are distortions.

5. **D** The purpose of the last paragraph of the passage is to show the benefits that art therapy has on the individual (D). (A), (B), and (E) are all out of scope. (C) is an extreme.

6. **B** The author of the passage disagrees with other translators who think that technical skill is all that is required for translating properly (B). (C) and (E) are distortions. (D) is out of the scope of the passage, while (A) is too narrow in scope to answer the question.

7. **C** (C) is the only answer that contains both technical skills and creativity in the answer. All of the rest of the answers are out of the scope of the passage—either too broad or too narrow.

8. **A** The tone of the first paragraph is humorous. The author is making fun of people who take a complicated problem like morality and try to simplify it into geographic locations (A). (C) is out of scope, while all of the rest (B), (D), and (E) are all misused details.

9. **D** In the paragraph after the one about English women, he immediately accounts for the morality of American women (D). (A), (B), and (E) are out of scope. (C) is a misused detail.

10. **A** The last point the author makes is to say that the question of how morality is formed in a society is not a simple question to answer, but that he believes that it has something to do with the equality instituted in certain societies (A). (B) and (E) are extremes, while (C) and (D) are misused details.

Paired Passages

DIFFICULTY: ★ ★ ★ ★

FREQUENCY: ★ ★

SURPRISE FACTOR: ★ ★

● INTRODUCTION TO PAIRED PASSAGES QUESTIONS

Paired Passage sets provide two passages that deal with the same topic or related topics on the SAT. Some of the questions ask about only one of the passages, while others ask you to consider both. The SAT should include one long and one short set of paired passages.

Many students find this question type particularly challenging for two reasons. The first is because incorrect answer choices can often refer to the wrong passage. You can see how these wrong-answer choices can be avoided in the Trap Door section of this lesson. Second, some questions ask you to compare and contrast the viewpoints of the two authors. Be sure to look carefully at the Performance Techniques section of this chapter to see how to best approach this challenging Paired Passage question.

There's good news, though. On average, as many as 70 percent of the questions in a Paired Passage set deal with only one passage. So, there won't be too many Compare and Contrast questions to decipher. When you do get to the Compare and Contrast questions, note that most authors in paired passage sets agree on some points and disagree on others. Some of the most challenging Paired Passage questions ask you to infer how one author would react to the ideas of the other.

Besides the Compare and Contrast questions, you'll see all of the other question types that you've seen in previous chapters: Inference, Detail, Global, Vocabulary-in-Context, and Function. If you need additional help on any of these question types, simply refer to the other lessons that deal with each of these passage-based questions.

● THE TRAP DOOR
Steering Clear of Answer Traps

For answering the questions in Paired Passage sets, you will need to stay on the lookout for all of the previously mentioned traps for reading comprehension. Refer to the introduction to Critical Reading, where you can find all of the potential traps for each question type.

However, another trap door lurks in Paired Passage questions. Many of the questions that only deal with the first passage will contain wrong answer choices that come from the second passage. Likewise, Passage 2 questions will have wrong answers that come from Passage 1. If you follow the strategy outlined in Performance Techniques, though, you can avoid this trap door on Test Day.

● PERFORMANCE TECHNIQUES
Key Formulas and Rules

In order to answer Paired Passage questions effectively, you must read the first passage only and then deal with the questions that relate to Passage 1. After you've answered those questions, then move on to the second passage. Read it, and then answer the questions that deal with Passage 2.

You're still following the Kaplan Method for Reading Comprehension. You'll just be doing the steps—(1) read the passage, taking notes; (2) examine the question stem; and (3) predict and select—for each passage and its accompanying questions one at a time. Once you've answered the questions that deal with each passage individually, then you can take a look at the compare and contrast questions that address both of the authors' viewpoints. This strategy will help you *keep straight who said what*.

● DRESS REHEARSAL
Sample Questions and Detailed Explanations

The following paired passage set and its accompanying questions have been divided in such a way as to make it easy for you to see how to follow the Kaplan Method for Reading Comprehension. The format of this passage is not how it will appear in the test booklet when you take the SAT. However, it is important to break down each step of the method before putting it all back together in the Final Act at the end of the chapter. The passages and questions that you see in that practice quiz will more closely resemble what you will see on Test Day.

Questions 1–4 are based on the following passages.

Step 1: Read the passage, taking notes.

Passage 1

People who work closely with animals readily acknowledge that they observe emotions in, or attribute emotions to, the animals they work with. Though this idea is
(5) derided by some in the scientific community, it is important to note that the most successful animal trainers are the ones who understand the "mood" of an animal—who are comfortable reading the emotional state of their charges. A horse trainer had better know
(10) whether a horse will take coaxing or commanding on a given day, and any trainer will tell you that different approaches are effective with different individuals, even those from the same breed. These trainers attribute the difference to the animals' emotional tendencies.

> Remember to read and take brief notes quickly! You have a limited amount of time on each section.

Step 2: Examine the question stem. (Only look at questions that deal with Passage 1.)

1. In line 5, the word *derided* is best understood as meaning

Step 3: Predict an answer

Made fun of, not believed true

and **select** the answer that best matches your prediction.

(A) argued

(B) ridiculed

(C) hated

(D) disturbed

(E) maligned

Here you have a Vocabulary-in-Context question. Remember to treat this question type like a sentence completion. Gather contextual clues that will help you make a strong prediction. From the context we can figure out that scientists feel differently about the subject matter than animal trainers do. So if animal trainers find that recognizing animal behavior is valid and beneficial, scientists would feel the opposite of that—NOT valid or beneficial. Look at your answer choices and then choose the answer that best matches your prediction. **Answer (B) is the correct choice.** You don't need to read any of Passage 2 in order to answer this question.

Repeat Step 1: Read the passage, taking notes.

Passage 2

The Oxford Companion to Animal Behavior advises animal behavior-
(15) ists: "One is well advised to study the behavior [of an animal], rather than attempting to get at any underlying emotion." Whether or not animals experience emotions similar to those that humans do, the fact is that there is no scientific way to quantify and categorize them. If animals do experience emotion, it is certain that they do not express
(20) it in the same way we do. Accordingly, making any conclusions about emotions based on behavior amounts to nothing more than guess-work and wishful anthropomorphizing.

Repeat Step 2: Examine the question stem.

2. In lines 15–16, the author uses the quotation primarily to

Repeat Step 3: Predict an answer

_____

_____

and **select** the answer that best matches your prediction.

(A) provide an example of an animal trainer's abilities

(B) question the assumption that is made by the author

(C) emphasize that animals are capable of experiencing emotion

(D) lend strong support to the author's argument

(E) convey an outside opinion that contrasts with the beliefs of the author

Why does the author put this quotation into the passage? Without any support this argument would be quite weak. By quoting a trusted source the author has strengthened the argument. Look for an answer that matches that prediction and you will see that **(D) is a great match!** (A) and (C) are typical wrong answers found in Paired Passage sets. They both come from Passage 1. (B) and (E) are opposite answers of this function question.

Now take a look at the Compare and Contrast questions.

Repeat Step 2: Examine the question stem.

3. How would the author of Passage 2 most likely respond to the assertion made by the author of Passage 1 that "successful animal trainers" understand the mood of their animals (lines 6–9)?

Before predicting this answer, consider the viewpoint of Author 2. Now think about how Author 2 would respond to Author 1's statement. Then, move on to predicting an answer.

Repeat Step 3: Predict an answer

you can't sci. under the word or animal

and **select** the answer that best matches your prediction.

(A) There is no scientific method for evaluating any animal's emotions.

(B) Animals are not capable of feeling emotion.

(C) Human beings can recognize emotion in animals because of our own intuitive nature.

(D) We are incapable of understanding how an animal behaves and why it acts the way it does.

(E) People should not waste their time with animals.

The correct answer is (A). (A) might appear at first to be an extreme answer; however, there is specific information in the passage that supports this answer. The author says, *Whether or not animals experience emotions similar to those that humans do, the fact is that there is no scientific way to quantify and categorize them.* The author uses the word NO and then goes on to say how ridiculous it would be to try to do something that to him seems like wishful thinking on the part of humans. (B) is a distortion. (C) is from Passage 1 author's point-of-view. (D) is also a distortion—one of the half right, all wrong answers. (E) is a complete opposite.

Repeat Step 2: Examine the question stem.

4. Which statement best describes how the authors of the two passages differ in their views on how animals experience emotion?

Before predicting this answer, consider the differences in the main arguments of each author. What was the main purpose of each passage? Then, move on to predicting an answer.

Repeat Step 3: Predict an answer

and **select** the answer that best matches your prediction.

(A) The author of Passage 1 is critical of animals' capacity to have emotions, whereas the author of Passage 2 considers it to be a necessary trial.

(B) The author of Passage 1 considers its social impact, whereas the author of Passage 2 examines its technical merits.

(C) The author of Passage 1 is concerned with the emotions that animals feel, whereas the author of Passage 2 believes it is unclear whether or not animals feel emotions at all.

(D) The author of Passage 1 praises the efforts of scientists, whereas the author of Passage 2 is critical of those efforts.

(E) The author of Passage 1 concludes that it is a matter of fact, whereas the author of Passage 2 considers it a matter of opinion.

(A), (B), and (E) are all distortions. These answer choices distort the perspective of one or both authors. (D) is an opposite, since there is no support for either of these statements. **(C) is the correct answer** since it is the only one that captures the opinions of both authors. Since Author 1 is convinced that animal trainers are not only capable of understanding the mood of an animal but also that animals are capable of feeling something, that author's perspective is very different from Author 2. Author 2 doesn't believe that we know whether or not animals experience emotion.

● **THE FINAL ACT**
Self-Check Quiz

Questions 1–10 refer to both of the following passages.

Passage 1
Money + Theater = Disaster: The Crisis of American Theater

Theater is being destroyed—which is evil—and like so many evils, money is at the root of it. To create a valuable, important and healthy theater, we must remove the profit motive from the core of the American theater and replace it with something better. Only then
(5) will theater artists be able to bring the American theater back to its former glory. We need to let our artists concentrate on art that asks big questions about human nature and social issues, not art that asks only the small question of how to make a buck.

If a theater company wants to survive in America, there are two
(10) practical options. Either it can create shows that draw a mass audience and support its financial needs with ticket-sales. Or it can apply to foundations and major corporations for charitable contributions.

In the first case, artists are totally dependent on the fickle tastes of the public and the almighty dollar. This means that instead of cre-
(15) ating work that investigates the human condition, asking the major philosophical questions of the soul, theater companies must chase the latest theatrical fads and guess which topics will interest a mass audience. It's a losing battle. So, as a result of profit-centered theater, we get vapid musical revues repackaging the works of Billy Joel or
(20) sitcom-style romantic comedies.

In the second case, a theater is beholden to major corporations that fund its artistic efforts. Corporate-funded theater is fearful, conservative and unwilling to challenge the status quo. Great theater should be fearless and radical, asking impertinent questions. Instead,
(25) it cowers before corporate boards and stodgy foundations.

In Europe, people recognize the value in theater that isn't related to its box office returns. The government subsidizes the arts to an extraordinary degree. France, for example, has given a lifetime of funding to acclaimed director Peter Brook. His only responsibility: do
(30) theater that interests him! So he creates brilliant theatrical explorations that touch on the major themes of the human condition: love, death, the relationship of the individual to society. His original pieces draw on a global theatrical tradition and are universally recognized by the critical establishment as works of shining genius.

(35)   Even here in the U.S., we once experienced a time when the theater operated on government subsidies; during the Depression, the WPA created the Federal Theater Project, giving thousands of dollars to actors, directors, and writers to create vital and important theatrical work. We can return to that mindset! But our politicians must have
(40) the courage to support this vital art and voters must let their representatives know that the state of the theater is unhealthy and needs them to recover!

Passage 2
Theater: It Makes Economical Sense

Theater is an essential part of any community. Without theater, our local economy would not be as strong as it is presently. Because of
(45) the wide range of theater companies in our city, we are able to attract tourists throughout the country and even internationally. These theater companies not only bring jobs to the actors, directors, designers, and technicians in the city, but also augment other entertainment and socially related businesses. Restaurants, parking garages and
(50) hotels see increased business on the days when there are theatrical productions running in their neighborhoods. Despite all of these great advances in our economy, there are still many public leaders that do not see theater as a worthy place to spend our tax dollars.

Many states have begun to give tax breaks to film production
(55) companies that bring in business to shoot films. Trying to attract these big budget films has become big business because city and state governments can easily see the amount of revenue being generated from

these commercial film productions. However, the theater that is being created throughout our city has not been given nearly the amount of
(60) tax breaks that film has been given. Our commercial theater industry, as well as the not-for-profit sector, is beginning to suffer.

Commercial theaters are having a difficult time convincing Broadway-bound musicals and plays to come to our fair city for their out-of-town tryouts because there are relatively few advantages to
(65) previewing a show here. Outside of sophisticated theater audiences, the city is not offering much in the way of outside assistance from the local and state government level—not in tax breaks, nor in other incentives.

Our local businesses are hurt, and the out-of-work artists and
(70) technicians stay unemployed, which creates another drain on our economy. If local government would spend more money supporting the commercial theater industry with tax incentives and spend more money on grants for not-for-profit theater companies, we could see revitalization in the theater that hasn't been seen since the Golden
(75) Age of the Broadway musical.

Only with the help of local government can the theater really begin to reach the next level of achievement. If city and state officials could see what a substantial effect the theater has on our economy, we may have an easier time convincing our elected servants to sup-
(80) port us in our theatrical endeavors. Money is what talks in our society, so start talking with your local and state government leaders about the economic benefits the theater can bring to our city.

1. In Passage 1, the critique at the end of the first paragraph primarily serves to

    (A) emphasize how profit-centered thinking is hurting the theater

    (B) provide a definition for arts funding

    (C) show how the government could use taxes to fund theater

    (D) argue for a different kind of leadership in government

    (E) illustrate the ways that theater effects our economy

2. In lines 9–12, the author of Passage 1 states that the two ways that theater companies can survive in America are through

    (A) taxes and private funding

    (B) charitable giving and producing shows with commercial appeal

(C) creative planning and suitable programming

(D) corporate foundations and private contributions

(E) ticket sales and commercial productions

3. In line 36, the word *subsidies* most closely means

(A) extra amenities

(B) tax gifts

(C) monetary contributions

(D) food stamps

(E) secret intelligence

4. From lines 39–42, it can be inferred that the American government

(A) hates the theater, while France gives money to Peter Brook to create new works for the theater

(B) neglects the theater, but once it supported it through a multitude of governmental programs

(C) abandoned theater artists, instead of helping them choose their productions

(D) uses few of its resources for theater; however, Europe generously supports the theater arts

(E) shuns the theater world, while Europe creates the most brilliant productions of our time

5. The author of Passage 2 most likely mentions "theater as a worthy place" in order to

(A) encourage public officials to stop slandering the theater

(B) discourage the public from attending commercial theatrical events

(C) describe this art form as the most deserving of public funds

(D) dissuade tourists from seeing only plays

(E) praise the art and make it more attractive to public leaders

6. Judging from lines 45–51, which of the following is not a positive aspect of the theater?

(A) The opportunity for growth in the tourism industry

(B) The revenue it helps generate for local restaurants

(C) The additional business at parking garages on nights of performances

(D) The exposure that is brought to social issues

(E) The jobs provided to theater artists

7. The author of Passage 1 would probably object to the statement that the "commercial theater industry" is beginning to suffer on the grounds that

(A) public officials are unwilling to increase taxes in order to create a bigger budget for the theater

(B) the theater's problems do not stem from commercial entertainment

(C) there are more important issues at stake for the theater than whether or not a show is commercially successful

(D) commercial theater is mindless entertainment that has its greatest stake in ticket sales

(E) commercial productions face an enormous risk of failing

8. The authors of both passages would probably agree that

(A) theater is evil since it is rooted in greed

(B) the government should be providing theaters with more money to create art

(C) theater is the most important of all the art forms

(D) many people are capable of producing a commercially successful show

(E) the theater is flawed due to its inability to be self-sufficient

9. How would the author of Passage 2 respond to the assertion of the author of Passage 1 at the end of the third paragraph?

(A) There is no evidence supporting the idea that theater companies turn out empty entertainment.

(B) The growth of the theater industry is waning due to a lack of support from the government.

(C) This argument is based on a misrepresentation of the validity of commercial theater.

(D) Commercial theater has indeed had a detrimental effect on the art as a whole.

(E) This view was asserted prematurely by younger theater artists.

10. Which statement best expresses the objection that the author of Passage 2 would make about Passage 1's argument regarding "profit motive" being removed from the American theater (lines 2–4)?

(A) It distorts the actual views of past theater historical experts.

(B) It is weak because the theater has been the subject of many different and often contradictory interpretations.

(C) It summarizes the long-held ideas that theater has proved to be a difficult art to fund properly.

(D) It is unfounded because the theater does not exhibit any of the qualities of greed.

(E) It makes little sense because we live in an economy-driven society from which the theater industry cannot be separated.

● ANSWERS AND EXPLANATIONS

1. **A**   The purpose of the first paragraph is to establish the author's point of view, that he does not agree with profit-based theater. The critique at the end of the paragraph just emphasizes that point (A). (B) is the opposite. (C), (D), and (E) are all distortions that come from Passage 2.

2. **B**   The second paragraph states there are two ways for a theater to survive in America. *Either it can create shows that draw a mass audience and support its financial needs with ticket-sales. Or it can apply to foundations and major corporations for charitable contributions.* This is a great prediction and (B) matches very well. (A) comes from Passage 2. (C), (D), and (E) are all distortions.

3. **C**   Subsidies are usually gifts of a monetary nature, but (B) is a tempting wrong answer meant to throw you off of the trail of the correct answer (C). (B) uses the language found in Passage 2. The author of Passage 1 does not mention taxes, ever. The rest of the choices (A), (D), and (E) don't make much sense in the context of the sentence.

4. **D** This author rants against the American government's lack of support for the theater. Then, he uses the Europeans as a shining example of how government spending can support the theater (D). (A), (B), and (C) are distortions. And (E) is an extreme answer.

5. **E** The word *worthy* serves as a big clue. The author is drawing attention to the merits of theater in this paragraph and why public leaders should support it (E). (A) is out of scope. (B) and (D) are distortions. (C) is an extreme.

6. **D** All of these things can be found in the first paragraph, except for (D). (D) comes to us courtesy of Passage 1, not Passage 2.

7. **D** The author of Passage 1 accuses the commercial theater of only being profit driven, not caring what kind of theater it creates so long as it makes money (D). (A) comes from the viewpoint of the author of Passage 2. (B) is a distortion. (C) is a misused detail. And (E) is an extreme.

8. **B** The only thing that both authors truly agree on is that the government should be spending money supporting the theater (B). (A) and (E) are distortions. (C) is an extreme. (D) is out of the scope of the passage.

9. **C** The author of Passage 1 says that the commercial, or profit-driven, theater creates *vapid...repackages* of *theatrical fads*. The author of Passage 2 never says anything to slight commercial theater. In fact, she wants the government to support the commercial theater industry, as well as the not-for-profit sector. She would likely respond to the author of Passage 1 by saying that he is missing the point and misrepresenting the art form in order to make a strong point (C). (A) and (D) are both extremes. (B) is a misused detail. (E) is out of scope.

10. **E** Since the author of Passage 2 bases her argument on the economical advantages of having theater in her city, we can assume that she would not agree with the author of the first passage when he says that money is the root of all the evils beleaguering the theater (E). (A), (B), and (C) are all out of the scope of the passage. (D) is a distortion.

Writing

SAT Writing Basics

The Writing section is made up of two main parts: the essay section and two multiple-choice sections. The multiple-choice section contains three different question types. The first is called *Improving Sentences.*

● IMPROVING SENTENCES QUESTIONS

Over half, or 25, of the 49 multiple-choice questions are of this type. Let's examine a typical Improving Sentences question to see how it's set up:

> Example 1: By the year 2020, our entertainment choices have been much wider than they are now.
>
> (A) have been much wider than they are now.
>
> (B) will be much wider than they are now.
>
> (C) having been much wider than they are now.
>
> (D) will be much wider than they currently are **being.**
>
> (E) being much wider than they are now.

In Improving Sentences questions, a portion of the sentence (or, occasionally, the whole sentence) is underlined. The sentence is followed by five multiple choice answer options. Option (A) always restates the underlined part of the sentence in its original wording. Options (B) through (E) make various revisions to the underlined part. You must determine which of these five possible answer choices gives the most correct and effective wording of the sentence. Choose the answer that is clearest and most precise, avoiding awkwardness and ambiguity. Any part of the sentence that is not underlined cannot be changed, so the answer you select should be the one that sounds best with the nonunderlined part. If the entire sentence is underlined, suspect a problem with the ordering of phrases or with sentence structure.

In the most common question setup, in which part of the sentence is underlined and part is not, *pay attention to the nonunderlined part!* Recall the approach for Sentence Completion questions: you read through the sentence, looking for clues. It's helpful to think of Improving Sentences questions in a similar way. Read the sentence slowly, paying attention to the context.

Though the writing chapters that follow point out particular answer traps for some error types, the most common answer trap is not set up by the test-maker. Instead, it's a trap you set up for yourself by taking the wrong approach. Many students struggle through the Writing section focusing too closely on the underlined part of the sentence. Your approach should be the opposite. To determine what, if anything, is wrong with the underlined part of the sentence, you need to look at the nonunderlined part. Remember, you don't have the option of changing anything in the nonunderlined part of the sentence, and therefore that part contains words that dictate how the underlined part should be phrased. Developing the habit of "thinking with your pencil" (marking important nonunderlined words) will help you keep your focus where it should be.

Let's look at how you can apply this advice to Example 1. The nonunderlined part of the sentence contains a reference to a time in the future, *by the year 2020.* This phrase is your clue that the sentence needs a future tense verb. In option (A), *have been* is incorrect because it's in the past tense. Options (C) and (E) don't provide future tense verbs. Options (B) and (D) do, but option (D) introduces a new verb error by adding "**being**" at the end of the sentence. Option (B) is the best answer because it corrects the error in the original sentence and does not introduce any other errors. In this example, the clue in the nonunderlined part of the sentence is circled. Bold text indicates an error not present in the original sentence but introduced by an answer choice.

● IDENTIFYING SENTENCE ERRORS QUESTIONS

The second type of multiple-choice writing question is called *Identifying Sentence Errors*. Each question is made up of a single sentence that has four words or phrases underlined. You must determine whether any of these underlined parts of the sentence is wrong. A fifth answer choice, "No Error," is offered in case the sentence is correct as written. Here's an example:

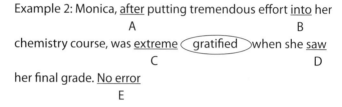

Example 2: Monica, <u>after</u> putting tremendous effort <u>into</u> her
          A   B
chemistry course, was <u>extreme</u> ⟨gratified⟩ when she <u>saw</u>
                            C   D
her final grade. <u>No error</u>
                   E

In Identifying Sentence Errors questions, you must look at each underlined word and think about how it works with the nonunderlined words in the sentence. Here, option (C) uses *extreme*, an adjective, to modify the word *gratified*. Because *gratified* is a verb, it requires an adverb as a modifier. Option (C) is wrong because the word should be *extremely*. Though an error like this is not difficult to understand, it may be tough to recognize if you read too quickly through the Writing questions. It can be helpful to think about the different ways you read on the SAT.

For most questions in the Writing section, you need to read with an editor's eye. Reading to edit is different from reading to understand content material. When you read a passage in the critical reading section, you focus on the main idea, rather than the details, on your first reading. Your goal is to get an idea of what the passage is about and pick up any information you can about the author's attitude toward the subject.

On the other hand, think about how you read for the Sentence Completions questions in the Critical Reading section. Here, details *are* crucial. You work with one sentence at a time, and your task is to figure out which parts of the sentence serve as clues to help you predict a meaning for the blank. The words you identify as clues are the crucial details. Likewise, in the writing section, Improving Sentences questions and Identifying Sentence Errors questions both demand that you concentrate on one sentence at a time. You get to the right answer by determining which nonunderlined words can serve as clues. If a verb is underlined, check for its subject. If a pronoun is underlined, check for the word it refers to. Context is crucial for Improving Sentences and Identifying Sentence Errors questions.

● IMPROVING PARAGRAPHS QUESTIONS

The third type of Writing multiple-choice question is Improving Paragraphs. A passage of three or four paragraphs is followed by six questions. The passage is considered a rough draft, so it will contain errors. Some questions will address these errors. (The passage may also contain errors that aren't addressed by questions. Avoid getting distracted by these.) Questions that address errors are similar to Improving Sentences questions and require you to read like an editor. Other questions, however, are similar to questions in the Critical Reading section. For these questions, you need to take more of a big-picture approach and apply your reading comprehension skills. These questions may ask about strategies the writer uses and whether or not a particular sentence should be added to or deleted from the essay. Using your active reading skills to determine the main idea of a paragraph will help you answer questions involving adding and deleting sentences.

With the exception of these Improving Paragraphs questions, however, most of the reading you do in the SAT Writing section will involve reading as an editor and focusing on details. Don't be overwhelmed. Keep in mind that the SAT Writing section tests only a limited number of topics. That's the beauty of a standardized test: predictable topics are tested in predictable ways. Verb usage, pronouns, and sentence structure are tested frequently; other topics are tested less frequently. Wordiness shows up frequently in wrong answer choices, so being alert for wordiness can help you eliminate wrong answers. Knowing what to expect is half the battle.

While there are some specific traps associated with particular writing topics, the most important trap is one of awareness. You need to know which topics are tested most frequently and be aware of words that serve as clues that let you determine whether an error is present. Don't spend a long time staring at the underlined words asking yourself what may be wrong with them. Instead, *look closely at the nonunderlined words and ask yourself how the underlined and nonunderlined words work together.* As you work through the practice quizzes in this book, get in the habit of noticing and circling clues.

Use the rankings to help you focus your study. In addition, look for examples of different phrasings, some correct, some incorrect. An icon will identify each: 👎 👎. You can skim through the section looking at these examples. When you see an example that is incorrect and you're not sure why, that indicates a topic you should study carefully.

● HOW MULTIPLE-CHOICE QUESTIONS ARE SCORED

If you get a multiple-choice question right, you earn 1 point. If you get a multiple-choice question wrong, you lose ¼ of a point. If you omit a multiple-choice question, you neither gain nor lose any points.

Your raw score for the multiple-choice questions is converted into a scaled score ranging from 200–800. This scaled score will account for two-thirds of your total Writing score.

Verb Usage

DIFFICULTY: ★

FREQUENCY: ★ ★ ★ ★

SURPRISE FACTOR: ★ ★

● INTRODUCTION TO VERB USAGE QUESTIONS

Verbs are the most frequently tested topic on the SAT writing section. This isn't surprising, since every sentence, by definition, contains a verb. Frequency is therefore the most important factor. Verb usage is not a very difficult topic because it is governed by predictable rules, all of which you're intuitively familiar with. In addition, the SAT tests a limited number of verb error types. Fortunately, you don't have to know every rule in the grammar book to do well on Verb Usage questions!

While verb usage follows rules, you should still exercise caution—the test-maker uses some deliberate traps that make verb questions tricky and can mislead you into choosing an incorrect answer. Have no fear, though; when you become aware of the traps and learn how to apply the rules in the Performance Techniques section of this lesson, you can be confident that you'll be able to handle nearly every Verb Usage question that you're likely to encounter on the test.

You'll find questions that involve verb issues in both the Improving Sentences and Identifying Sentence Errors questions. With both of these question types, you should always consider the possibility of an error in verb usage whenever you see an underlined verb. Most Improving Paragraphs questions test issues other than verbs. There is, however, one Verb Usage question type that is specific to the Improving Paragraphs section. This is verb tense consistency, and it's explained in Verb Usage Rule 5.

Characteristics of Verb Usage Questions

Understanding two key concepts, tense and subject-verb agreement, will enable you to handle most Verb Usage questions effectively. The first concept is tense, and the second is subject-verb agreement. Whenever you see an underlined verb, you should consider both tense and agreement to determine whether or not the verb is being used correctly. The rules in the Performance Techniques section also discuss some other verb problems you will see on the SAT, including the incorrect use of *being* and other verb forms ending in *–ing*.

Most Common Types of Verb Usage Questions

There are two commonly tested types of Verb Usage questions. The first involves tense. Verbs convey two types of information: *what* the action is and *when* the action occurs. The *when* aspect of the verb is called the verb's **tense**. Here are the three tenses and some examples:

Present tense—the verb expresses an action happening currently

I walk; she is walking

Past tense—the verb expresses an action that occurred at some earlier time

He walked; they have walked, you had walked

Future tense—the verb expresses an action that will occur at some future time

She will walk; they will have walked

You don't need to worry much about the grammatical classification of verb tenses in order to do well on the SAT. You simply need to make sure that verb tenses are used accurately and logically within the sentences (in Identifying Sentence Errors and Improving Sentences) and consistently within the whole passage (in Improving Paragraphs).

A second commonly tested verb issue is subject-verb agreement. You know that every sentence must have a subject and a verb. The verb expresses either an action or a state of being. The subject is the person or thing that does or receives the action. (Most often, the subject does the action.)

In a grammatically correct sentence, the subject agrees with the verb. That means you need to choose the correct form of the verb to correspond with (to "agree" with) the subject. In short simple sentences, your ordinary knowledge of English guides you to recognize correct subject-verb agreement. Here are two short sentences with correct subject-verb agreement:

👍| The *box is* upstairs in the attic.

👍| The old *magazines are* upstairs in the attic.

Subject-verb agreement does get a little trickier in longer sentences. The discussion of traps below will help you identify correct subject-verb agreement even in more complicated situations.

● THE TRAP DOOR
Steering Clear of Verb Usage Answer Traps

For errors in verb tense, certain words in the nonunderlined part of the sentence serve as clues that indicate which verb form should be used in the underlined part of the sentence. You can read more about these clues in the Performance Techniques section later in this lesson.

However, questions testing subject-verb agreement often use a couple of traps that seem to be set deliberately by the test-maker. Once you know what you need to look for, these traps will be very easy to spot.

Subject-Verb Agreement Trap 1: A prepositional phrase or two comes between the subject and the verb.

Before we look at an example, let's review prepositions. A preposition, by definition, is a word that expresses a relationship between two nouns. The preposition and the words that follow it make up what is called a **prepositional phrase.** A prepositional phrase always starts with the preposition and ends with the noun that follows it. The prepositional phrase in this sentence is shown in bold:

🗨 Susan bought a carton **of eggs**.

The word *of* is a preposition, and its object is *eggs*. The word *of* is used to express the relationship between the two nouns *carton* and *eggs*. In other words, the prepositional phrase *of eggs* describes the carton by stating what it contains. You can refer to the accompanying box for some examples of prepositions.

Examples of Prepositions				
at	for	near	over	under
between	from	of	to	with

Prepositional phrases are used frequently in English, but you're probably not accustomed to paying much attention to them. As you read through the sentences in the Writing section, get in the habit of noticing any prepositional phrases that appear *immediately before an underlined verb.* Whenever you spot this situation, always suspect a possible error in subject-verb agreement.

Now let's look at a specific example of Subject-Verb Agreement Trap 1. With this trap, the subject of the sentence is followed by a prepositional phrase whose object differs in number from that of the subject. This sounds more complicated than it is. Remember that the *number* of the subject is either singular or plural. See if you can spot the trap here:

Learn Your Lines

🗨 The **box** of old magazines **are** upstairs in the attic.
it if you cover it, it does make sense! Duh!

The subject of this sentence is *box*, not *magazines*. Since *box* is singular, the verb in this sentence should be *is*. Your ear tells you that *the box is* is correct. You would never say *the box are*. The prepositional phrase *of old magazines* describes the subject, *box*. You need to think analytically about this sentence to recognize that *magazines* is *not* the subject. Here is how the sentence should read:

🗨 The **box** of old magazines **is** upstairs in the attic.

You can easily avoid this trap by making sure you pause at every underlined verb to ask yourself, "What is the subject that corresponds to this verb?" Don't fall for the trap of letting the verb agree with the object of a preposition. Remember that in any given sentence, the object of a preposition can never be the same word as the subject of the sentence, and the verb must agree with the subject.

Subject-Verb Agreement Trap 2: Part of the verb appears before the subject in the sentence.

In English the subject usually precedes the verb in a sentence, though there is no grammatical rule that requires this order. When you encounter a sentence on Test Day that puts part of the verb first, the sentence will probably sound strange or formal to you. Since we don't generally put the verb first in ordinary conversation, it can be easy to fall into the trap of thinking that a noun that comes immediately before a verb must be its subject. Look at this example:

> ➤ Also **included** in the planning stages of the project **was** the **architect and** a design **consultant**.

In this sentence the verb is made up of two words that aren't next to each other: *was* and *included*. To find the subject, ask yourself, Who or what was included? It's not *the project*, but the *architect…and…consultant*. Since the subject is plural, the verb should be *were* rather than *was*:

> ➤ Also **included** in the planning stages of the project **were** the **architect and** a design **consultant**.

If you find yourself struggling with a question like this, it can help to mentally rephrase the sentence, placing the subject before the verb:

> ➤ The **architect and** a design **consultant was** also **included** in the planning stages of the project.

In this rephrasing, the very same words are used; they are simply arranged according to the more common pattern that places the subject before the verb. With this more conventional word order, it's not difficult to identify the subject and recognize it as plural. Making the correction becomes much easier:

➡ The **architect and** a design **consultant were** also **included** in the planning stages of the project.

If you encounter a sentence that seems to use strange wording, remember to ask yourself if the verb comes before the subject. If so, don't be afraid to rearrange the word order in your mind in order to determine if the sentence uses correct subject-verb agreement.

Handling a Sentence with Unconventional Word Order

Do not assume that a sentence has an error simply because it uses unconventional word order and sounds formal or unusual to you. Try rearranging the sentence so that the subject comes before the verb. If you do this and your ear tells you that the subject and verb agree, then the sentence is correct in the area of subject-verb agreement. Remember that "No error" will sometimes be the correct answer for Identifying Sentence Errors questions. A sentence is not necessarily wrong just because the verb appears before the subject. Agreement between subject and verb is what matters. (See Sample Question 2.)

While you're learning to avoid the subject-verb agreement traps, it's a good idea to keep your pencil in hand as you read through the sentences. You can either circle the subject or draw brackets around any prepositional phrases that come between the subject and the verb.

Find the Subject!

Both subject-verb agreement traps can be avoided by following one simple guideline: **Don't be fooled into thinking that whatever noun comes just before the verb is necessarily the subject of that verb!**

● **PERFORMANCE TECHNIQUES**
Key Formulas and Rules

This section is not a comprehensive treatment of verbs. Instead, it presents five specific rules that cover nearly all of the verb errors you'll see on the SAT. In reading about these rules, you should focus on learning which kinds of words in the nonunderlined part of a sentence function as clues that guide you in the process of identifying and correcting verb usage errors.

In addition to the five rules, this section presents some examples of two verb forms that are sometimes misused, the infinitive and the gerund. There is no general rule that applies in all cases, but your ear will usually determine which form is more appropriate in a particular case.

Verb Usage Rule 1: A verb must agree with its subject.

You find the subject of a sentence by starting with the verb and asking the question, Who or what? before the verb. For example:

☞❙ The library's **collection** of CDs **is** quite extensive.

The verb in this sentence is *is*. To find the subject, ask yourself, "Who or what *is extensive?*" The answer to this question is *collection. CDs* cannot be the subject because the word *CDs* is the object of the preposition *of*. Remember to be on the lookout for the subject-verb agreement traps described above.

Verb Usage Rule 2: The tense of a verb must make sense in relation to any other verbs that may appear in the sentence. In addition, a verb's tense must be logically consistent with any time-related phrases that appear in the sentence.

If a sentence contains two verbs, only one of them will be underlined. The verb that is not underlined is not open to change and therefore serves as a clue that indicates what the correct tense of the underlined verb will be. Consider this example:

The treatment <u>that</u> <u>is being used</u> by doctors for a century was
     A   B   C
finally shown to be <u>ineffective</u>. <u>No error</u>
                    D   E

In this sentence, the nonunderlined verb *was…shown* is in a past tense, while the underlined verb *is being used* is in a present tense. Since the nonunderlined verb cannot be changed, you must identify the underlined verb as an error, because the two verbs in the sentence are not logically consistent. The sentence would be correct if the wording of option B were changed to *had been used*.

You can apply Rule 2 simply by using your ordinary knowledge of English and your common sense. Just think in terms of when one action takes place in relation to another. Your ear should help you spot the error in this sentence:

👎 Ms. Howard, though she *is working* at Midland High for only one year, *received* the award for "Favorite Coach" from the senior class at graduation last week.

Here, one verb, *is working,* is in a present tense, and the other, *received*, is in a past tense. Logically, this doesn't make sense. The problem can be corrected by changing *is working* to a past tense:

👍 Ms. Howard, though she *has worked* at Midland High for only one year, *received* the award for "Favorite Coach" from the senior class at graduation last week.

In addition to considering the relationship between the two verbs in this sentence, you should notice that the sentence contains two phrases relating to time: *for only one year* and *last week*. When you see a time-related phrase, especially in the Identifying Sentence Errors questions, think of it as a clue that prompts you to consider an error related to verb tense. You will see time-related phrases that serve as clues even in identifying sentence errors questions that contain only one verb.

Here is a one-verb sentence in which a time-related phrase indicates an error in verb tense:

➡ *Before 1985,* fewer than half of all Americans will use a computer at home.

The phrase *before 1985* should alert you that the verb in this sentence requires the past tense. The verb *will use* is in the future tense and so is not consistent with the phrase indicating that the action took place at an earlier time. The sentence can be corrected with a past tense verb:

➡ *Before 1985,* fewer than half of all Americans *used* a computer at home.

Other examples of time-related phrases are **after 1588, before 1950, by the end of the week, forty years ago,** and **last month.**

Verb Usage Rule 3: The verb form ending in "-ing" cannot be used alone as the main verb of a clause or a sentence.

A clause is a group of words that contains both a subject and a verb. (You can read more about clauses in Lesson 20, Sentence Structure.)

If the main verb in a clause or a sentence ends in *-ing,* another verb word, sometimes called a *helping verb* (such as *have, has, had, is,* etc.) must also be included. Look at this sentence:

➡ *Hiking through the woods,* Steven noticed an amazing variety of birds.

In this sentence, the main verb is *noticed.* The subject is *Steven. Hiking through the woods* is a phrase (not a clause) that modifies, that is, provides more information about, Steven. This sentence is correct, because here the *-ing* form *hiking* is not the main verb of a clause.

In contrast, look at this example:

➡ On her vacation, Sherri *hiking through the woods.*

This doesn't sound quite right, does it? Something is missing. To be correct, this sentence needs a helping verb such as *has been, is,* or *was.* Here's an example of a correction:

➡️ On her vacation, Sherri *was hiking* through the woods.

Particularly in the Improving Sentences questions, you should be on the lookout for clauses that contain an *-ing* verb form without a helping verb. These clauses will always require a revision. Being aware of this rule can also help you eliminate wrong answer choices.

Verb Usage Rule 4: Do not use the phrases "being as" or "being that" to mean "because."

This rule overlaps the topics of verb usage and word choice. The phrases *being as* and *being that* will never be correct on the SAT. You may use or hear these phrases in conversation, but they aren't correct according to the rules of formal writing, which is what the SAT tests. Notice the incorrect usage in this example:

➡️ *Being as* she got stuck in a traffic jam, Susan missed the first 15 minutes of the movie.

Changing *being as* to *because* corrects the problem:

➡️ *Because* she got stuck in a traffic jam, Susan missed the first 15 minutes of the movie.

Remember that the *being* will not necessarily be incorrect every time you see it on the SAT, but there's a high likelihood that it will be wrong. Therefore, whenever you see *being* under-lined, always take note of it and determine whether or not it's used correctly in context.

Verb Usage Rule 5: In Improving Paragraphs questions, choose a verb tense that matches the tense used most consistently throughout the passage.

This rule will guide you for an Improving Paragraphs question that asks you to make a revision or add a sentence to the essay. A new or revised sentence can be correct only if its verb is in the same tense as most of the other verbs in the passage. Usually passages are written in the past tense, but you may see a passage written in the present tense. Your task is to identify the predominant tense in the passage and select an answer choice that uses the same tense. Notice the verb tenses in these three sentences:

> **(1)** Many famous scientists **were** not academic stars during their childhoods. **(2)** Albert Einstein, for example, **leaves** school as a teen-ager before he **received** his diploma. **(3)** This situation, however, did not **prevent** him from becoming one of the most famous scientists of all time.

Because the other verbs in Sentences 1 and 2 are in the past tense, the present tense verb *leaves* in Sentence 2 is incorrect. To be consistent with the other verbs, the past tense verb *left* should be used here instead of *leaves*.

> **Guideline for Gerunds and Infinitives: Whenever a gerund (a verb form ending in "-ing") or an infinitive (a verb form used after the word "to") is underlined, take note of it. Some Identifying Sentence Errors questions test whether the gerund or infinitive is appropriate in a particular context.**

There isn't a general rule that lets you determine when a gerund is best and when an infinitive is called for instead. Sometimes the two are interchangeable; sometimes they're not. Your ear should be a reliable guide in determining which is appropriate. Let's consider some examples. First, notice that in these examples, the infinitive and gerund are interchangeable:

> 👍 Miranda began *studying* algebra in eighth grade.
> 👍 Miranda began *to study* algebra in eighth grade.
> 👍 Aaron likes *playing* frisbee.
> 👍 Aaron likes *to play* frisbee.

Here are some examples in which the infinitive is necessary, and the gerund is incorrect:

> 👎 John has decided *pursuing* an acting career.
> 👍 John has decided *to pursue* an acting career.
> 👎 The visitors are expected *arriving* by noon.
> 👍 The visitors are expected *to arrive* by noon.

In the following examples, on the other hand, the infinitive is wrong, and the gerund is necessary:

👎 The child did not deny *to hit* her brother.
👍 The child did not deny *hitting* her brother.
👎 Many people detest *to eat* liver.
👍 Many people detest *eating* liver.

Gerunds and infinitives aren't a huge issue on the SAT, and, as the examples above show, you can rely on your ear. Just keep in mind that a gerund or infinitive won't necessarily be used erroneously every time you see it underlined.

● DRESS REHEARSAL
Sample Questions and Detailed Explanations

All the examples in this section are either Improving Sentences or Identifying Sentence Errors questions, because these are the question categories in which most verb issues are tested. Remember that consistency of verb tense is occasionally tested in an Improving Paragraphs question. (See question 10 in the Final Act section for an example.)

Sample Question 1: Prepositional Phrase Appears between the Subject and Verb

The <u>unhealthy</u> effects of a sedentary lifestyle <u>becomes</u>
    A   B

<u>more obvious</u> to people as <u>they</u> age. <u>No error</u>
  C   D   E

The correct answer is B. If you don't see an error right away, remember that verbs are tested frequently so start by finding the verb. In this sentence option B contains the verb *becomes.* Remember Rule 1: A verb must agree with its subject. What is the subject here? Ask yourself, "What is it that *becomes more obvious*?" It is not simply *a sedentary lifestyle,* but the *effects* of that lifestyle. *Effects* is the subject of this sentence. Thus, subject-verb agreement is the error here. Option B should read *become* instead of *becomes.*

Sample Question 2: Part of the Main Verb Appears before the Subject

Also participating in the panel discussion about the
    A   B

controversial new ruling was the mayor and five city
    C   D

council members. No error
                   E

The correct answer is D. This sentence probably sounds a little strange to you. What is it that's odd? Look at option A. *Also participating* sounds unusual, but it doesn't actually constitute an error. It's part of a trap. Look at option B. *A discussion about the ruling* is the correct idiomatic usage. In option C, *controversial* correctly modifies *ruling*. Now look at option D. *Ruling was* sounds correct; this is a trap. Sometimes the verb appears before the subject. The verb in this sentence isn't simply *was*. It's *was participating*. To find the subject ask yourself, Who or what was participating? It wasn't *the ruling* that *was participating*. It was *the mayor and five city council members* that *was participating*. Your ear tells you that's wrong. Correct agreement is *the mayor and five city council members **were** participating*. It turns out that you don't have to be concerned about the wording of option A even if you think it sounds funny, because option D clearly contains a verb usage error.

Sample Question 3: Sentence Contains a Time-Related Phrase as Clue

By the end of the 1970s, many veterans of World War II
    A   B

are becoming grandparents. No error
       C   D   E

The correct answer is C. This sentence should sound a little strange to you. Can you put your finger on why? Let's see what happens when we consider each underlined part in relation to the rest of the sentence. Look at option A. *By the end is* idiomatically correct. Look at what follows it though: *By the end of the 1970s*. This is a time-related phrase, which is a clue to help you determine the right verb tense. The verb in this sentence is *are becoming* (option C), which is in a present tense.

That's not appropriate here, because *by the end of the 1970s* refers to a time in the past. Therefore, the verb in this sentence should be in the past tense, and option C is the error. Note that in option B, *many* correctly modifies *veterans*. Option D is correct because *grandparents* is a plural noun that appropriately matches the plural noun *veterans* in the nonunderlined part of the sentence.

Sample Question 4: Underlined Verb Doesn't Relate Logically to a Nonunderlined Verb

To successfully complete a large project such as a research paper, one must plan carefully, breaking the project into manageable tasks that had been accomplished in small time increments.

(A) that had been accomplished in small time increments

(B) that you can accomplish in small time increments

(C) that can be accomplished in small time increments

(D) that can be accomplished in a much less amount of time

(E) that one can be accomplishing in small time increments

The correct answer is option (C). When you read option (A), your ear should tell you that something is off. The nonunderlined phrases *to successfully complete* and *one must plan* are clues that a future tense verb is needed in this context. Therefore, option (A), which uses a past tense *had been accomplished,* can't be correct.

Option (B) doesn't sound bad at first. It changes the verb to "can accomplish," which fits the context of the sentence nicely. However, while correcting the verb tense, option (B) also incorrectly introduces the pronoun "you." Since the nonunderlined part of the sentence uses the pronoun "one," the correct revision cannot include the pronoun "you."

Option (C) corrects the verb tense without introducing any new errors. This seems like a good answer, but you should still consider the remaining two options. Option (D) corrects the verb tense but introduces a new error. The phrase *a much lesser amount of time* is wordy and uses an incorrect idiom. Option (E) correctly uses the pronoun *one,* which is necessary to fit the context of the nonunderlined part of this sentence. Look at the verb, though. There is no need for the verb to end in -*ing* here. The verb *can be accomplishing* does not logically relate to the other verbs in this sentence. Thus, as we expected, option (C) turns out to be the best revision for this sentence.

Sample Question 5: Underlined Verb Doesn't Relate Logically to a Nonunderlined Verb

Although the Victorian writer Thomas Hardy wished to be remembered for his poetry, he is best known by his contemporaries for his tragic novels.

(A) he is best known by his contemporaries for his tragic novels

(B) he is best known by his contemporaries as one who wrote tragic novels

(C) he will be best known by his contemporaries for his tragic novels

(D) he was best known by his contemporaries for his tragic novels

(E) he was best knowing by his contemporaries as a writer of tragic novels

The correct answer is option (D). Let's start by examining the nonunderlined part of the sentence for clues. *Victorian* is a time reference that suggests a past time, and sure enough, the verb in the nonunderlined part of the sentence, *wished to be remembered* is in a past tense. This past tense verb in the nonunderlined part of the sentence indicates that the verb in the underlined part of the sentence must be in a past tense. Options (A) and (B) both include the present tense, verb *is known,* so they are both wrong. Option (C) uses a future tense, which doesn't match the past-tense verb in the nonunderlined part of the sentence.

Options (D) and (E) both use a past tense. To determine which option is more appropriate, carefully read the whole sentence with each wording. Option (E) uses a past tense with an –*ing* ending, which is not logical here. In addition, option (E) uses the phrase *as a writer of* tragic novels, which is wordy. Option (D), on the other hand, uses a past tense that is logical in the context of the sentence, and this option is less wordy. Therefore option (D) is the best choice.

● THE FINAL ACT
Self-Check Quiz

1. Written by Charles Darwin in 1859, *The Origin of Species* remains profoundly influential even though some of the arguments it makes have been modified by later research.

   (A) Written by Charles Darwin in 1859, *The Origin of Species* remains

   (B) Charles Darwin having written it in 1859, *The Origin of Species* remains

   (C) *The Origin of Species*, being written in 1859 by Charles Darwin, remains

   (D) Written by Charles Darwin in 1859, *The Origin of Species* continues remaining

   (E) Despite Charles Darwin writing it in 1859, *The Origin of Species* remaining

2. The sociologist clearly argues that changes in family structure has not been nearly as influential as changes in the economy.

   (A) has not been nearly as influential as changes in the economy

   (B) has not been as influential as in the economy

   (C) have not been nearly as influential as changes in the economy

   (D) have not been more influential as changes in the economy

   (E) have not been more influencing as changes to the economy

3. The new professor with expertise in several fields have been hired to rejuvenate the history department's curriculum.

   (A) have been hired to rejuvenate the history department's curriculum

   (B) have been hired for the purpose of rejuvenating the history department's curriculum

   (C) have been hired to renovate the history department's curriculum

   (D) has been hired to rejuvenate the history department's curriculum

   (E) has been hiring himself to rejuvenate the history department's curriculum

4. <u>Also performing</u> in tonight's concert <u>is</u> two friends, both of
    A   B

   <u>whom</u> studied music at the conservatory with me <u>many years</u>
    C   D

   ago. <u>No error</u>
           E

5. Jane was reluctant <u>to try</u> the <u>heavily</u> spiced potatoes; she
                          A   B

   <u>worried</u> that the dish would not agree <u>with</u> her. <u>No error</u>.
    C   D   E

6. Four years after my grandfather died, my father <u>will decide</u> to
                                              A

   start a new life <u>by</u> emigrating <u>from</u> his native country <u>of Italy</u>.
               B   C   D

   <u>No error</u>
    E

7. Because Jessica <u>is</u> sick <u>with pneumonia</u> for the last two weeks
                     A   B

   <u>of August,</u> she missed the first three of <u>her team's</u> soccer
     C   D

   games. <u>No error</u>
          E

8. Two years after <u>the publication of</u> the first edition <u>of</u> *Lyrical*
                   A

   Ballads, William Wordsworth <u>will be writing</u> a new preface <u>that</u>
                                  B   C

   became <u>the manifesto of</u> the Romantic movement. <u>No error</u>
               D   E

9. The juror did not begin <u>to question</u> the <u>defendant's innocence</u>
                             A   B

   until after the prosecution's third witness <u>testifies</u> about what
                                      C

   happened <u>on the night of</u> the alleged crime. <u>No error</u>
              D   E

10. **(1)** Government officials are concerned that many citizens are no longer making an effort to go to the polls to vote. **(2)** Some observers believe that as a nation, we are becoming more apathetic.

In context, which of the following is the best sentence to be inserted between sentences 1 and 2?

(A) The exact causes of this situation were unclear.

(B) Many causes for this had been suggested.

(C) The precise causes of this situation are unclear.

(D) The precise reasons in this case can not entirely be made clear.

(E) What might be causing this could not even be clarified.

● ANSWERS AND EXPLANATIONS

1. **A** The underlined part of the sentence contains two verbs. *Written* is used correctly to introduce a phrase that describes the book, *The Origin of Species.* The main verb, *remains,* is in the present tense. The nonunderlined part of the sentence contains yet another verb, *have been modified.* Even though this verb is in a past tense, the present tense verb *remains* works logically with it. Option (A) seems like a good choice, but you should still consider the other options.

Option (B) is incorrect because the verb *having written* doesn't work logically here. Option (C) is wrong because the verb form *being written* is inappropriate here. If the word *being* were omitted, then option (C) would be an acceptable way to phrase this sentence. Option (D) is wrong because it introduces a wordiness error. Either *continues* or *remains* would be acceptable here, but *continues remaining* is not. Option (E) is wrong because it uses the *–ing* verb form by itself as the main verb of a clause.

2. **C** Option (A) contains a verb that doesn't agree with its subject. The prepositional phrase *in family structure* in the nonunderlined part of the sentence serves as a clue that a subject-verb agreement trap is at work here. The noun *structure* is not the subject; it is the object of the preposition *in.* The subject is

changes, so the correct verb here is *have not been.* This tells you that option (B) cannot possibly be correct. Option (C) sounds good, but you should look at the other choices. Option (D) introduces a word choice error. The word *more* is used incorrectly. The word *as* is called for here. Option (E) introduces two other word choice errors. The verb *influencing* should be changed to *influential.* Because the nonunderlined part of the sentence uses the phrasing *changes **in** family structure,* option (E) is incorrect in switching to the phrasing *changes **to** the economy.*

3. **D** Because the underlined part of the sentence contains a verb, you should determine its subject and check for subject-verb agreement. The subject of *have been hired* is *professor.* The verb, therefore, should be changed to ***has** been hired.* The sentence sets up a subject-verb agreement trap by using two prepositional phrases *with expertise* and *in several fields* between the subject and the verb. Having identified the trap, you can eliminate options (A), (B), and (C). Option (E) is wrong because it inappropriately uses the *–ing* verb *hiring,* and includes the word *himself.* (The professor did not hire *himself.*)

4. **B** This sentence uses Subject-Verb Agreement Trap 2 because part of the main verb, *performing,* appears before the subject. The verb *is* constitutes an error, because the subject, *friends,* is plural. Mentally reorder part of the sentence as *two friends **is** performing.* Your ear tells you that this wording is wrong. Option B should contain the verb *are* instead of *is.* Option C correctly uses the object pronoun *whom* as the object of the preposition *of.* Option D is idiomatically correct.

5. **E** Option A is a correct use of the infinitive *to try.* Option B correctly uses an adverb to modify the adjective *spiced.* Option C uses a past tense, *worried,* which is consistent with the past tense verb *was* in the nonunderlined part of the sentence. Option D is used correctly as part of the idiomatic expression *agree with.*

6. **A** The time-related phrase *four years after* and the nonunderlined past tense verb *died* are clues that this sentence requires a past tense verb. The wording in option A should be *decided.* Option B is a correct use of the preposition *by* with the

verb *emigrating.* Option C correctly uses the preposition *from* to follow *emigrating.* Option D correctly uses the prepositional phrase *of Italy* to describe *country.*

7. **A** The time-related phrase *the last two weeks* and the non-underlined past tense verb *missed* serve as clues that a past tense verb is required here. Option A should be changed from *is* to *was.* Option B is a correct idiomatic expression. Option C correctly uses a prepositional phrase to describe *weeks.* Option D is a correct use of the possessive *her team's* before the noun *games.*

8. **B** The time-related phrase *two years after* is a clue that this sentence is testing verb tense. Option B contains a future tense verb, *will be writing,* which is incorrect in this context. The non-underlined past tense verb *became* indicates that a past tense verb is required. Thus, option B should be changed from *will be writing* to *wrote.* Option C correctly uses *that* to introduce a dependent clause. Option D uses appropriate word choice.

9. **C** *Testifies* is a present tense verb, which is not correct in this context. The time-related phrase *until after* and the nonunderlined past tense verb *did not begin* are clues that a past tense verb is needed. Therefore, option C should be changed from *testifies* to *testified.* Option A correctly uses the infinitive *to question.* (You should note here, though, that the infinitive *questioning* would also be correct in this context.) Option B is a correct use of the possessive. Option D uses an idiomatically correct expression.

10. **C** Notice that sentence 1 contains the present tense verb *are concerned* and sentence 2 contains the present tense verb *believe.* Therefore, any sentence added to the passage must also be in the present tense in order be consistent. This fact allows you to rule out some answer choices. Option (A), which contains *were,* and option (B), which contains *had been,* are wrong because they use past instead of present tense. Option (C)uses the present tense *causes,* and this is the best answer. Option (D) doesn't have an error in verb tense, but it isn't as concise as option (C). Option (E) is wrong because it uses the past tense verb *could not be clarified.*

Pronouns

DIFFICULTY: ★ ★

FREQUENCY: ★ ★ ★ ★

SURPRISE FACTOR: ★

● INTRODUCTION TO PRONOUNS QUESTIONS

Pronouns are one of the two most frequently tested topics on the SAT. Verb usage is the only other topic that is tested as heavily as pronouns.

Remember that a **pronoun** is a word that refers to a noun or another pronoun. This noun or pronoun that is referred to is called the pronoun's *antecedent*. The use of pronouns is governed by some very specific grammatical rules. The good news is that you already know most of these rules and apply them unconsciously in your everyday speech. Understanding all the different types of Pronouns questions, however, does require familiarity with some grammatical terms that you may not have thought about for a while. This lesson will help you learn or reacquaint yourself with the concepts that you need to succeed with Pronouns questions on the SAT.

The fact that pronouns are tested so frequently offers you some predictability. If you see a pronoun in an underlined part of the sentence, you should *always* check for an error because you know that pronouns are tested frequently. You shouldn't be caught off guard by Pronouns questions.

Characteristics of Pronouns Questions

The most important part of identifying and correcting pronoun errors is making sure that you know how to recognize pronouns. This lesson identifies the pronouns that are tested most frequently on the SAT. But first, let's review some grammatical terms that will help you understand how to use pronouns correctly.

Like nouns, pronouns can be either singular or plural. A **singular** pronoun refers to only one person or thing. A **plural** pronoun refers to two or more people or things. We use the word *number* to describe whether a pronoun is singular or plural. For example, the pronoun *me* is singular, while the pronoun *us* is plural.

A pronoun's **case** is determined by how the pronoun functions in a sentence. When a pronoun serves as the subject of sentence, it should be in the **subjective case.** A pronoun that functions as an object, whether an object of a verb or an object of a preposition, must be in the **objective case**. For example, *she* is a subjective pronoun; you would say, "*She* works hard." The pronoun *her* is objective; you would say, "Dad gave the book to *her*." A **possessive case** pronoun is used to show ownership. This sentence uses two possessive pronouns: "The computer used to be *his*, but now it is *mine*." Pronoun case errors on the SAT will usually involve the subjective or objective case.

Pronouns are also described in terms of **person.** A *first* person pronoun refers to the person who is speaking (I, me, we, us). A *second* person pronoun refers to a person who is being spoken to (you). A *third* person pronoun refers to someone or something that is being spoken about (he, she, it, him, her, they, them). The only time you need to be concerned with pronoun person on the SAT is to detect the *one-you* shift, which is described later in the Most Common Types of Pronouns Questions section. Familiarize yourself with the chart in this lesson so that you can recognize pronouns quickly. You may want to refer to this chart as you read the rules in the Performance Techniques section.

Personal Pronouns

	Subjective Case	Objective Case	Possessive Case
1st person singular	I	me	my, mine
1st person plural	we	us	our, ours
2nd person singular	you	you	your, yours
2nd person plural	you	you	your, yours
3rd person singular	he, she, it	him, her, them	his, her, hers, its
3rd person plural	they	them	their, theirs

A **personal pronoun** stands for a person, place, thing, or idea. Other types of pronouns tested on the SAT are **relative pronouns** and **demonstrative pronouns.** Relative pronouns are used to relate, or connect, one phrase or clause to another phrase or clause. A relative pronoun introduces a dependent clause and can function as either the subject or an object in that clause. The relative pronouns tested on the SAT are *who, whom, which,* and *that.* A demonstrative pronoun points to and identifies a noun or pronoun. Demonstrative pronouns include *this, that, these,* and *those.* The pronouns *this* and *these* refer to things that are close to the speaker in either space or time. The pronouns *that* and *those* refer to things that are farther away. A demonstrative pronoun takes the same form whether it's used as a subject or an object, so you don't have to worry about case.

Demonstrative Pronouns

	For something near	For something far
Singular	this	that
Plural	these	those

Most Common Types of Pronouns Questions

Two of the most common types of pronoun errors on the SAT revolve around case and number. These are grammatical errors that will often sound wrong to you on a first reading. Even if they don't sound wrong immediately, if you notice that the underlined part of the sentence contains a pronoun and you think about the traps described below, you will easily detect the error.

Another common type of pronoun error is called **ambiguity.** This problem occurs when a pronoun either does not have an antecedent or does not have a clearly defined antecedent. Remember, an antecedent is the noun or pronoun that a pronoun refers to. Rules 2 and 3 discussed in the Performance Techniques section below will help you handle problems with antecedents and ambiguity.

Another pronoun error you're likely to see on the SAT is called the *one-you* shift. This error involves inconsistency of person. *You* is a second person pronoun, but *one* is a noun and so is in the third person. Remember that, in using *you,* the speaker is addressing the listener, whereas in using *one,* the speaker is talking about a third person, that is, someone different from the speaker or the listener. You can read more about this issue of pronoun consistency in the discussion of Rule 4 in Performance Techniques.

● THE TRAP DOOR
Steering Clear of Answer Traps

Remember that many of the Pronoun questions you'll see on the SAT do not involve traps at all. Frequency is the most important factor for pronouns. Not every underlined pronoun you see will be used erroneously, but many will be.

Developing a keen awareness of pronouns will help you be sensitive to a trap the test-maker sets up on the SAT. This trap is the use of a conjunction such as *and* or *or* in a Pronouns question. When the test-makers pair a conjunction with a pronoun, they can make it harder for your ear to detect an error in pronoun case. Let's look at some examples:

☞ *Him* or Carlie will go next.

☞ Jonah should have sent a copy to Martha and *she*.

If you were to see the above sentences without *or* or *and*, you would easily hear the errors. You would never say "Him will go" or "Send a copy to she." When you see a pronoun used near a conjunction, be alert to the possibility of an error in case. Using your pencil to make notations on the test booklet can help you think through a problem like this. In the following corrections, see how the parentheses can help you focus.

👍 *He* (or Carlie) will go next.

　He is the subject of *will go*.

👍 Jonah should have sent a copy to (Martha and) *her*.

　Her is the object of the preposition *to*.

Don't be afraid to write in your SAT test booklet as you identify clues and traps. Marking up the test questions when you recognize clues and traps helps you stay focused.

● PERFORMANCE TECHNIQUES
Key Formulas and Rules

Five rules are presented here to help you handle all the Pronoun Questions you'll see on the SAT. The trap described above relates only to the first rule, which concerns pronoun case.

Rule 1: Pronoun Case

A pronoun's case is determined by the function of the pronoun within the sentence. Use subject case pronouns (I, you, he, she, it, we, they) for the subject of a verb. Use objective case pronouns (me, you, him, her, it, them, us) for objects, whether the object of a verb or the object of a preposition.

Ordinarily this rule is not difficult to apply because a sentence will sound wrong to you if a pronoun is in the wrong case. Be careful, though. Take note when you see a personal pronoun underlined when it's near the word *and* or *or*. Remember that the pronoun trap described above makes it a little more challenging for your ear to detect an error in pronoun case.

Rule 2: Pronoun Antecedent
A pronoun must have a clear and unambiguous antecedent.

Remember that an antecedent is a specific noun or pronoun that a given pronoun refers to. Be especially careful when you notice that the personal pronoun *they* is underlined on the SAT. This pronoun is often used without an antecedent, as in this sentence:

> ☞ In the article, *they* say that eating vegetables promotes health.

Here the pronoun *they* has no antecedent. It doesn't logically refer either to *the article* or to *vegetables*. Therefore, it's unclear exactly whom the writer means by *they*. To correct an error like this, the pronoun that lacks an antecedent must be replaced by a noun. Here are two acceptable revisions:

> ☞ In the article, the *author* says that eating vegetables promotes health.
> ☞ In the article, many nutrition *experts* who are quoted say that eating vegetables promotes health.

Both of these corrections provide a specific noun to take the place of *they* in the original sentence.

Note that Rule 2 contains two requirements: (1) a pronoun must have an antecedent and (2) there must be only one possible antecedent for the pronoun. If a pronoun can possibly refer to more then one word, the pronoun is ambiguous. Look for the ambiguity in this sentence:

> ☞ After studying with *Mike and Terrence*, Joe gave *him* a ride home.

Here, the reader has no way of knowing whether *him* refers to Mike or Terence. To avoid ambiguity, the appropriate person's name must be restated. You can expect to find ambiguous pronoun errors like this one in the Identifying Sentence Errors questions. In the last example, the word *him* would appear as one of the underlined choices, and that choice should be identified as the error.

(Audition Again)

Rule 3: Pronoun Agreement

A pronoun must agree with its antecedent in person and number.

On the SAT you will see sentences in which pronouns conflict with their antecedents in both person and number. In this example, number agreement is lacking:

> 👎 Each *athlete* does *their* best.

You may encounter sentences like this one frequently in ordinary conversation and informal writing. On the SAT, however, this sentence must be considered an error, since it doesn't follow the rules of standard English. The sentence contains an error in number agreement. The pronoun *their* is plural, but its antecedent, *athlete,* is singular. Depending on whether the athletes in question are males, females, or males and females, there are three acceptable ways to correct this sentence:

> 👍 Each *athlete* does *his* best.
> 👍 Each *athlete* does *her* best.
> 👍 Each *athlete* does *his or her* best.

On the SAT, you're most likely to see an error like this in the Identifying Sentence Errors questions, with *their* underlined. Thus, you wouldn't be required to actually correct the error but only to notice that the pronoun doesn't agree with its antecedent.

Here is an example of an error in which the pronoun does not agree with its antecedent in person:

> 👎 Most *people* know that when *they* travel outside the country, *you* will need passports.

Here the pronoun *they* agrees with *people,* because both are in the third person. The pronoun, *you,* however, is in the second person and so does not agree with the antecedent *people.* This sentence can be corrected as:

> 👍 Most *people* know that when *they* travel outside the country, *they* will need passports.

This revision consistently uses only the plural pronoun *they* to refer to *people*. This sentence, in addition to illustrating the rule of pronoun agreement, also provides an example of correct noun-noun agreement. Notice that the object *passports* is plural, making it agree with the plural subject *people*. See the tip below for another example of noun-noun agreement.

Noun-Noun Agreement on the SAT

Number agreement between two nouns is sometimes tested on the SAT. If a subject is plural, logic may dictate that an object in the sentence must also be plural. Look at this example:

👎 Students who do not have *their book* in class will be allowed to do this assignment at home.

Unless the students are sharing a single book, it is illogical to refer to the singular book with the plural students. This sentence should be revised as:

👍 *Students* who do not have *their books* in class will be allowed to do this assignment at home.

Sentences that test noun-noun agreement don't occur with high frequency on the SAT, but there's a good chance you'll see one among the Identifying Sentence Errors questions.

Rule 4: The One-You Shift
Avoid shifting between one and you in a sentence or an essay.

This rule describes a specific way of applying Rule 3 about pronoun agreement. You are highly likely to see the *one-you* shift on the SAT, almost certainly in the Identifying Sentence Errors questions and perhaps also in an Improving Sentences question. Whenever the word *one* or *you* is underlined in a sentence, check to see if it is used consistently. Here is a typical error:

👎 If *you're* not fond of spicy foods, *one* should be careful when ordering in restaurants.

A shift such as this must always be considered an error on the SAT. Here are two acceptable ways to correct this mistake:

👍❙ If *you're* not fond of spicy foods, *you* should be careful when ordering in restaurants.

👍❙ If *one is* not fond of spicy foods, *one* should be careful when ordering in restaurants.

Notice that each of these revisions is internally consistent. Remember, *you* is a second person pronoun and should be used only when addressing the reader or listener. The noun *one* requires a third person pronoun. If a nonunderlined part of the sentence uses the word *one* to refer to a person, then *you* should not be used in the sentence to refer to that person.

Rule 5: Relative Pronouns
To refer to people, use *who* (for a subject) or *whom* (for an object). Do not use *which* to refer to people.

In this sentence, the relative pronoun which is used incorrectly:

👎❙ My brother, *which* is still in college, will graduate next spring.

Because the relative pronoun refers to the noun *brother*, a person, the pronoun required here is either *who* or *whom*. To determine whether *who* or *whom* should replace *which* here, see whether *he* or *him* sounds correct in context. If *he* sounds correct, then use *who*, because both are subjective case pronouns. If *him* sounds correct in context, use *whom*, because both are objective case pronouns. Here, you would never say "*him* is in college." You would say "*he* is in college." Because the subjective case pronoun *he* is appropriate, the correct pronoun in this case is *who*:

👍❙ My brother, *who* is still in college, will graduate next spring.

Here's another example:

👎❙ The student teacher, *which* you will be meeting next week, will be starting with the unit on medieval history.

Here the pronoun *which* is not correct because it refers to the *teacher*, a person. To determine whether *which* should be replaced by *who* or *whom*, you have to determine how the pronoun functions in the sentence. Is it a subject or an object?

To find out, mentally reword the sentence: *you will be meeting* which *next week*. Ask yourself whether *she* or *her* should replace *which* here. Your ear tells you that the correct pronoun is *her: you will be meeting* her *next week*. Because the objective case personal pronoun *her* sounds best, the objective case relative pronoun *whom* is needed here. Therefore, the original sentence should be corrected as:

> ☜ The student teacher, *whom* you will be meeting next week, will be starting with the unit on medieval history.

To reiterate, decide between *who* and *whom* by determining whether the pronoun functions in its clause as a subject or an object. If *him* or *her* sounds correct, then choose *who*. If *he* or *she* sounds correct, then choose *whom*.

● **DRESS REHEARSAL**
Sample Questions and Detailed Explanations

As you read through the sample questions, remember to pay attention to any underlined pronoun and refer to the non-underlined part of the sentence to see if the pronoun is used correctly in context.

Sample Question 1: Pronoun without a Clear Antecedent

Melissa felt <u>quite</u> certain that, given the opportunity <u>to tour</u>
         A   B

the continent <u>on foot</u>, she would be more than eager to <u>do it</u>.
            C   D

<u>No error</u>
 E

The correct answer is D. On a quick reading, this sentence may sound correct. You can easily understand the meaning. Knowing that the SAT tests pronouns frequently, though, you should pause to think about option D. Notice the pronoun *it*, and ask yourself what noun it refers to. The only nouns in the sentence are *Melissa, opportunity, continent,* and *foot*. None of these nouns is what *it* refers to. Therefore, the pronoun *it* lacks an antecedent, and option D is an error.

Option A correctly uses the adverb *quite* to modify the adjective *certain*. Option B correctly uses the infinitive *to tour* following *opportunity*. Option C is a correct idiomatic expression.

Sample Question 2: *Which* Used Incorrectly to Refer to People

Many violin teachers believe that the students <u>who</u> will go the
                                                  A
farthest are not those who have remarkable talent, <u>but</u> those
                                                     B
✗ <u>which</u> are willing to practice <u>regularly</u>. <u>No error</u>
    C   D   E

The correct answer is C. Whenever you see *which* underlined, take note. Remember that *which* should not be used to refer to people. In this sentence, *which* refers to the pronoun *those*, and *those* is used in this sentence to refer to *students*, who are people. Therefore the use of *which* here is an error. The correct wording for option C is *who*.

Option A correctly uses the subjective pronoun *who* as the subject of the verb *will go*. Option B correctly uses the transition *but* to express the contrast in this sentence. Option D correctly uses the adverb *regularly* to modify the verb *practice*.

Sample Question 3: Wrong Case for Subject

After my lab partner and I spent three afternoons <u>trying</u> to get
                                                    A
the experiment right, <u>him and myself</u> were able <u>to complete</u>
                        B   C
the lab report <u>relatively</u> quickly. <u>No error</u>
                 D   E

The correct answer is B. This sentence may sound wrong to you. Even if it doesn't, you know that you should pay attention to any underlined pronouns and think carefully about how they are used in the sentence. Option B contains two pronouns. Thinking about sentence structure, you should see that the phrase *him and myself* functions as the subject of the verb *were*. Therefore, the subjective case pronouns *he* and *I* are necessary here.

Option A correctly uses the –*ing* verb form following the verb *spent*. Option C correctly uses the infinitive *to complete* following the verb phrase *were able*. Option D correctly uses the adverb *relatively* to modify the adverb *quickly*.

Sample Question 4: Pronoun after *Than*

No one on the team could have been <u>more happier than me</u> when my final shot landed in the basket.

(A) more happier than me

(B) more happy than myself

(C) as happy like I was

(D) happier than me

(E) happier than I

The correct answer is (E). Notice that the underlined phrase contains the pronoun *me*. Remember that whenever you see an underlined pronoun, you should make sure that it's used correctly in context. The underlined phrase involves a comparison, indicated by the word *than*. The sentence as written contains two errors, a pronoun case error and a word choice error. The word *more* is redundant here because the –*er* ending of *happier* already expresses the comparison. It is also incorrect to use the objective case pronoun *me* after the word *than* in this context. The correct expression is *no one could have been happier than I [was happy]*. The words in brackets with the clause completed as implied show that the subjective pronoun *I* is required here. Option E corrects both the pronoun case and the word choice errors.

Like option (A), option (B) contains both word choice and pronoun errors. The phrase *more happy* should be *happier* and the reflexive pronoun *myself* should be the subjective pronoun *I*. Option (C) is incorrect because it contains a word choice error. When the word *as* begins a comparison phrase, the adjective, here *happier*, should be followed by *as* rather than *like*. Option (D) is incorrect because although it corrects the word choice error, it still incorrectly uses the objective pronoun *me*.

Sample Question 5: Demonstrative Pronouns in Improving Paragraphs Questions

(1) My new hockey coach, determined to reverse the team's poor record, has required that all players do individual training six days a week. **(2)** This has gotten many parents concerned.

In context, Sentence 2 is best worded in which of the following ways?

(A) This has gotten many parents concerned.

(B) This has resulted in many parents becoming concerned.

(C) It has caused many parents to become concerned.

(D) This requirement has caused concern for many parents.

(E) Consequently, this has gotten many parents concerned.

The correct answer is (D). Notice that the underlined part of the sentence contains the demonstrative pronoun *this*. Be careful when you see *this, that, these,* or *them* on the SAT. These pronouns are often used erroneously. Sentence 1 contains six nouns, *coach, record, players, training, days,* and *week.* None of these nouns, however, is what the word *this* in sentence 2 refers to. A specific noun must be provided to go with the pronoun *this.* Option (D) fills this need by adding the word *requirement.* Option (D) also improves the wording by changing the expression *gotten many parents concerned* to *caused concern for many parents.*

Options (B) and (E) leave *this* without a specific word to refer to. Option (C) switches the pronoun from *this* to *it,* but sentence 1 doesn't contain an antecedent for *it.*

● THE FINAL ACT
Self-Check Quiz

1. If you read the article about the city's new parking rule, <u>you will see that they no longer allow overnight parking on the street</u> during the winter.

  (A) you will see that they no longer allow overnight parking on the street

  (B) you will see that they are now forbidding overnight parking on the street

(C) one will see that overnight parking on the street is now forbidden

(D) you will see that they are no longer allowing the parking of cars on the street overnight

(E) you will see that the city no longer allows overnight parking on the street

2. <u>It is not uncommon for one becoming frustrated with new electronic products</u>, especially when you find that the directions don't seem to make sense.

(A) It is not uncommon for one becoming frustrated with new electronic products

(B) It is not uncommon for one to become frustrated with new electronic products

(C) One becoming commonly frustrated with new electronic products

(D) It is not uncommon to become frustrated with new electronic products

(E) Commonly, one can become frustrated with new electronic products

3. Because they were getting older and no longer wanted to face the challenges of winter in the <u>northeast, this inspired my grandparents to move to Florida</u>.

(A) northeast, this inspired my grandparents to move to Florida

(B) northeast is the reason why my grandparents were inspired to move to Florida

(C) northeast, it inspired my grandparents to move to Florida

(D) northeast, this gave my grandparents the inspiration for moving to Florida

(E) northeast, my grandparents were inspired to move to Florida

4. This season's symphony schedule includes a large number of famous musicians as well as some <u>performers which are not well-known to many people</u>.

(A) performers which are not well-known to many people

(B) less well-known performers

(C) less well-known performers are included

(D) less well-known performers also

(E) performers being less well-known to many people

5. Large dogs <u>owned by</u> busy people who live <u>in small</u>
                        A   B
    <u>apartments</u> are not always the <u>healthiest</u> because
           B   C
    <u>it needs</u> daily exercise in a large area. <u>No error</u>
         D   E

6. <u>Almost</u> every teacher I have ever <u>met</u> has a genuine
         A   B
    <u>concern for</u> and appreciation of <u>their</u> students. <u>No error</u>
           C   D   E

7. My maternal grandparents, <u>who</u> are originally <u>from China,</u>
                                  A   B
    <u>have been living</u> in the United States for <u>more than</u> twenty
              C   D
    years. <u>No error</u>.
              E

8. If you like to play soccer, you <u>ought to</u> remember that
                                        A
    <u>wearing</u> shin guards can help prevent <u>one</u> <u>from</u> getting
         B   C   D
    injured. <u>No error</u>
                E

9. I <u>would appreciate</u> it if, <u>when</u> you have finished reading the
             A   B
    book, <u>you</u> would save it for my sister Allison <u>and I</u>. <u>No error</u>
              C   D   E

10. After <u>allowing</u> Jessica and Chelsea to go ahead <u>of me</u> in the
              A   B
    line, I <u>certainly</u> expected that <u>she</u> would acknowledge my
                C   D
    consideration. <u>No error</u>
                        E

● ANSWERS AND EXPLANATIONS

1. **E**   The underlined part of the sentence contains a pronoun that lacks an antecedent. There are no plural nouns anywhere in the sentence, so the pronoun *they* can't possibly be correct. Option (E) substitutes *the city* for *they*.

Options (B) and (D), like option A, use *they* without an antecedent. Option (C) removes *they*, thus correcting the pronoun without an antecedent. This option, however, introduces a new pronoun error, the *one-you* shift. Because the nonunderlined part of the sentence uses *you*, the use of the word *one* in option (C) is incorrect.

2. **D**   The pronoun error in this sentence is the *one-you* shift. Because the nonunderlined part of the sentence contains the pronoun *you*, the underlined part of the sentence should not contain the noun *one*. In addition to this pronoun error, there is also a problem with verb usage: the gerund *becoming* is used in a context where the infinitive *to become* is required. Option (D) corrects both the pronoun and the verb usage errors.

Option (B) corrects the verb usage error by substituting *to become* for *becoming,* but it doesn't get rid of the word *one*. Option (C) changes the underlined version, an independent clause, into a fragment, which cannot be combined with the nonunderlined part of the sentence to make a correctly formed sentence. Option (E)does supply an independent clause, but it keeps the word *one* and so does not correct the *one-you* shift.

3. **E**   The sentence as written contains an incorrect use of the pronoun *this*. The nonunderlined part of the sentence is a dependent clause containing the transition word *because,* so it's not necessary to use the demonstrative pronoun *this* to start the independent clause. Option (E) rewords the sentence to avoid using *this.*

Option (B) is redundant. A sentence that starts with *because* should not also contain the phrase *is the reason why.* This phrase repeats the idea contained in the word *because.* Option (C) incorrectly uses the pronoun *it.* There is no antecedent for *it* in the nonunderlined part of the sentence. Option

(D) uses slightly different wording than option (A) does, but option (D) still contains the incorrect use of the demonstrative pronoun *this.*

4. **B**   The most obvious error in the sentence as written is that the pronoun *which* is incorrectly used to refer to people. In addition to the pronoun error, the underlined version of the sentence is wordy. Option (B) gets rid of the incorrect use of *which* and uses more concise wording.

Option (C) does not contain a pronoun error but introduces a parallelism error. The nonunderlined part of the sentence contains the phrase *as well as,* which indicates that parallelism is required. A noun to parallel *a large number* is called for here. Option (C) provides a clause instead of the necessary noun phrase. Option (D) is incorrect because the word *also* is repetitive: the nonunderlined part of the sentence contains that phrase *as well as.* Option (E) is wrong because it incorrectly uses the verb *being.* With the phrase *to many people,* option (E) also retains the wordiness error present in option (A).

5. **D**   You should recognize that option D contains the pronoun *it.* In this sentence *it* refers to *dogs,* which is plural. The correct pronoun to refer to a plural noun is *they.*

Option A correctly uses the preposition *by.* Option B correctly uses the preposition *in.* Option C correctly uses the superlative form in referring to *dogs,* a group implicitly larger than two here.

6. **D**   You should notice the pronoun *their.* This is a plural pronoun that is incorrectly used here to refer to the singular noun *teacher.* The word *their* could be correctly replaced by either *his,* or *her,* or *his or her.*

Option B uses a past tense, which is correct in context. Option C correctly uses the preposition *for.*

7. **E**   Option A correctly uses the pronoun *who* to refer to people. Option B is a correct use of the preposition *from.* Option C uses the correct verb tense for an action that is continuing. Option D is idiomatically correct.

8. **C** The nonunderlined part of the sentence contains the second person pronoun *you,* so the third person noun *one* is incorrect here.

Option A is idiomatically correct. Option B correctly uses the *–ing* form of the verb as a noun. Option D is an idiomatically correct use of the preposition *from* with the verb *prevent.*

9. **D** Here the subjective pronoun *I* is used as the object of the preposition *for.* The objective pronoun *me* should be used instead of *I.*

Option A correctly uses the conditional phrasing *would* before a clause that begins with *if.* Option B correctly uses *when* to refer to time. Option C correctly uses *you* to be consistent with the other use of *you* in the sentence.

10. **D** The use of the pronoun *she* here results in ambiguity. It is not clear whether *she* is intended to refer to *Jessica* or to *Chelsea.* The appropriate name must be restated to correct the ambiguity. If the pronoun is meant to refer to both *Jessica and Chelsea,* then the plural pronoun *they* should be used here.

Option B correctly uses the objective pronoun *me* as the object of the preposition *of.* Option C correctly uses an adverb to modify the verb *expected.* Option D correctly uses the subjective pronoun *she* as the subject of the verb *would acknowledge.*

Sentence Structure

DIFFICULTY: ★ ★ ★ ★

FREQUENCY: ★

SURPRISE FACTOR: ★ ★

● INTRODUCTION TO SENTENCE STRUCTURE QUESTIONS

Sentence Structure questions are considered difficult because you need to be comfortable with quite a bit of grammatical terminology to understand this topic. In addition, there is usually more than one way to correct a sentence structure error. You need to be familiar with several possible corrections. This lesson will help you gain a good understanding of how to apply the principles of proper sentence structure. You will also find that some of the material in Lesson 23, Transitions, can increase your understanding of how clauses fit together to form correct sentences.

Sentence structure is tested primarily in Improving Sentences questions. In this question type, remember, all or part of the sentence is underlined. Option (A) always repeats the wording used in the original sentence. Options (B) through (E) offer four different wordings, and you have to choose the best one. Even though a sentence structure error may not exist in option (A) (say, for example, option (A) contains only a parallelism error), one or more of the other four options may introduce a sentence structure error.

Despite their relative difficulty, sentence structure is not often the tested issue in sentence structure questions. In other words, the error in the original wording of an Improving Sentences question (the option (A) version) doesn't frequently contain a sentence structure error. Errors involving other topics, such as parallelism, modifiers, and transitions, are more likely to appear in the option (A) wording. Sentence structure is also tested, but to a much lesser extent, in Identifying Sentence Errors questions.

Characteristics of Sentence Structure Questions

Sentence Structure questions have to do with how words are put together to form grammatically correct sentences. Here are some questions you can ask to help you identify errors in sentence structure:

1. Does the sentence seem incomplete in some way? If so, check to see if it contains both a subject and a verb.

2. Does the sentence contain a word that shows a logical relationship? (See the accompanying box for examples.) If so, the sentence probably contains a dependent clause, which must be combined with an independent clause to complete the thought.

3. Do any of the underlined choices contain a semicolon? If so, consider the possibility of an error in sentence structure.

**Relationship Words That Can Introduce
a Dependent Clause**

after	because	where	which	while
before	that	whereas	who	

Most Common Types of Sentence Structure Questions

Most sentence structure errors that show up on the SAT involve one of two problems, the **fragment** or the **comma splice.** A **sentence fragment** is a group of words that cannot stand alone as a sentence. The most common fragment type you will see on the SAT is a dependent clause that is not properly connected to an independent clause. Look at this example:

👎 *Because* the sun was shining.

The relationship word *because* sets up the expectation of a logical consequence. Therefore, more information is required to make this group of words a complete thought. To be correct, this sentence needs to convey *what resulted because the sun was shining*. The revisions below include the additional information and form a complete sentence:

👍 *Because* the sun was shining, we decided to eat outside.
👍 We decided to eat outside *because* the sun was shining.

As these revisions illustrate, it doesn't matter if the relationship word *because* is placed at the beginning of the sentence or in the middle. The important thing is that the additional information *we decided to eat outside* is included to complete the thought introduced by *because*.

A **comma splice** occurs when a comma is used incorrectly to *splice*, or join, two independent clauses. A comma splice is sometimes referred to as a **run-on sentence.** Here is an example:

👎 William Shakespeare lived in England during the reign of Queen Elizabeth I**, [note comma here]** he was a famous playwright.

There are several ways to correct a comma splice. One is to join the two independent clauses with a semicolon as in this revision:

👍 William Shakespeare lived in England during the reign of Queen Elizabeth I**; [note semicolon here]** he was a famous playwright.

Another way to correct the comma splice is to add the conjunction *and* after the comma:

👍 William Shakespeare lived in England during the reign of Queen Elizabeth I**, and** he was a famous playwright.

Still another way to correct this comma splice is to rewrite the sentence as one independent clause that contains a noun phrase describing the subject:

▇▌ William Shakespeare, **a famous playwright,** lived in England during the reign of Queen Elizabeth.

Any one of the above corrections can be acceptable. Context may dictate that one is preferable. On the SAT, context is considered to be the words in the sentence that are not underlined, since they must remain as written.

● **THE TRAP DOOR**
Steering Clear of Answer Traps

There are no sentence structure traps that are deliberately set up by the test-maker. The only trap for sentence structure is a lack of awareness on your part. You need to develop a good understanding of the principles of correct sentence structure and learn to recognize situations in which they're not applied.

Recall the three questions presented earlier: Does the sentence feel incomplete? Does it contain a relationship word? Does at least one of the answer choices contain a semicolon? The answers to these questions can give you clues that sentence structure may be a tested error. Observing these clues is crucial to success.

● **PERFORMANCE TECHNIQUES**
Key Formulas and Rules

Before we look at the rules, let's clarify the technical terms you need to understand in order to think about Sentence Structure.

A **clause** is a group of words that contains both a subject and a verb. A clause is either **independent** or **dependent**.

A **dependent clause** is a group of words that contains a subject and a verb but also includes another word that expresses a relationship between ideas. This type of clause is *dependent* on some information outside itself to express a complete thought. A dependent clause cannot stand alone as a sentence. Within a sentence, a dependent clause is sometimes used to modify, or describe, another word in the sentence.

An **independent clause** is a group of words that contains a subject and a verb and expresses a complete thought by itself. An independent clause can stand alone as a sentence.

A **main verb** is a verb form (which may be made up of a single word, such as *goes* or several words, such as *will be going*) that is associated with the subject to express the action or state of being in a clause.

A **helping verb** is a verb such as *are* or *has* that is sometimes used with another verb form, usually one ending in *–ed* or *–ing*.

Here are four rules to help you apply the principles of correct sentence structure. The first two relate to the wording of sentences, while the second two address punctuation.

Sentence Structure Rule 1: A sentence must contain at least one independent clause.

Just because a group of words starts with a capital letter and ends with a period, it doesn't necessarily constitute a grammatically correct sentence. Look at this example:

👎 Driving to the store.

This example is not a sentence because it doesn't contain an independent clause. There is a verb, *driving,* but no subject. We don't know *who* was *driving to the store.* Look at this revision:

👍 *Anthony* was driving to the store.

Adding a subject clears up the mystery of *who* and creates an independent clause, which, by definition, can form a complete sentence.

Sentence Structure Rule 2: The "–ing" verb form used by itself cannot function as the main verb in an independent clause.

Remember, the main verb is the one that is associated with the subject, that is, tells what the subject does or is. Some sentences include verbs other than the main verb, but every independent clause, by definition, contains a main verb. Look at this example, which does not violate Rule 2:

👎I Quickly *grasping* the toddler's hand, the babysitter *led* the child away from the open drain.

In this sentence, *grasping* is a verb, but it is not the main verb of a clause. The independent clause is *the babysitter led the child away from the open drain*. The main verb here is *led*. The words *quickly grasping the toddler's hand* form a phrase, not a clause, so *grasping* is not a main verb, and therefore the sentence is correct.

Here is another example, one that does, in fact, break Rule 2:

👎I A doctor who smokes cigarettes *setting* a bad example.

In this sentence, *who smokes cigarettes* is a dependent clause that describes *doctor*. Reading the sentence without that clause, we're left with *A doctor setting a bad example*. This is not an independent clause until we add a helping verb as in this revision:

👍I A doctor who smokes cigarettes *is setting* a bad example.

Using the verb *sets* also creates an independent clause:

👍I A doctor who smokes cigarettes *sets* a bad example.

The key point here is that a verb ending in *–ing* can't be used as the main verb of a clause unless a helping verb is used with it. You can expect to see sentences that test this rule in the Identifying Sentence Errors questions.

Sentence Structure Rule 3: Two independent clauses can be joined by a comma and a FANBOYS word to form a sentence.

You may already be familiar with FANBOYS words. If not, don't worry. FANBOYS is simply an acronym to help you remember the seven conjunctions that can be used with a comma to connect two independent clauses. They are **F**or, **A**nd, **N**or, **B**ut, **O**r, **Y**es, and **S**o.

Notice that Rule 3 doesn't state that a comma followed by a FANBOYS word is the *only* correct way to join two independent clauses in one sentence. Rule 3 describes one possibility for combining two independent clauses. Rule 4, below, offers a different possibility. The key to Rule 3 is that the comma and the FANBOYS words work together. You can't use one without the other; both are necessary. Here's a sentence that correctly applies Rule 3:

> 👎| Julio admired his older sister, *yet* he found some of her habits annoying.

If either the comma or the word *yet* is removed, the result is a run-on sentence:

> 👎| Julio admired his older sister **[no comma] yet** he found some of her habits annoying.

> 👎| Julio admired his older sister, **[notice lack of FANBOYS word]** he found some of her habits annoying.

Remember, commas and FANBOYS words work together to combine two independent clauses in one sentence.

Sentence Structure Rule 4: Two independent clauses that are closely related in content can be joined either by a semicolon alone or by a semicolon and a transition word that is not a FANBOYS word.

Understanding the correct use of the semicolon will greatly enhance your ability to spot incorrect answer choices in the Improving Sentences questions. Rule 4 describes the *only* correct use of the semicolon that you'll see on the SAT. This means that whenever you see a semicolon in an answer choice, that choice can be correct only if the semicolon is used to join two *independent* clauses.

Notice that a FANBOYS word must not be used with a semicolon. There are, however, some words that can be used after a semicolon. You will encounter these words again in Lesson 23, Transitions. Not every transition word can be used after a semicolon. The box below lists some that can be.

Some Transition Words That Can Follow a Semicolon to Join Two Independent Clauses

however	nevertheless	therefore
moreover	nonetheless	thus

Let's look at how Rule 4 offers another correct way to rewrite the sentence presented above:

👍 Julio admired his older sister**; [note semicolon]** *however,* he found some of her habits annoying.

Together, Rules 3 and 4 suggest that if the semicolon were changed to a comma, the sentence would be incorrect:

👎 Julio admired his older sister, **[note comma]** *however* he found some of her habits annoying.

This sentence is incorrect because a comma can't be used to join two independent clauses unless it's followed by a FAN-BOYS word.

● DRESS REHEARSAL
Sample Questions and Detailed Explanations

Three of the five questions in this section are Improving Sentences questions, because this is the category that tests sentence structure most frequently. When sentence structure is tested in identifying sentence errors, an error might be present because the sentence contains too many words (as in Question 4 below) or too few words (as in Question 5 below).

Sample Question 1: Comma Splice

Not everyone <u>who becomes famous was a successful student in school, Einstein is just one example</u>.

(A) who becomes famous was a successful student in school, Einstein is just one example

(B) becoming famous was successful in school, Einstein is just one example

(C) who becomes famous was a successful student in school; Einstein is just one example

(D) who becomes famous was a successful student in school; for example, Einstein

(E) who becomes famous was a successful student in school, take Einstein for example

The correct answer is (C). Option (A) is a comma splice. It is made up of two independent clauses joined by a comma. There are two acceptable ways two fix this. We can either add a FANBOYS word after the comma (Rule 3), or we can simply change the comma to a semicolon (Rule 4). Option (C) makes the correction by adding the semicolon. Option (B) does not correct the comma splice, and it introduces a new error by changing "who becomes" to *becoming*. Option (D) substitutes a semicolon for the comma, and adds the transition phrase *for example*, but this option is incorrect because what follows the semicolon is not an independent clause. In option (E), what follows the comma is an independent clause (the subject is the implied *you*), so it cannot be correctly joined to the preceding independent clause by only a comma.

Sample Question 2: Sentence Is Correct as Written

William Shakespeare may be best known today as an author <u>of plays, but in his own time he was involved in many aspects</u> of producing them as well.

(A) of plays, but in his own time he was involved in many aspects

(B) who created plays, but in his own time he was also involved in many aspects

(C) of plays, however in his own time he was involved in many aspects

(D) of plays; but in his own time he was involved in many aspects

(E) of plays, but in his own time he was being involved in many aspects

The correct answer is (A). Option (A) correctly joins two independent clauses with a comma followed by the FAN-BOYS word *but* (Rule 3). Option (B) introduces the problem of wordiness. An author, by definition, creates, so changing *an author of plays* to *an author who created plays* is redundant. The introduction of *also* in option (B) is another example of redundancy, because it repeats the idea conveyed by *as well* in the nonunderlined portion of the sentence. Option (C) consists of two independent clauses incorrectly joined. To be correct, the transition word *however* **must** be preceded by a semicolon rather than a comma (Rule 4). Option (D) incorrectly uses the FANBOYS word *but* together with a semicolon to join two independent clauses. Option (E) correctly uses *but* preceded by a comma to join two independent clauses, but it incorrectly changes *was involved* to *was being involved.*

Sample Question 3: Incorrect Use of FANBOYS Word to Join Dependent and Independent Clauses

In spite of <u>following a strict regimen of exercise and nutrition, but Gianna still got the flu just before her vacation started</u>.

(A) following a strict regimen of exercise and nutrition, but Gianna still got the flu just before her vacation started

(B) her following a strict regimen of exercise and nutrition, Gianna still got the flu anyway just before her vacation started

(C) her having followed a strict regimen of exercise and nutrition, Gianna still got the flu just before her vacation started

(D) following a strict regimen of exercise and nutrition, because Gianna still got the flu just before her vacation started

(E) following a strict regimen of exercise and nutrition, Gianna got the flu just before her vacation started

The correct answer is (E). The problem with option (A) is that the two clauses in this sentence are both dependent clauses. This situation violates Rule 1. It can be easily corrected by simply removing the word *but* from the middle of the sentence. Option (E) does this. Option (B) introduces two new problems, adding the unnecessary *her* before *following* and adding the word *anyway*, which repeats the idea conveyed by *still*. Option (C) incorrectly changes the verb *following* to *having followed*. Option (D) incorrectly introduces *because*, a transition word that shows cause and effect and is therefore inappropriate in a sentence that already contains the transition phrase *in spite of.*

Sample Question 4: Comma Splice

Scientists still have <u>a lot</u> to learn about <u>fibromyalgia</u>, <u>this is</u> a
                           A   B   C
condition <u>that</u> causes pain and fatigue. <u>No error</u>
          D   E

The correct answer is C. The inclusion of *this is* makes the sentence a comma splice. Simply deleting these words corrects the sentence. Then, the end of the sentence *a condition that causes pain and fatigue* becomes a phrase which correctly modifies the word *fibromyalgia*. Option A, *a lot* is idiomatically correct. Option B, *fibromyalgia* is a word that may or may not be familiar to you, but you should be able to infer from the context that fibromyalgia is some kind of medical condition. In Identifying Sentence Errors questions, do not assume that just because a word is not known to you, it is necessarily incorrect. Examine the other underlined parts of the sentence to check for error types that you should be familiar with. Option D correctly uses *that* to introduce a dependent clause that modifies the word *condition.*

Sample Question 5: An "-ing" Verb Used Incorrectly as Main Verb in Clause

Sonia frequently <u>driving</u> one hundred miles <u>or more</u> to visit old
                     A   B
friends <u>whom</u> she has known <u>since</u> she was a child. <u>No error</u>
        C   D   E

The correct answer is A. Option A violates Rule 2 by using the *–ing* form of the verb as the main verb in the clause whose subject is *Sonia*. Option B, *or more*, is an idiomatically correct expression. Option C correctly uses *whom* as the object of the verb in the dependent clause *whom she has known*. Option D is an idiomatically correct use of *since.*

● THE FINAL ACT
Self-Check Quiz

1. Because I am a great fan of classical music <u>so my parents gave me a subscription to the symphony</u> for the upcoming season.

   (A) so my parents gave me a subscription to the symphony
   (B) so my parents had given me a subscription for
   (C) that is why my parents gave me a subscription to the symphony
   (D) my parents gave me a subscription to the symphony
   (E) therefore my parents were giving me a subscription from the symphony

2. By watching for sales and shopping at different stores, my grand-mother kept her grocery expenditures to a minimum, <u>this was a necessity when living on a limited budget.</u>

   (A) this was a necessity when living on a limited budget
   (B) a necessity for those who lived on a limited budget
   (C) this was necessary when you were living on a limited budget
   (D) this was essential when living on a limited budget
   (E) being necessary when living on a limited budget

3. Marya explained to her great-grandfather that she was saving money to purchase a digital camera, <u>it lets you take pictures without film.</u>

   (A) it lets you take pictures without film
   (B) which lets you take pictures without film
   (C) allowing the taking of pictures without the use of film
   (D) it allowing the taking of pictures without film
   (E) whereby it lets you take pictures without even using film

4. <u>Mihaly Csikszentmihalyi, a contemporary scholar doing ground-breaking work in the area he calls flow</u>; he describes flow as a state in which a person is so absorbed in an activity that he or she loses awareness of time.

   (A) Mihaly Csikszentmihalyi, a contemporary scholar doing groundbreaking work in the area he calls flow

   (B) Mihaly Csikszentmihalyi is a contemporary scholar doing groundbreaking work in the area he calls flow

   (C) A contemporary scholar doing groundbreaking work in the area he calls flow, Mihaly Csikszentmihalyi

   (D) Mihaly Csikszentmihalyi being a contemporary scholar doing groundbreaking work in the area he calls flow

   (E) A contemporary scholar, Mihaly Csikszentmihalyi, doing groundbreaking work in the area he calls flow

5. Administrators hope <u>for improvements in test scores this year, they will be as large</u> as the district has ever seen.

   (A) for improvements in test scores this year, they will be as large

   (B) that improvements in test scores this year will be as large

   (C) for improvements in test scores this year to be as larger

   (D) for improvements in test scores this year to be as the largest

   (E) for test score improvements to be becoming as large

6. Young doctors, although they may be lacking in experience, <u>their understanding of new technologies is usually impressive</u>.

   (A) their understanding of new technologies is usually impressive

   (B) usually possess an impressive understanding of new technologies

   (C) understand impressive things about new technologies

   (D) their understanding of new technologies will be impressive

   (E) they possess an impressive understanding of new technologies

7. While some teens are now applying to <u>as many as</u> 15 or 20
                                           A
   colleges, <u>yet</u> many <u>prefer to</u> narrow <u>their</u> choices to a much
           B   C   D
   smaller number. <u>No error</u>
                   E

8. As a consequence of staying out <u>way past</u> his curfew,
                                  A
   <u>therefore</u> Nicholas is not allowed to use <u>his father's car</u> again
     B   C
   <u>for a month</u>. <u>No error</u>
     D   E

9. Because <u>running the marathon</u> will certainly deplete your
                   A
   strength, <u>is why</u> you should pay careful attention <u>to</u> nutrition
           B   C
   well <u>in advance</u> of the race. <u>No error</u>
        D   E

10. <u>Young</u> children, although they <u>enjoy</u> asserting their
      A   B
    independence, <u>they</u> need frequent reassurance from their
                   C
    parents <u>in order to</u> feel secure. <u>No error</u>
          D   E

● **ANSWERS AND EXPLANATIONS**

1. **D** All of the other options incorrectly repeat the cause and effect idea that is conveyed by the word *because* in the non-underlined part of the sentence. Option (B) also introduces a verb usage error in *had given*. This tense should be used only to express an action that occurs *before* another action. Option (C) incorrectly uses *that is why,* which repeats *because.* Option (E) incorrectly uses *therefore,* which repeats *because.* Option (E) also introduces a verb tense error in *were giving.* This tense is used to express an action that goes on continually rather than an action that happens once and is completed.

2. **B** Because the nonunderlined part of the sentence is an independent clause followed by a comma, the rest of the sentence cannot consist of an independent clause without a FANBOYS word. Only option (B) fits. Options (A), (C), and (D) are all independent clauses. Option (E) is wrong because it incorrectly uses *being* to mean *which was*.

Option (C) introduces an error in pronoun usage as well. Because the subject of the nonunderlined part of the sentence is *grandmother*, it's incorrect to use the pronoun *you* in the middle of this sentence. Option (D) is only slightly different from option (A). Changing *a necessity* to *essential* would be acceptable but does nothing to correct the sentence structure error. Option (E) incorrectly uses the verb *being* to mean *which was*. It is incorrect to use *being* in this way.

3. **B** Since the nonunderlined part of the sentence is an independent clause followed by a comma, the rest of the sentence cannot consist of an independent clause without a FANBOYS word. Option (B) uses a dependent clause to modify *camera*. This is the only acceptable option because *camera* is followed by a comma in the nonunderlined part of the sentence.

Option (A) is unacceptable only because it joins two independent clauses with a comma rather than a semicolon. Option (C) is confusing because it starts with *allowing* and uses two –*ing* verb forms so close together. Option (D) is wrong because, in addition to retaining the sentence structure error that option (A) has, it also uses the wrong verb form, *allowing*. The –*ing* form cannot be used by itself as the main verb in a clause. Option (E) uses incorrect diction. The word *whereby* is inappropriate in this context.

4. **B** This sentence requires a careful reading to notice that the semicolon that follows the underlined part of the sentence is *not* underlined. Therefore, the semicolon must be appropriate with whichever option you choose. This means that your answer must be an independent clause. Only option (B) meets this requirement.

Option (A) is wrong because, although it is lengthy, it does not constitute an independent clause. The underlined words following the comma all form a descriptive phrase. There is no main verb. Option (C) consists of an introductory modifying phrase and a possible subject, but because there is no verb to follow the subject, option (C) is not an independent clause. Option (D) is wrong because it uses *being* incorrectly. Option (E) is wrong because it's not an independent clause. The verb form *doing* cannot be correctly used as the main verb in an independent clause.

5. **B** The sentence as written is incorrect because it is a run-on. Two independent clauses are joined by a comma instead of a semicolon. Option (B) is best because it corrects the sentence structure problem and also eliminates the wordiness of option (A). Option (C) does correct the sentence structure error, but it introduces a new error with the word *larger*. Because the nonunderlined part of the sentence contains the comparative phrase *as the district has ever seen*, the word *large* is appropriate here instead of *larger*. Like option (C), option (D) corrects the sentence structure error but introduces an error in how the comparison is described. The phrase *as the largest* is incorrect word choice. Option (E) is similar to the correct answer, option B, but the use of *becoming* in option E makes it incorrect.

6. **B** In the sentence as written, sentence structure is incorrect because the underlined part of the sentence is an independent clause. What is needed here is a verb to go along with the nonunderlined subject *doctors*. Option (B) fills this need by adding *possess*.

Option (C) uses correct sentence structure, but it's not the best answer here because it introduces the nonspecific word *things*, thereby distorting the meaning of the original sentence. Option (D), like option (A), consists of an independent clause rather than a verb to go with the subject *doctors*. Option (E) is similar to the correct answer, option (B), but it incorrectly repeats the subject by introducing the word *they*.

7. **B** The word *yet* is unnecessary because the idea of contrast is already expressed by the nonunderlined word *while*. Also, since the part of the sentence *before* the comma is a dependent clause, the part of the sentence *after* the comma should not be introduced by a FANBOYS conjunction.

Option A is idiomatically correct. Option D correctly uses the preposition *to* with *prefer.* Option D correctly uses the plural pronoun *their* to refer to the plural noun *teens.*

8. **B** The word *therefore* incorrectly repeats the idea of cause and effect which is expressed by *as a consequence of* in the nonunderlined part of the sentence. Simply removing *therefore* establishes correct sentence structure.

Option A is idiomatically correct. Option C correctly uses the possessive. Option D is idiomatically correct.

9. **B** The phrase *is why* is used incorrectly. It repeats the logic already expressed by the word *because* in the nonunderlined part of the sentence.

Option A uses a verb tense that corresponds correctly with the other verb in the sentence, *should pay.* Option C uses the correct preposition in the idiom *pay attention to.* Option D is idiomatically correct here.

10. **C** The word *children* in the nonunderlined part of the sentence is the subject of the verb *need.* Repeating the pronoun *they* here unnecessarily repeats the subject, creating incorrect sentence structure.

Option A correctly uses an adjective to modify the noun *children.* Option B is the correct form of the verb; it agrees with the subject *they.* Option D is idiomatically correct.

Modifiers

DIFFICULTY: ★ ★

FREQUENCY: ★ ★

SURPRISE FACTOR: ★ ★ ★ ★

● INTRODUCTION TO MODIFIERS QUESTIONS

A **modifier** is a word or a group of words that *modifies*, that is, gives more information about, another word. Two parts of speech, adjectives and adverbs, are used as modifiers. A phrase or a clause can also be used as a modifier.

Most students aren't aware of how modifiers are tested on the SAT. In fact, the general public isn't in tune with the logic of modifiers. You will frequently see or hear modifiers used incorrectly even in published materials and broadcast media. Therefore, when you encounter a modifier error in a sentence on the SAT, it often won't *sound* wrong to you even if you read the sentence aloud.

Although modifiers show up fairly frequently on the SAT, they aren't tested nearly as much as verb usage and pronouns. Fortunately, when you understand the rules for modifiers, it's quite easy to spot errors. Therefore, difficulty is the last thing you need to worry about. It's awareness that matters most.

Characteristics of Modifiers Questions

On the SAT, you'll see modifiers as both single words and phrases. In the Identifying Sentence Errors questions, you should check for a modifier error whenever you see a single adjective underlined. In the Improving Sentences questions, be alert whenever a sentence begins with a descriptive phrase, especially one that starts with a verb form that ends in –*ed* or –*ing*. Often this opening descriptive phrase is not underlined. This situation serves as a clue that you need to consider a modifier error.

Most Common Types of Modifiers Questions

There are only two kinds of modifier errors tested on the SAT, and you can easily learn to spot them. It helps that each one tends to appear in only one of the Writing question types. You'll find single-word modifiers, that is, adjectives and adverbs, in Identifying Sentence Errors questions. Modifying phrases, on the other hand, will show up in Improving Sentences questions.

Remember back in grade school when you learned these definitions? An **adjective** modifies or describes a noun or pronoun. An **adverb** modifies a verb, an adjective, or another adverb. You also learned that adverbs are often formed by adding the suffix –*ly* to an adjective. There is nothing complicated about this; you simply need to be aware that you'll sometimes see an adjective where an adverb is required on the SAT, particularly in the Identifying Sentence Errors questions. Remember to watch for any underlined adverb or adjective and make sure that it's used correctly.

Like adjectives, most modifying phrases on the SAT will be describing nouns. Expect to see modifying phrases tested in a recognizable format in Improving Sentences questions. Usually a modifying phrase will be followed by a comma, and the words following this phrase will be underlined. If the modifying phrase is used incorrectly, it will be because the next noun after the modifying phrase is *not* the word the phrase describes. Often, a sentence with this error will evoke a funny mental image that doesn't make sense if you think about it. Here's an example:

➡️ *Walking* quickly through the crowd, *my papers* flew away.

This wording suggests that the papers are walking, definitely an illogical image. The sentence makes more sense this way:

➡️ *As I walked* quickly through the crowd, my papers flew away.

You might be tempted to protest, "But I *know* it was a person, and not papers, doing the walking!" This is a good point, but you need to remember that on the SAT, modifying phrases must be associated with, that is placed next to, the particular word that they modify.

● THE TRAP DOOR
Steering Clear of Answer Traps

For modifiers, the traps are external to the test. You don't need to worry about the test-maker wording sentences in a way that will trick you. Rather, you simply need to keep in mind that modifiers—both single words and phrases—will show up on the SAT. Remember that these errors may not *sound* wrong to you at first.

Trap 1: The Single-word Modifier Trap

Stay alert and take note of any underlined adjectives. You may think that using an adjective where an adverb is called for is too simple an error type to be tested on the SAT. It's not! On some Identifying Sentence Errors questions, the error is merely that an adjective needs to have *–ly* added to it.

While the test-makers don't deliberately try to trick you about this, your own brain can actually trick you. You may know that single-word modifiers are tested on the SAT and still fail to spot one. This happens because, when you read, your brain tries to make sense of the words. Since you know that an adverb must be used to modify a verb, your brain may actually read *Josie walked home quick* as *Josie walked home quickly.*

You can avoid this trap by reading carefully and deliberately as you work through the writing section. Especially when your initial impression is that a sentence contains no errors, go back and check each underlined part of the sentence in a systematic way. If you see a single adjective underlined, ask yourself which word in the sentence the adjective describes. Remember that an adjective can modify only a noun or a pronoun.

Trap 2: The Modifying Phrase Trap

This trap is similar to the first one in that the test-maker doesn't do anything with the wording of the sentence to make this error type tricky. The only trap is not reading carefully enough to know when you're dealing with a modifying phrase.

Recognizing Modifying Phrases

Most modifying phrases tested on the SAT come at the beginning of the sentence and start with a verb that ends in *–ed* or *–ing*. Sometimes another word, such as *before* or *after*, comes before the verb, as in *before attempting* or *after driving*.

Train yourself to watch for verbs at the very beginning of a sentence. The first step in handling modifying phrases correctly is simply to know that you're dealing with one. The second step is to ask yourself what word the modifying phrase describes. Third, make sure that word immediately follows the modifying phrase.

After studying the examples in this lesson, you can be confident that you will know how to recognize modifying phrases whether they're underlined or not. You will learn to pay attention to the logic of the sentence in order to easily determine whether or not a modifying phrase is used correctly.

● PERFORMANCE TECHNIQUES
Key Formulas and Rules

There are only two rules here, one for single-word modifiers and one for modifying phrases. These rules restate ideas presented above in the discussion of traps.

Modifier Rule 1: An adjective can modify only a noun or a pronoun. An adverb is needed to modify a verb, adjective, or another adverb.

This is a rule you're almost certainly familiar with. Remember to pay attention to any underlined adjective. Notice the adjective in this sentence:

◀▎ Joanna could *see clear* that she had made a serious mistake.

Here, *clear* is used incorrectly to modify the verb *see*. Simply changing the adjective to an adverb corrects the sentence:

◀▎ Joanna could *see clearly* that she had made a serious mistake.

This sentence is correct because it uses an adverb to modify a verb.

Modifier Rule 2: A modifying phrase should be placed immediately next to the word described by the phrase.

Many of the modifying phrases you will see on the SAT will be introductory modifiers. An introductory modifier is one that appears at the very beginning of the sentence. Therefore, you should always pay careful attention when you see a sentence with a descriptive phrase at the beginning. A modifying phrase will usually be followed by a comma. Rule 2 tells you that the very next noun after the comma must be the word the phrase describes. Look at this example:

◀▎ *Injured during the game*, the paramedics carried *the player* off the field.

This sentence opens with a modifying phrase, *injured during the game*. To apply Rule 2, ask yourself, Who or what was injured during the game? The answer is clearly *the player*. Therefore, this sentence is not correct. There are two ways to revise it. The first keeps the introductory modifying phrase but places the word it modifies immediately following the modifying phrase:

◀▎ *Injured during the game, the player* was carried off the field by the paramedics.

The second revision moves the information previously contained in the introductory modifier, placing it in the middle of the sentence and adding the words *who was*. Notice that the modifying phrase is now right next to the word it modifies:

◀▎ The paramedics carried *the player, who was injured during the game*, off the field.

You should be aware that either of these revisions is acceptable. You might see either type of revision, but certainly not both for the same question, as the correct answer for an Improving Sentences question.

● DRESS REHEARSAL
Sample Questions and Detailed Explanations

Because you're probably more familiar with single-word modifiers, only one of the following sample question includes one. You probably have less experience thinking about modifying phrases, so four of the five questions below include those. Remember that with modifying phrases you need to pay attention to the logic of the sentence; you can't rely on your ear alone.

Sample Question 1: Adjective Used Instead of Adverb

<u>Though</u> the proposal to establish a drama program
   A

<u>for young children</u> was written carefully and researched
     B

<u>thorough</u>, the cultural commissioner refused to <u>allocate</u>
   C   D

funding for it. <u>No error</u>
            E

The correct answer is C. The word *thorough* is an adjective. Since it's used here to modify the verb *researched,* it is incorrect. Because *researched* is a verb, it must be modified by the adverb *thoroughly.*

Option A is correct because *though* properly introduces the dependent clause at the beginning of this sentence. Option B is a correct use of a prepositional phrase. Option D is the correct word in this context.

Sample Question 2: Introductory Modifier Followed by Wrong Noun

Wanting to please her new teacher, <u>the math problems were done carefully by the diligent student</u>

(A) the math problems were done carefully by the diligent student

(B) it was in a careful way that the diligent student did the math problems

(C) the diligent student did the math problems carefully

(D) the math problems having been done carefully by the diligent student

(E) the math problems that were done carefully by the diligent student

The correct answer is (C). You should notice that the sentence opens with an introductory modifying phrase. The *–ing* ending of the first word in the sentence is a good clue here. Ask yourself who or what the modifier is describing. It is *the diligent student* here who wants to please the new teacher. The correct answer will be worded in a way that makes *student* the first noun following the introductory modifier. Only option (C) correctly places *the diligent student* immediately after its modifying phrase.

Option (B) starts with *it was,* still incorrectly separating the modifier *wanting to please her new teacher* from the noun it modifies. Options (D) and (E), like option (A), incorrectly use *problems* as the first noun following the modifying phrase.

Using Modifying Phrases to Eliminate Wrong Answer Choices
On introductory modifying phrase questions, often you don't even have to read through all of the answer choices. It's likely that only one or two answer choices will start with the noun that is modified by the introductory phrase. One of those two options must be the correct answer.

Sample Question 3: Introductory Modifier Followed by Wrong Noun

Before entering into a legally binding contract, <u>all aspects of the agreement must be carefully reviewed by both parties</u>

(A) all aspects of the agreement must be carefully reviewed by both parties

(B) the agreement must be carefully reviewed by both parties regarding all aspects

(C) a careful review of all aspects of the agreement must be done by both parties

(D) the agreement that must be carefully reviewed in all aspects by both parties

(E) both parties must carefully review all aspects of the agreement

The correct answer is (E). This sentence contains the *-ing* verb form that is often a clue to the presence of an introductory modifier. Don't miss this clue just because the sentence starts with *Before*. Ask yourself, Who or what is entering into a legally binding contract? The answer is *both parties*. Therefore, *parties*, not *aspects*, is the noun that should immediately follow the modifying phrase. Option (E) is the only answer choice that includes this revision.

Options (B) and (D) are incorrect because it is not *the agreement* that is *entering into a legally binding contract*. Likewise, option (C) is wrong because *review* is not the noun that is modified by the introductory phrase.

Sample Question 4: Introductory Modifier Combined with Sentence Structure Error

Allowing the consumer much greater control of snapshots, <u>digital cameras, they quickly became popular.</u>

(A) digital cameras, they quickly became popular

(B) digital cameras, they have quickly become popular

(C) the popularity of digital cameras was established quickly

(D) they quickly became popular

(E) digital cameras quickly became popular

The correct answer is (E). This sentence starts with a modifying phrase, *allowing the consumer much greater control of snapshots,* and this phrase is correctly followed by *digital cameras,* which the phrase modifies. There is still a problem, however. The underlined part of the sentence does not use correct sentence structure. The verb *became* appears to have two subjects: *digital cameras* and *they.* The pronoun *they* incorrectly repeats the subject *digital cameras,* so the pronoun must be deleted. Option (E) does this.

Option (B) merely changes the verb tense that is used in option (A), but it doesn't correct the sentence structure error. Option (C) is wrong because it moves *digital cameras* away from the introductory modifier. Option (D) is wrong because, although it eliminates the problem of two subjects for *became,* it uses the pronoun *they* without an antecedent.

Sample Question 5: Modifying Phrase in Sentence Containing Verb Error

The results of the survey, the most extensive ever done by the company, being disputed by managers in the production and sales departments.

(A) The results of the survey, the most extensive ever done by the company, being disputed

(B) The most extensive ever done by the company, the survey's results are being disputed

(C) The results of the survey, being the most extensive ever done by the company, are disputed

(D) The results of the most extensive survey ever done by the company being in dispute

(E) The results of the survey, the most extensive ever done by the company, are being disputed

The correct answer is (E). The modifier in this sentence is the phrase *the most extensive ever done by the company.* The modifier is not introductory; it appears in the middle of the sentence. Its location is correct, because it immediately follows the noun that it modifies, *the survey.* The problem here is with verb usage. It's easy to identify the problem if you read the sentence without the modifier: *The results of the survey being* *disputed by managers in the production and sales departments.* Correcting the verb usage problem requires adding a helping verb before *being*. Option (E) does this.

Option (B) is wrong because it creates a modifier error that wasn't present in the original sentence. This revision moves the modifying phrase to the beginning of the sentence, thus making *results* rather than *survey* the next noun. Option (C) is incorrect because it unnecessarily uses *being* to introduce the modifying phrase. Option (D) starts out well, acceptably putting *most extensive* before *survey*, but this change is followed by an error in verb usage. Remember that the word *being* by itself can never serve as the main verb of a clause.

● **THE FINAL ACT**
  Self-Check Quiz

 who was?

1. <u>Leading the orchestra with passion and energy</u> the baton was dropped by the conductor, to her great embarrassment.
   must come after

   (A) the baton was dropped by the conductor, to her great embarrassment

   (B) the baton, to her great embarrassment, was dropped by the conductor

   (C) the baton had been dropped by the conductor, to her great embarrassment

   (D) the conductor was dropping the baton, to her great embarrassment

   (E) the conductor, to her great embarrassment, dropped the baton

2. <u>Tremendously excited at the prospect of her first overseas trip, it was impossible for Jenna to sleep on the night before her departure.</u>

   (A) Tremendously excited at the prospect of her first overseas trip, it was impossible for Jenna to sleep on the night before her departure.

   (B) Jenna could not sleep on the night before her departure because she was tremendously excited at the prospect of her first overseas trip.

(C) Jenna, tremendously excited at the prospect of her first over-seas trip, it was impossible to sleep on the night before her departure.

(D) Tremendously excited at the prospect of her first overseas trip, Jenna's problem was not sleeping on the night before her departure.

(E) Jenna, going overseas for the first time and being tremendously excited at this prospect, found that sleeping was an impossibility for her on the night before her departure.

3. Revisiting the office building where he had worked for so many years, <u>the retired executive found many memories flooding his consciousness</u>.

  (A) the retired executive found many memories flooding his consciousness

  (B) many memories flooded the consciousness of the retired executive

  (C) it was a flood of many memories that the retired executive was aware of

  (D) many memories came flooding back to the retired executive

  (E) the retired executive found his consciousness filled with a flood of many memories

4. Led by the principal, <u>the faculty and staff of Marlin Elementary have made huge strides in creating a positive learning environment this year</u>.

  (A) the faculty and staff of Marlin Elementary have made huge strides in creating a positive learning environment this year

  (B) huge strides have been made by the faculty and staff in creating a positive learning environment at Marlin Elementary this year

  (C) a positive learning environment has been created this year by the faculty and staff of Marlin Elementary

  (D) this year's strides in the creation of a positive learning environment by the faculty and staff have been huge at Marlin Elementary

  (E) huge improvements have been made this year by the faculty and staff as regards the creation of a positive learning environment at Marlin Elementary

5. Arguing that diet has a significant influence on health, <u>the effect of Dr. Andrew Weil's popular books has been to make people far more conscious of the types of food they consume</u>.

   (A) the effect of Dr. Andrew Weil's popular books has been to make people far more conscious of the types of food they consume

   (B) people have become far more conscious of the types of food they consume after reading Dr. Andrew Weil's popular books

   (C) the types of food they consume have risen in their consciousness after people have read the popular books of Dr. Andrew Weil

   (D) Dr. Andrew Weil's popular books have made people far more conscious of the types of food they consume

   (E) the effect of Dr. Andrew Weil's popular books has been making people far more conscious of the types of food they consume

6. <u>Fuel-efficient cars, distressed by rising gasoline prices, are in demand by consumers.</u>

   (A) Fuel-efficient cars, distressed by rising gasoline prices, are in demand by consumers.

   (B) Consumers, distressed by rising gasoline prices, are demanding fuel-efficient cars.

   (C) Cars that are fuel-efficient are being demanded by distressed consumers because of the price of gasoline.

   (D) Distressed by rising gasoline prices, consumers are currently demanding cars that would use fuel efficiently.

   (E) Consumers, distressed by rising gasoline prices, are demanding cars primarily for its efficiency of fuel use.

7. Worn beyond repair, <u>Derek was finally forced to replace the tires on his bicycle.</u>

   (A) Derek was finally forced to replace the tires on his bicycle.

   (B) Derek was finally forced into replacing the tires on his bicycle.

   (C) it finally became a necessity to replace the tires on Derek's bicycle.

   (D) the tires on Derek's bicycle finally needed to be replaced.

   (E) it was out of necessity that Derek finally was forced to replace the tires on his bicycle.

8. Frightened by the sound of his baby's gasping, the young
      A   B

   father instantly picked up the phone to call the paramedics.
            C   D

   No error
    E

9. Given the high winds that had been predicted for the day, I
    A   B

   was quite surprised at how smooth we sailed during our
                         C

   cruise on the bay. No error
         D   E

10. Although the broker had expected the price of the stock to
                   A

    increase eventually, she was amazed by the surprising large
                 B   C

    jump that occurred over the course of a week. No error
                  D   E

● ANSWERS AND EXPLANATIONS

1. **E** You should notice that the first word of the sentence is a verb ending in *–ing*. This is a clue that you're dealing with an introductory modifier. The noun described by this introductory modifier is *the conductor,* so this noun should immediately follow. Therefore only options (D) or (E) can possibly be correct. Option (D), however, introduces a verb error by using a verb ending in *–ing* for an action that is not continuing. Option (D) also moves the phrase *to her great embarrassment,* which describes *conductor,* next to *baton.* Option (E) correctly places *conductor* immediately after the introductory modifier and retains the correct verb tense, *dropped.*

Options (A), (B), and (C) are all incorrect because *baton* is not the noun described by the introductory modifier.

2. **B** In option (A), you should notice the verb ending in *–ed.* Even though *excited* is not the first word of the sentence, it is near the beginning; you should recognize the verb ending in *–ed* as a clue that this is an introductory modifier. In this case,

the entire sentence is underlined, suggesting that the best answer choice may not necessarily keep the modifier at the beginning of the sentence. Option (B) restructures the sentence using a dependent clause starting with *because* to convey the information that option A includes in the introductory modifier.

Option (C) introduces a problem with sentence structure. *Jenna* is used as though it is a subject, but no corresponding verb follows. Instead *Jenna* and the modifier are followed by an independent clause. Option (D) is wrong because it keeps the introductory modifier but follows it with the noun *problem*, which is not the noun the modifier describes. Option (E) does not contain any modifier or sentence structure errors, but it is wordy.

3. **A** The *–ing* verb, *revisiting*, is a clue that the sentence opens with a modifier. The noun it describes, *executive*, follows immediately, so this sentence contains a correct use of an introductory modifier.

Option (B) is incorrect because *memories*, the first noun following the modifier, is not the noun described by the modifier. Option (C) is incorrect because the introductory modifier is immediately followed by an independent clause rather than the noun described by the modifier. Option (D) is wrong because, as in option (B), the wrong noun follows the modifier. Option (E), which starts like option (A), does not contain a modifier error. Option (E), because it is wordy, is a less desirable choice than option (A).

4. **A** The first word in the sentence, *Led,* is a past participle, a hint that an introductory modifier is present. The modifier is used correctly here because it is immediately followed by the two nouns it modifies: *faculty and staff.*

Option (B) is incorrect because *strides*, the first noun after the introductory modifier, is not the word described by that modifier. Option (C) is likewise incorrect because *environment* is not what is described by the modifier. Option (D) is wrong for a similar reason. Like options (B), (C), and (D), Option (E) uses the wrong noun to follow the introductory modifier and, in addition, is wordy in using the phrase *as regards the creation of.*

5. **D**   The *–ing* ending of the first word in the sentence is your clue that the sentence opens with a modifier. The word described by this modifier, *arguing that diet has a significant influence on health,* is *books.* Option (D) correctly makes *books* the first noun after the modifier. Option (A) is incorrect because the noun *effect* is not what is described by the modifier.

Options (B), (C), and (E) are also incorrect because they place the wrong noun immediately after the introductory modifier. In addition, option (C) is wordy in using the phrase *have risen in their consciousness.* In option (E), the construction *effect…has been making* is also wordy.

6. **B**   When an entire sentence is underlined, you should suspect that the sentence needs its components rearranged. This sentence, though it doesn't open with a modifier, does contain an error in modifier placement. The phrase set off by commas, *distressed by rising gasoline prices,* describes *consumers* rather than *cars.* Therefore this phrase must be placed next to the word *consumers.* Options (B), (D), and (E) all place this noun next to its modifier. Option (B) is best because options (D) and (E) introduce other types of errors. Option (D) is wordy in unnecessarily adding the adverb *currently.* Option (D) also introduces a verb usage error by unnecessarily using the conditional *would.* Option (E) introduces a pronoun error in using the singular *its* to refer to the plural *cars.* In addition, option (E) uses a wordy construction.

Option (C) is incorrect because it uses a confusing word order. It doesn't make sense to separate the adjective *distressed* from the phrase *price of gasoline.*

7. **D**   The sentence opens with a modifier. The verb *worn* does not end with *–ing* or *–ed,* but it is like an *–ed* verb in that it is a past participle. This is your clue that an introductory modifier is present. This question becomes very easy when you ask the question you always need to ask for introductory modifiers. Here the question is, "Who or what was *worn beyond repair?*"

The answer is *the tires*. Notice that only option (D) starts with *the tires*. If you recognize the modifier and ask the right question, you don't even have to carefully read the rest of the answer choices.

Options (A) and (B) start with *Derek* and therefore are not correct because *Derek* is not what is being described by the introductory modifier. Options (C) and (E) introduce the problem of wordiness and do not correct the modifier error.

8. **E** Option A correctly uses a verb with an *–ed* ending to start an introductory modifier. Option B correctly uses the preposition *of*. Option C correctly uses the adverb *instantly* to modify the verb *picked*. Option D correctly uses the infinitive *to call* after the verb phrase *picked up the phone*.

9. **C** Remember to pay attention to any underlined adjective and see if it is used to modify a noun or a pronoun. Here, the adjective *smooth* is incorrectly used to modify the verb *sailed*. The adverb *smoothly* is required here.

Option A is a correct use of the past participle *given*. Option B is a correct use of the past tense in the context of this sentence. Option D correctly uses the preposition *on* in the idiomatic expression.

10. **C** You should note that *surprising* is an adjective that is used here to modify the adjective *large*. This is incorrect because the adverb *surprisingly* is required to modify an adjective.

Option A correctly uses the past perfect tense *had expected* to express an action that occurred before another action. Option B correctly uses the singular pronoun *she* to refer to the singular noun *broker*. Option D is an idiomatically correct expression.

PARALLELISM

DIFFICULTY: ★ ★

FREQUENCY: ★ ★

SURPRISE FACTOR: ★ ★ ★

● INTRODUCTION TO PARALLELISM QUESTIONS

Parallelism means expressing grammatically similar things in the same form. This concept is easier to understand if you look at an example:

> 🖒 My plans for the day include *running* three miles, *doing* homework, and *watching* a movie.

This sentence contains a list, and each item in the list is expressed in the same form—in this case, a verb with the *–ing* ending. If the beginning of the sentence were changed slightly, it would be correct to express each item of the list as a verb starting with *to,* as in this sentence:

> 🖒 My plans for the day are *to run* three miles, *to do* homework, and *to watch* a movie.

Both of the above sentences correctly use parallelism because a consistent form is used to express each item in a list. Mixing the *–ing* verb form and the verb form starting with *to* creates an error in parallelism:

> 🖓 My plans for the day include *running* three miles, *doing* homework, and *to watch* a movie.

In this sentence, mixing the –*ing* verb forms with the infinitive form *to watch* creates a parallelism error. This lesson will help you become aware of situations that require parallelism.

Detecting parallelism errors can be tricky, since they may not necessarily sound wrong to you. Once you recognize that a sentence requires parallelism, identifying the correct phrasing is fairly easy, however. Parallelism isn't tested nearly as often as other writing topics, such as verb usage and pronouns.

Characteristics of Parallelism Questions

Now you know that using parallelism involves using parallel (consistent) phrasing for parts of a sentence that are grammatically alike. Recognizing parts of a sentence that are grammatically similar is your biggest challenge. It's not difficult, though, if you learn to look for clues indicating that a sentence requires parallelism.

Parallelism errors often involve mixing the gerund (a verb with the –*ing* ending used as a noun) with the infinitive form (the verb following the word *to*). Whenever you notice these two grammatical forms in the same sentence, ask yourself if they serve grammatically similar functions. This combination is often a clue that a parallelism error is present.

Another clue that parallelism is being tested in a particular question is the presence of any words that indicate comparison. See the following box for some examples.

Comparison Words and Phrases				
better	less	more	rather	the same as
different	like	prefer	than	worse

Also any comparative form of an adjective, for example:

greater	lesser	older	smaller	younger

Note that it doesn't matter what the adjective is. It's the –*er* ending that is your clue that a comparison is present.

Most Common Types of Parallelism Questions

The two most common situations requiring parallelism on the SAT are:

1. Items in a series
2. Items being compared

Errors involving items in a series often mix verb forms. For example, here are two gerunds with an infinitive verb form trying to sneak in at the end of the series:

> ✍ My favorite sports are *running, playing* basketball, and *to go* hiking.

To correct this parallelism error, you must use the same grammatical form for each of the three items in the series. Here, simply removing the words *to go* accomplishes this:

> 👍 My favorite sports are *running, playing* basketball, and *hiking.*

Like questions that test parallelism of items in a series, questions that test parallelism in comparisons can also involve mixing a gerund with an infinitive. See if you can identify what's wrong with this sentence:

> ✍ Active *listening* requires more than simply *to hear* the words spoken.

Here, the gerund "listening" is paired with the infinitive "to hear." Parallelism is established by substituting "hearing" for "to hear":

> 👍 Active *listening* requires more than simply *hearing the words spoken.*

Notice that the comparison word *more* is your clue that the sentence requires Parallelism.

● THE TRAP DOOR
Steering Clear of Answer Traps

The test-maker doesn't set any deliberate traps for Parallelism questions. The only trap here is one of your own making: failing to recognize a grammatical structure that requires parallelism.

You can avoid this trap by paying special attention to the words in the two boxes in this lesson. As you read through the writing section, you need to constantly be on the lookout for words that indicate either grammatical or logical parallelism is required.

It also helps to keep in mind that in your everyday speech you probably hear and use phrasing that lacks parallelism. An error in parallelism will not necessarily sound wrong to your ear. You need to think carefully about the structure of the sentence and the relationships within it in order to notice a situation that calls for parallelism.

● PERFORMANCE TECHNIQUES
Key Formulas and Rules

In addition to three rules, this section presents a list of words that serve as clues to help you notice situations that require parallelism.

Rule 1: Items in a series must be expressed in the same grammatical form.

It doesn't matter how the series itself functions in the sentence. See if you can spot the error in this sentence in which the subject comprises a series:

> 🖎 *Persistence, effort,* and *being self-disciplined* contribute to success in college.

The series is made up of two nouns and a gerund. Though the gerund form, *being*, functions technically as a noun, it is not needed here, because the word which follows it can be phrased as the noun *self-discipline*:

☞ *Persistence, effort,* and *self-discipline* contribute to success in college.

Sometimes a series functions grammatically as the object of a preposition. In the next example: look for the preposition, and see if you can identify the error in parallelism:

☞ Many young children are afraid *of spiders, thunderstorms,* and *being left alone.*

In this sentence, parallelism can be established by making the third item, a phrase, into a single noun, to make it parallel to the first two items:

☞ Many young children are afraid *of spiders, thunderstorms,* and *abandonment.*

Rule 2: Items in a comparison must be expressed in the same grammatical form.

Remember to watch for words that suggest comparison. In this sentence, the construction *prefer…to* is a clue that a comparison is being made:

☞ Ajay *prefers dining* in restaurants *to home-cooked meals.*

Think about this sentence logically. What two things are being compared here? The answer is *dining in restaurants* and *home-cooked meals.* The first is a verb phrase, while the second is a noun preceded by an adjective. There are two ways to correct the parallelism here. One is to express both parts of the comparison as gerunds:

☞ Ajay prefers *dining* in restaurants to *eating* home-cooked meals.

Here the parallelism of *dining* and *eating* reflects the logic of the comparison. Another way to correctly express this parallelism is to express both items being compared as nouns:

☞ Ajay prefers *restaurant meals* to *home-cooked meals.*

Rule 3: Items being compared must be logically similar.

While Rule 2 states that items being compared must be *grammatically* similar, Rule 3 refers to the *logical* parallelism of items in a comparison. What does it mean to say that items in a comparison must be *logically* similar? The answer has to do with an old saying you may be familiar with, "You can't compare apples to oranges." On the SAT you're unlikely to encounter sentences comparing fruits. You are, however, likely to see comparisons of items such as paintings, books, or movies. Errors in comparisons like this can be hard to spot unless you're on the lookout for them. Read carefully to determine what makes this comparison incorrect:

⇒❙ The *paintings of El Greco* tend to be much darker than *Monet*.

Logically speaking, this sentence is comparing paintings to a painter. That's like comparing apples to oranges; it's not allowed on the SAT. To be logically correct, you must phrase the sentence in a way that compares the *works* of one artist to the *works* of the other artist. There are several ways to make this correction. One is to add the phrase *the paintings of*:

👍❙ The *paintings of El Greco* tend to be much darker than *the paintings of Monet*.

It would also be acceptable to add the phrase *those of* instead of repeating the word *paintings:*

👍❙ The *paintings* of El Greco tend to be much darker than *those of* Monet.

You could even use the possessive and let the word *paintings* be implied:

👍❙ The *paintings of El Greco* tend to be much darker than *Monet's*.

The common thread that runs through all three of the above corrections is that each compares *works of art* to *works of art* rather than comparing *works of art* to *an artist*.

Memorizing common phrases that set up a situation that requires parallelism will make it easy for you to apply the above rules.

Recognizing a Clue for Logical Comparisons Questions

If you see the phrase *those of* or *that of* in an answer choice for an Improving Sentences question, check to see if the sentence is testing logical comparison. If so, the answer choice using *those of* or *that of* is probably the correct answer.

Phrasings that Require Parallelism and Logical Comparisons

as…as	both…and	the more…the less
neither…nor	the more…the more	the less...the more
either…or	the less…the less	not only…but also

● **DRESS REHEARSAL**
Sample Questions and Detailed Explanations

Each of the sample questions below is labeled in a way that points out which words in the sentence serve as clues that parallelism is required.

Sample Question 1: Clue Phrasing Is "as…as"

Southside Prep's debate team does not have <u>as impressive a record as Roosevelt High</u>.

(A) as impressive a record as Roosevelt High

(B) a record being as impressive as Roosevelt High

(C) as impressive a record as Roosevelt High's

(D) as impressive a record than Roosevelt High's

(E) a record as impressive as Roosevelt High

The correct answer is (C). The words *as impressive a record as* should alert you that a comparison is being made here. Think carefully about the logic of the sentence to determine what things are being compared. The sentence as worded in option A compares Southside Prep's *debate team* to *a school*, Roosevelt High. We need to apply Rule 3 here: compare one debate team to another, *not* a debate team to a high school. Option (C) does this, using the possessive *Roosevelt High's* with *debate team* being unstated but implied. Option (B) fails to correct the illogical comparison and also incorrectly introduces *being*. Option (D) does use the possessive *Roosevelt High's*, but it incorrectly substitutes *as* for *than*. Option (E) differs only slightly from option (A), changing *as impressive a record as* to *a record as impressive as*. This wording in option (E) could be acceptable, but option (E) fails to correct the illogical comparison.

Sample Question 2: Clue Phrasing Is "as...as"

The exhausted freshman eventually realized that staying up all night to write a paper is not as efficient as <u>to plan ahead and work steadily over a period of time</u>.

(A) to plan ahead and work steadily over a period of time

(B) planning ahead and working steadily over a period of time

(C) to plan ahead steadily and work over a period of time

(D) having planned ahead and working steadily over a period of time

(E) to plan in advance and work steadily for a period of time

The correct answer is (B). When you first read this sentence, you should notice the construction *not as...as*, which indicates a comparison. Think about the sentence carefully, and ask yourself what is being compared here. The verbs used in the comparison are *staying up* and *to plan...and work*. Since *staying* is in the part of the sentence that is not underlined, you must convert the other verbs to their gerund forms to match *staying*. A quick glance through the first words in each answer choice tells you that only option (B) uses *planning*. Having identified the problem in option (A) as lack of parallelism in a comparison, you can be almost certain at this point that Option (B) is the best answer. You should still quickly check the other choices. Option (C) moves the adverb *steadily*, but it does nothing to correct the parallelism problem. Option (D) incorrectly uses the past tense *having planned* instead of the gerund *planning*. Option (E) merely changes the word *ahead* to *in advance*, which would be acceptable, but it fails to correct the parallelism error.

Sample Question 3: Clue Is Preposition

Meal preparation involves a great deal of effort; <u>time must be spent on menu-planning, the need to go shopping, the actual preparation of the food</u>, and cleaning up the kitchen.

(A) time must be spent on menu-planning, the need to go shopping, the actual preparation of the food

(B) time must be spent on thinking up the menu, the need to go shopping, the actual preparation of food

(C) you have to plan the menu, go shopping, prepare the food

(D) time must be spent on menu planning, shopping, actually preparing the food

(E) it takes time to do menu-planning, go shopping, the actual preparation of the food

The correct answer is (D). This sentence requires close observation to determine the structure that requires parallelism. The part of the sentence that is not underlined is an independent clause. Look at the part of the sentence following the semicolon. Ask yourself how this second independent clause works. Notice the preposition *on.* The object of this preposition is a series stating what activities are involved in meal preparation. Looking at the series as written in option (A) and reducing it to the basic nouns, we see, *planning,…the need…, the…preparation….* You should notice that *cleaning,* in the nonunderlined part of the sentence, is the final item in this series. Since we can't change *cleaning,* we need to phrase the other three items in the series to be parallel to *cleaning.* Option (D) does this by phrasing all items of the series in –*ing* form. Option (B) uses the gerund *thinking* for the first item of the series but does not remove *the need to* in the second item or change *preparation* to *preparing.* Option (E) changes the original wording *time must be spent on* to *it takes time to do,* which doesn't work well with the nonunderlined part of the sentence *cleaning up the kitchen,* but, even more important, option (E) fails to correct the error in parallelism in the underlined part of the sentence.

Sample Question 4: Clue Is Gerund in Nonunderlined Part of Sentence

Wearing a seatbelt can be a good way to avoid getting <u>injured</u>
                                                         A
in a car accident; <u>to drive</u> defensively, <u>though</u>, can prevent an
                        B   C
accident <u>from</u> happening in the first place. <u>No error</u>
          D   E

The correct answer is B. This sentence consists of two independent clauses joined by a semicolon. The subject of the first clause is *wearing*. The subject of the second clause is *to drive*. Substituting *driving* for *to drive* is necessary to make the two clauses parallel. Option A is correct because the past participle is appropriate here. Option C uses the transition word *though*, correctly conveying contrast here, since preventing an accident is preferable to merely avoiding injury. Option D is an idiomatically correct use of *from* with *prevent*.

Sample Question 5: Clue Phrasing Is "neither...nor"

Children <u>who</u> enter kindergarten should <u>thoroughly</u>
          A   B
understand that <u>they</u> will be allowed neither to kick other
                     C
children nor <u>the use of</u> disrespectful language. <u>No error</u>
                  D   E

The correct answer is D. Notice the construction *neither... nor* in this sentence. Remember that this is on the list of words that set up a situation in which parallelism is required. What follows *neither* here is an infinitive, *to kick*, so the principle of parallelism requires *nor* to be followed by an infinitive also. Therefore, Option D is incorrect and should read "to use." Option A correctly uses the pronoun *who* as the subject of a dependent clause. Option B correctly uses the adverb *thoroughly* to modify the verb *understand*. Option C uses *they*, the correct form of the pronoun to serve as the subject of the clause.

● **THE FINAL ACT**
Self-Check Quiz

It'd don't match

1. The store manager asserted that items sold in the electronics department <u>become outdated more quickly than the furniture department</u>.

   (A) become outdated more quickly than the furniture department

   (B) have became outdated more quickly than the furniture department

   (C) become outdated more quickly than the products in the furniture department

   (D) become more quickly outdated than the furniture department

   (E) becoming outdated more quickly than the products in the furniture department

those stories from

2. The short stories of William Faulkner, <u>like Ernest Hemingway, often appear on</u> required reading lists for high school English classes.

   (A) like Ernest Hemingway, often appear on

   (B) like those of Ernest Hemingway, often appear on

   (C) as with Ernest Hemingway, often appear on

   (D) like those of Ernest Hemingway, are often being present on

   (E) similar to Ernest Hemingway, appearing often on

3. The degree of success you can achieve in playing a musical instrument often depends more upon patience and self-discipline than upon <u>innate musical talent</u>.

   (A) innate musical talent

   (B) how much innate musical talent you have

   (C) how talented you may be musically

   (D) musical talent which is innate

   (E) whether you are innately musically talented

4. The ability to draw well is probably more useful to an architect than <u>either an accountant or a writer.</u>

   (A) either an accountant or a writer

   (B) to either an accountant or to a writer

   (C) to either an accountant or a writer

   (D) either an accountant or to a writer

   (E) either to an accountant or a writer

5. Educators encourage the use of computers in the classroom because they promote research skills, <u>provide immediate feedback to students, and enthusiasm is generated for learning.</u>

   (A) provide immediate feedback to students, and enthusiasm is generated for learning

   (B) providing immediate feedback to students, and generating enthusiasm for learning

   (C) provide immediate feedback to students, and generate enthusiasm for learning

   (D) immediate feedback is provided, and generating enthusiasm for learning

   (E) provide feedback immediately to students, and producing enthusiasm for learning

6. Now that I have learned ancient Greek, I would rather read the Odes of Pindar <u>in the original than if they are translated.</u>

   (A) in the original than if they are translated

   (B) in the original than in translation

   (C) as originally written not as being translated

   (D) in original form than if they are translated

   (E) in the original than as they are translated

7. The buildings designed by Frank Lloyd Wright are often considered <u>to be more innovative than other architects.</u>

   (A) to be more innovative than other architects

   (B) to be more innovative than the buildings of other architects

   (C) as being more innovative than other architects

   (D) to be increasing in innovation than other architects

   (E) for their greater innovation than other architects

8. Phil <u>expects</u> that, <u>over</u> the long weekend, he will have <u>more</u>
          A   B   C
   homework in history than in either physics or <u>in economics.</u>
                                                        D

   <u>No error</u>
      E

9. <u>At one time</u>, executives in the movie industry feared that
          A
   <u>people</u> would rather watch movies <u>in</u> their own homes than
          B   C
   <u>going</u> out to the cinema. <u>No error</u>
      D   E

10. <u>I'm afraid</u> it will be impossible for <u>me</u> to both complete my
           A   B
    paper <u>on time</u> and <u>the production of</u> my best work. <u>No error</u>
              C   D   E

● **ANSWERS AND EXPLANATIONS**

1. **C**   The phrase *more...than* should clue you in to the comparison here. The two parts of the comparison are *items sold in the electronics department* and *the furniture department.* Parallelism calls for comparing *what is sold* in one department with *what is sold* in the other department. Option (C) does this by comparing *items* from one department with *products* from the other department.

Option (A) lacks parallelism, as described above. Option (B) starts off badly by using an incorrect form of the past tense *have became* and still does not correct the parallelism problem. Option (D) makes a change that is acceptable but inconsequential, moving the adverb *quickly.* Option (D) is definitely wrong, though, because it fails to correct the parallelism. Option (E) does correct the parallelism problem but creates an additional error by changing the verb *become* to *becoming.*

2. **B**   The word *like* is a clue that the sentence involves a comparison. Remember that a comparison must relate similar items. Option (A) compares the works of Faulkner to the writer Hemingway. Option (B) correctly inserts the phrase *those*

of in order to establish a comparison between the works of one writer and the works of another writer.

Option (C), like option (A), makes a comparison between works and a writer instead of between the works of one writer and the works of another. Option (D) gets off to a good start by inserting the phrase *those of* to establish a logical comparison, but introduces a new error in verb usage by changing *appear* to *are being present on*. Option (E) does not correct the logic of the comparison and introduces a new error in verb usage by changing *appear* to *appearing on*.

3. **A**   The words *more...than* are clues that you're dealing with a comparison in this sentence. The two items being compared are *patience and self-discipline,* used as a logical unit here, and *talent.* Since we have all nouns for both sides of the comparison, this sentence correctly applies the rule of parallelism.

Option B breaks the parallelism by using a clause instead of a noun for the second part of the comparison. Option (C), like option (B), also ends the sentence with a clause instead of a noun. Option (D) may seem reasonable in that it does use the noun, *talent,* but *which is innate* is wordy and therefore less desirable than the wording of option (A). Option (E), like options (C) and (D), destroys the parallelism by using a clause where a noun is called for.

4. **C**   The words *more...than* and *either...or* are clues that this sentence contains a comparison and so requires parallelism. In this case, the parallelism revolves around the use of the preposition *to.* The comparison has two parts, first, *an architect* and, second, a pair consisting of *an accountant* and *a writer,* which form a group. To establish parallelism, it's necessary to repeat the word *to* before *either.*

Option (A) is not parallel because *to* is not repeated before *either.* Option (B), by repeating the word *to* before *a writer,* breaks up the logical pairing of *accountant* and *writer* in this sentence. Option (D) does not include the word *to* before *accountant* as it does before *writer.* Option (E), since it includes the word *to* between *either* and before *an accountant,* would need to repeat the word *to* between *or* and *a writer* in order to establish parallelism.

5. **C** You need to think carefully about this sentence to real-ize that it includes a series. The first item in the series starts with the present tense verb *promote*. Because the verb *promote* appears in the nonunderlined part of the sentence, in order to establish parallelism each of the other items in the series must also start with a verb. In option (A), the second item correctly starts with *provide*, but the third item, *enthusiasm*, incorrectly starts with a noun. Option (C) correctly uses a verb, *generate*.

Option (A) lacks parallelism, as described above. Option (B) makes the second and third items of the series, *providing* and *generating*, parallel with each other, but these are incorrect in the context of the nonunderlined part of the sentence. Option (D) makes the noun *feedback* the second item of the series and the gerund *generating* the third item. Neither of these is paral-lel with the first item, *promote*. Option (E) changes the adjective *immediate* to the adverb *immediately*, which is acceptable. How-ever, by using *producing* instead of *produce* for the third item in the series, option (E) fails to establish parallelism.

6. **B** The expression *rather...than* is your clue that this sen-tence contains a comparison and therefore requires parallel-ism. The two things being compared are the Odes *in the origi-nal* and the Odes *if they are translated*. The first, *in the original*, is a prepositional phrase. The second, *if they are translated*, is a dependent clause. Option (B) establishes parallelism by phras-ing both parts of this comparison as prepositional phrases.

Option (A) lacks parallelism, as described above. Option (C) doesn't start out too badly, but the second part of the com-parison, *as being translated*, incorrectly introduces the verb *being* and is very awkward. Option (D), which is similar to option (A), lacks parallelism because *in the original form* is a prepo-sitional phrase, while *if they are translated* is a clause. Option (E) again incorrectly pairs a prepositional phrase *in the original* with a clause *as they are translated*, so there is no parallelism here.

7. **B** The expression *more...than* should alert you that a comparison is present in this sentence. The two things being compared in option (A) are *the buildings* designed by one ar-chitect, Wright, and the *other architects*. Parallelism requires us

to compare buildings to buildings, not buildings to people. Option (B) establishes parallelism by adding the phrase *the buildings of.*

Option (A) lacks parallelism, as described above. Option (C) starts off with the awkward wording *as being* instead of *to be,* and it lacks parallelism because it still compares buildings to architects, as option (A) does. Option (D) starts off by incorrectly using *increasing in innovation* instead of *more innovative,* and it does not correct the parallelism problem. Option (E) starts off with poor idiomatic expression in *for their greater innovation* and repeats the parallelism error that is also present in all options except option (B).

8. **D** The expressions *more...than* and *either...or* are your clues that parallelism is needed in this sentence. The two items compared are *history* and the pair *physics and economics.* Both items consist of nouns; the lack of parallelism occurs because of the way the preposition *in* is used here. Since *physics and economics* have a logical unity in this sentence, the preposition *in,* which appears before the word *either,* is sufficient. Repeating *in* immediately before *economics* is incorrect because it breaks down the linkage in this sentence between *physics* and *economics.*

Option A correctly uses the present tense for *expects.* Because the sentence later uses the future tense *will have,* the present tense for *expects* makes sense here. Option B is a correct idiomatic usage of *over.* Option C correctly uses *more* to coordinate with *than,* which appears later in the nonunderlined part of the sentence.

9. **D** The word *rather* is a clue that the sentence includes a comparison, so parallelism is required. The two parts of the comparison are *watch movies in their own homes* and *going out to the cinema.* To make these parallel, you must change *going* to *go.*

Option A is idiomatically correct. Option B correctly uses the plural noun *people* to correspond with the plural noun *their,* which is not underlined and so cannot be changed. Option C uses the preposition *in* correctly in the expression *in their own homes.*

10. **D** The word *both* in the nonunderlined part of the sentence is a clue that parallelism is required. The two items that here that must be parallel are *complete* and *the production of*. To establish parallelism, option D should be worded as *produce*.

Option A, *I'm afraid*, is used correctly here to mean *I'm concerned*. Option B correctly uses the pronoun *me* as the object of the preposition *for*. Option C, *on time*, is idiomatically correct.

LESSON 23

Transitions

DIFFICULTY: ★ ★

FREQUENCY: ★ ★

SURPRISE FACTOR: ★ ★ ★

● INTRODUCTION TO TRANSITIONS QUESTIONS

You're probably familiar with using transitions in writing. When you're writing a paper and you use a smooth transition between paragraphs, you make it easier for your reader to see the connection between one paragraph and the next.

On the SAT, you may see some questions that involve transitions between paragraphs. However, since there are only six Improving Paragraphs questions on the whole test, you won't be working with a great number of paragraph transitions.

The Improving Sentences questions on the SAT also test transitions. Though you may not have thought of it in this way before, transitions can be important even within sentences to show how two ideas are related. Identifying appropriate transitions requires you to think about logic. Two common logical relationships that you'll see in a sentence with more than one clause are contrast and cause and effect.

If you've already worked through the Critical Reading lessons on sentence completions, you'll recall that the logical relationship between parts of a sentence is important in mapping the sentence. The same words that you identify as context clues in the Sentence Completion questions are often the very same words you that appear in Transitions questions in the Writing section of the SAT.

If you're not aware of how transitions are tested on the SAT, you may get caught off guard. You should feel confident, though, that if you pay attention to the transitions words presented in this chapter, you will easily be able to recognize transitions errors.

You should expect to see several questions involving transitions in the Improving Sentences questions. You'll probably see at least one or two in the Improving Paragraphs questions also. Relative to other question types though, Transitions questions are infrequent in the multiple-choice writing section. On the SAT as a whole, however, the concept of transitions is crucial. Pay special attention to the tip in the Performance Techniques section of this lesson, because it describes the importance of transitions as a key topic that overlaps the essay, critical reading, and multiple choice writing sections of the SAT.

Characteristics of Transitions Questions

Transitions questions ask you to make sure that there is a smooth and logically correct connection between ideas. To do this, you need to think about the *meaning* of the sentences. In other words, you need to read differently than you do when you're handling other error types. For example, to identify a subject-verb agreement error, you read the sentence analytically. When you see an underlined verb, you read the sentence looking for the subject. This is a somewhat mechanical way to read. To handle a Transitions question, however, you have to read to *understand* the meaning. Paying attention to the meaning is necessary so that you can identify the logical relationship between ideas in the sentence.

Some of the same skills you use in the Critical Reading section of the SAT will help you on Transitions questions. You need to think about what the sentence means and how the parts relate to each other. Let's look at an example. Consider the logical relationship between the ideas in this sentence:

> 👎 I wanted to try out for the school play; *therefore* I couldn't because play practices were held at the same time as my soccer practices.

[handwritten annotation: transition word doesn't make sense]

Does a quick reading of this sentence leave you shaking your head in confusion? The sentence doesn't make sense because there's a contradiction between the idea expressed in the first clause, the desire to be in the play, and the idea in the second clause, the conflict between the schedules for the play and soccer. The transition word used here, *therefore*, is a word that expresses cause and effect. It's the wrong transition in this sentence, which needs a word that expresses contrast. This revision should make more sense to you:

> ➥ I wanted to try out for the school play; *however*, I couldn't because play practices were held at the same time as my soccer practices.

The word *however* correctly expresses the contrast in this sentence. For Transitions questions, you have to read for content. There is usually no single clue word you can point to in either clause that lets you know what the relationship between the clauses is. Transitions questions don't hinge on a single part of speech or a grammatical rule; an appropriate transition can be determined only by paying attention to the combined meaning of the words in each clause.

Most Common Types of Transitions Questions

The Improving Sentences questions that test transitions will be made up of more than one clause. You will notice, either in the sentence as it is written or in the answer choices, a word or words from the lists of transitions in the Performance Techniques section of this lesson. Whenever you see a word you recognize as a transition word, there's a good chance that the question will test transitions. You should take the presence of the transitions words as a clue that you need to read each clause carefully and think about the logical relationship between the two.

In the Identifying Sentence Errors questions, you may see questions similar to those described above, questions that test your understanding of how to correctly express the logical relationship between two clauses. In Improving Paragraphs questions, the logical relationship may be between two sentences. For these questions, you need to determine the appropriate transition, one that expresses the relationship and also fits in the given context. (For example, *while* and *but* both express contrast, but *while* is better if the transition word must fit in the beginning of the sentence. You can read more about this in the Performance Techniques section.)

In Improving Paragraphs questions, you may also see some unique question types that actually have more in common with the passage-based reading questions than with most of the other writing questions. These are questions that ask, for example, which sentence would be most appropriate to conclude the essay or where a new paragraph should begin. These types of questions demand that you use skills, such as determining main ideas, similar to those you use in answering reading comprehension questions.

When transitions between sentences are tested in an Improving Paragraphs question, it's important to remember the principles of correct sentence structure. Often, questions that ask you about the best way to combine sentences test not only the correct use of transitions words and phrases but also the correct ways of combining clauses into a complete sentence. Remember that two independent clauses may be combined by either a comma followed by a FANBOYS conjunction or by a semicolon if no FANBOYS word is used.

● **THE TRAP DOOR**
Steering Clear of Answer Traps

If you become familiar with the three categories of transition words and you pay attention to main ideas and logical relationships as you read the passage in Improving Paragraphs Questions, you should feel very comfortable handling transitions. There is, however, one small trap you need to be aware of for transitions: sometimes the best transition word or phrase is none at all! This trap occurs relatively infrequently. Refer to sample Question 2 that follows for an example.

● **PERFORMANCE TECHNIQUES**
Key Formulas and Rules

Two rules for transitions are presented here. As you read through the explanations and examples, you will enhance your understanding of how transitions and sentence structure errors frequently overlap. This section also includes a tip that can help you with certain kinds of Improving Paragraphs questions.

Rule 1: A transition word or phrase must correctly express the logical relationship between the two ideas it joins.

To apply this rule, you need to be aware of the different types of transitions. In the accompanying boxes, transitions are grouped into three categories. The most common transition types are cause-and-effect and contrast. The other category is an umbrella group of transitions that express continuity, emphasis, examples, explanation, and similarity.

If you study the three lists in the boxes below, you will be familiar with nearly all the transitions that you're likely to see on the SAT. You certainly won't see questions that test all of these words in the writing section, given the low frequency rating for transitions. Despite this, you should still spend some time becoming familiar with these words and practice using them in writing that you do for yourself and for school. Doing so will help you prepare for the essay section of the SAT. An effective use of transitions will make your essay easy to read. You can think of transition words and phrases as trail markers that help your reader figure out where your argument is going. The more precise you are in specifying the logical relationships among the ideas in your essay, the more likely you'll be to produce a strong, effective piece of writing.

Transitions That Show Cause and Effect		
as a consequence	consequently	therefore
as a result	resulting in	thus
because	so	

Transitions That Show Contrast

although	in contrast	though
but	nevertheless	whereas
despite	nonetheless	while
even though	on the other hand	yet
however	rather	

Transitions That Show Continuity, Emphasis, Examples, Explanation, or Similarity

additionally	in addition	likewise
certainly	in fact	moreover
for example	in other words	similarly
for instance	indeed	such as
furthermore		

You should note that even the words and phrases in a single box aren't necessarily interchangeable in a particular context. Let's look at two contrast transitions, *but* and *however*. These are both commonly used on the SAT writing section. Though both express contrast, each has a distinctive use. The transition *but,* you should remember from the sentence structure lesson, is a FANBOYS conjunction that can be used when preceded by a comma to join two independent clauses. Here is a correct use of this transition:

👍 I studied French for three years in school, *but* on my vacation, I found it difficult to understand the language as it is spoken in Paris.

The word *but* here correctly conveys the contrast between the two parts of this sentence. The second clause, not understanding the French spoken in Paris, expresses the opposite of what the first clause sets you up to expect. You would expect that, having studied French for so long, I would be able to use the language and understand it. The second clause contradicts this expectation. The word *but* conveys the contradiction, or contrast, correctly. It's certainly possible to use other words from the contrast list, but it might be necessary to restructure the sentence. Here are some other acceptable ways to express the idea of contrast:

> ➥ *While* I have studied French for three years in school, on my vacation, I found it difficult to understand the language as it is spoken in Paris.
> ➥ I have studied French for three years in school; *however,* on my vacation, I found it difficult to understand the language as it is spoken in Paris.

Note that the transition *however* is not a FANBOYS word. Therefore, when it is used to join two independent clauses, it must be preceded by a semicolon, not a comma. As the examples above illustrate, there is often more than one correct way to express a particular logical relationship. Rest assured, though, that if several acceptable phrasings exist, only one of them will be offered among the answer choices on the SAT. No question on the test can have two correct answers!

Rule 2: Use more than one transition in a sentence only when emphasis is desired and correct sentence structure can be maintained.

Sentence structure errors are frequently combined with transitions errors on the SAT. Let's look at an example to see how using two transitions causes a problem with sentence structure:

> ➥ *Though* Emily Dickinson was a recluse, *but* she *nonetheless* became a famous poet.

This sentence probably sounds wrong to you, because the transitions *though* and *but* shouldn't be used together. *Though* introduces a dependent clause, and *but*, a FANBOYS word, should be used with a comma to join two independent clauses. A third transition word, *nonetheless,* is also present here, but this is acceptable to emphasize the contrast if using it doesn't compromise sentence structure. Thus, the sentence can be revised as:

☜ *Though* Emily Dickinson was a recluse, she *nonetheless* became a famous poet.

This revision contains two transitions that work appropriately together.

Writers' Strategy in Improving Paragraphs Questions

Occasionally one of the Improving Paragraphs questions will ask about strategies used by writers. While these questions aren't directly related to transition words and phrases, answering them correctly requires the same skills you use for Transitions questions. Thinking about these questions may help you:

What is the main idea of the paragraph?
What is the main idea of the passage?
How does the author feel about this topic?
What does the writer want me to think about this topic?
How are the ideas in one paragraph related to the ideas in the other paragraphs?
What kinds of evidence does the writer provide to support the main ideas?

These questions are similar to those you ask yourself in doing active reading for the passage-based Critical Reading questions. You find the answers by paying attention to transition words and phrases. Being aware of the tremendous importance of transition words in both the Critical Reading and Writing sections of the SAT can help boost your score on both sections of the test.

● **DRESS REHEARSAL**
Sample Questions and Detailed Explanations

The sample questions in this dress rehearsal are all Improving Paragraphs questions. The Final Act for this lesson contains Improving Sentences and Identifying Sentence Errors questions. Remember that the passages that form the basis for Improving Paragraphs questions are likely to contain some errors that are not addressed by the questions. You should view the passage as a rough draft of an essay and focus your attention on making only the improvements called for by the particular questions.

Questions 1–5 are based on the following passage.

(1) The summer I was ten, my mother decided to expose us to the world of art. **(2)** My brother and I were not very excited when we heard what my mother meant. **(3)** She didn't mean we could take drawing classes or painting classes. **(4)** Therefore she meant that we were going to have to spend one afternoon a week with her at the Fine Arts Museum. **(5)** Before each visit to the museum, she made us read print-outs from a website about artists and painting styles. **(6)** It was, on the other hand, almost as bad as being in school. **(7)** Who wants to spend the summer thinking about artists when you could be with your friends at the pool?

(8) First we had to read about ancient Egyptians and their weird way of painting faces and then go look at them at the museum. **(9)** My 12-year-old brother thought this was fascinating, because I was not impressed. **(10)** Later we had to learn about artists in the Middle Ages who painted people wearing strange long clothing. **(11)** We had to look at pictures of fat babies with wings and curly hair and no clothes flying around the edges of paintings. **(12)** I certainly couldn't see what my mother thought was so great about art.

(13) On our last visit to the museum, something clicked when I saw this painting by a woman called Mary Cassatt. **(14)** In it, a woman was reading to a child. **(15)** The colors were soft and gentle, and you could tell by the mother's expression how happy she was just to be with the child. **(16)** I couldn't stop looking at this painting! **(17)** I wanted to see every painting Mary Cassatt had ever made. **(18)** It was definitely worth looking at so many paintings to find a painter I could relate to.

Sample Question 1: Combining Sentences That Express Contrast

1. Of the following, which is the best way to revise and combine sentences 3 and 4 (reproduced below)?

   She didn't mean we could take drawing classes or painting classes. Therefore she meant that we were going to have to spend one afternoon a week with her at the Fine Arts Museum.

(A) She didn't mean we could take drawing or painting classes, therefore, but that we would have to spend an afternoon a week with her at the Fine Arts Museum.

(B) Spending an afternoon a week with her at the Fine Arts Museum, in addition to taking drawing and painting classes, was what my mother had in mind.

(C) She didn't mean taking drawing or painting classes, but, rather, spending an afternoon each week with her at the Fine Arts Museum.

(D) It wasn't taking drawing or painting classes that she had in mind, but furthermore spending an afternoon each week with her at the Fine Arts Museum.

(E) Not drawing or painting classes, she had in mind, but spending one afternoon a week with her at the Fine Arts Museum.

The correct answer is (C). The two sentences you're asked to combine express contrasting ideas: it wasn't one thing, but another. The word *therefore,* because it expresses cause-and-effect, is the wrong transition here. In addition, the two sentences are wordy, unnecessarily using *she meant that we were going to* right after *she didn't mean we could.* The best revision will be one that avoids the wordiness and uses an appropriate contrast transition. Option (C) does this. The transition *rather* is correctly used to emphasize the contrast expressed by *but.* You should also note that this revision uses parallelism in the pairing of two *–ing* verb forms, *taking* and *spending.*

Option (A) is incorrect because it includes the cause-and-effect transition *therefore* and doesn't correct the wordiness. Option (B) is incorrect because it distorts the meaning of the original by using the transition *in addition to.* Option (D) is incorrect because it uses *furthermore,* a transition that shows continuity instead of contrast. Option (E) is incorrect because, although it correctly uses the contrast transition *but,* it does not use correct sentence structure in the first clause, *not drawing or painting classes, she had in mind.*

Sample Question 2: Determining When the Best Transition Is No Transition

2. In sentence 6, *on the other hand* is best replaced by

(A) (delete *on the other hand* and do not replace it with anything)

(B) as a result

(C) as a consequence

(D) rather

(E) however

The correct answer is (A). To determine the appropriate transition, ask yourself about the logical relationship between sentences 5 and 6. There is a connection between these two sentences: the writer feels that having to do the reading before visiting the museum makes the experience *almost as bad as being in school.* The relationship between the ideas is one of similarity. It would be acceptable, but not necessary, here to use a transition such as *in fact* to express the similarity. Notice, however, that *in fact* is not offered here as an answer choice. Options (B) and (C) both contain transitions expressing cause-and-effect, which is not the correct relationship in this context. Options (D) and (E) both contain contrast transitions, also not the correct relationship. Therefore, because none of the answer choices offers an appropriate type of transition word, the best choice here is to use no transition at all.

Sample Question 3: Using a Contrast Transition

3. In sentence 9, the word *because* should be replaced by

(A) consequently

(B) however

(C) on the other hand

(D) meanwhile

(E) but

The correct answer is (E). First, read the sentence carefully to determine the logical relationship between the two clauses. In this case, paying attention to specific words will help you identify the relationship. The words *fascinating* and *not impressed* indicate contrast. Three answer choices, options (B), (C), and (E), are contrast transitions. Option (B), *however,* will not work here, because it would require *fascinating* to be followed by a semicolon instead of the existing comma. The same is true for option (C): the use of *on the other hand* would require a semicolon after *fascinating*. Option (E), *but,* is correctly used to express contrast when two independent clauses are joined with a comma. Option (A) is incorrect because it is a cause-and-effect transition. Option (D) is incorrect because *meanwhile* relates to time and does not express the logical relationship of contrast.

Sample Question 4: Identifying a Writer's Strategy

4. A strategy that the writer uses in the third paragraph is

   (A) refuting the argument of another

   (B) using difficult vocabulary

   (C) drawing a conclusion based on experience

   (D) maintaining a disinterested tone

   (E) quoting published material to support a statement

The correct answer is (C). While this question doesn't ask specifically about transitions, the attention you've already given to transitions in answering the previous questions should help you answer this one. You may need a clarification of some of the vocabulary used in the answer choices. In option (A), *refuting* means giving evidence that argues against a particular position or *argument*. Option (A) is incorrect because, while the view of the writer's mother that looking at art is worthwhile is important to the essay, this view is not presented as an argument. Option (B) is incorrect because the vocabulary in this passage is quite easy to understand. Option (C) is the correct answer. The writer begins the essay describing reluctance to engage in the museum experience but concludes with a change of opinion, feeling after all that the experience has been valuable. In option (D), *a disinterested tone* refers to writing about something in an objective, matter-of-fact way, merely describing and not expressing a personal opinion about the topic. Option (D) is incorrect because the writer of this passage is personally involved with the topic. The essay is based on personal experience, and the writer's opinions are included, particularly in sentences 16, 17, and 18. Option (E) is incorrect because the author does not provide any quotations in this passage.

Sample Question 5: Providing an Effective Concluding Sentence

5. Which of the following sentences is the best to add as a conclusion, following sentence 18?

(A) I just wish I had been able to spend more time swimming.

(B) Finally, I knew, this was the excitement my mother was hoping I would find at the art museum that summer.

(C) It's too bad my mother's plan wasn't more of a learning experience for me.

(D) I think I would like to learn about the paintings of Marsden Hartley as well.

(E) I learned that Mary Cassatt did many painting of mothers and children.

The correct answer is (B). A concluding sentence can be considered a special kind of transition. To be effective, a concluding sentence must appropriately summarize or capture the main idea of the passage. It should also be consistent with the focus of the passage. A good concluding sentence will help the reader remember the main point of the passage.

Option (A) is incorrect because it picks up on one minor detail in the passage, sentence 7, and it also seems to contradict the writer's main point, that the art exposure was ultimately meaningful. Option (B) is the best answer because it sums up the passage. Option (C) is incorrect because it contradicts the main idea of the passage. The passage does indeed describe a learning experience, because the writer progresses from being uninterested in art to finding a painter who sparks an interest. Option (D) is incorrect because it brings up a new topic, another painter, rather than summarizing the passage. Option (E) is incorrect because it provides a detail about Mary Cassatt but does not summarize the main point of the passage.

● THE FINAL ACT
Self-Check Quiz

1. Both candidates would like to restructure the way public schools are financed; <u>however, they intend to accomplish this in similar ways.</u>

    (A) however, they intend to accomplish this in similar ways *showing dif. when there is none*

    (B) in contrast to one another, however, they intend to accomplish this in similar ways

    (C) moreover, they intend to accomplish this goal in similar ways

    (D) on the other hand, they intend to accomplish this in similar ways

    (E) moreover, they intend on accomplishing this in similar ways

2. Some doctors refuse to see patients who will not quit <u>smoking, the reason is that smoking has adverse effects on many systems of the body.</u>

    (A) smoking, the reason is that smoking has adverse effects on many systems of the body

    (B) smoking; the reason why is that smoking has adverse effects on many systems of the body

    (C) smoking because it has adverse effects on many systems of the body

    (D) their habit of smoking because it has adverse effects on many systems of the body

    (E) smoking for the reason that smoking has adverse effects on many systems of the body

3. The actress had been hoping she would be cast as the lead, <u>and the director did not find her appropriate for the part.</u>

    (A) and the director did not find her appropriate for the part

    (B) but the director did not find her appropriate for the part

    (C) however, the director did not find her appropriate for the part

    (D) but the director had not been finding her to be appropriate for the part

    (E) and the director did not agree that she was appropriate for the part

4. <u>Despite the jet lag and my lack of sleep,</u> I felt surprisingly ener-
   getic when my plane arrived in Moscow.

   (A) Despite the jet lag and my lack of sleep
   (B) Because of the jet lag and my lack of sleep
   (C) Despite the jet lag and my lack of sleep, however
   (D) Although the jet lag and my lack of sleep
   (E) Despite the problems of jet lag and my lacking in sleep

5. Though careful consideration of issues is crucial to a democracy,
   <u>yet many students graduate from high school having had very</u>
   <u>little preparation</u> for their role as voters.

   (A) yet many students graduate from high school having had
        very little preparation
   (B) but many students become high school graduates having
        had very little preparation
   (C) moreover, many students graduate from high school not
        well-prepared
   (D) many students with very little preparation graduate from
        high school
   (E) many students graduate from high school having had very
        little preparation

6. The incoming president wants the historical association

   <u>to shift</u> <u>its focus</u> to public <u>buildings, and</u> the longtime
     A   B   C
   members <u>prefer to keep</u> the focus on private residences.
              D
   <u>No error</u>
     E

7. Some students want <u>to leave</u> the school building immediately
                 A
   when <u>their</u> last class is over; others, <u>similarly,</u> enjoy staying
        B   C
   <u>into the evening</u> to participate in school activities. <u>No error</u>
        D   E

8. Though Ana had long thought she wanted to be a doctor,

   <u>whereas</u> she found <u>herself</u>, <u>after her first year</u> in college,
     A   B   C

   more <u>interested in</u> pursuing creative writing. <u>No error</u>
         D   E

9. <u>Because</u> some parents have been <u>known</u> to interfere during
     A   B

   games, league regulations now forbid parents <u>from</u> talking to
                                           C

   coaches while a game is <u>in progress</u>. <u>No error</u>
                        D   E

10. <u>Because</u> some critics bemoan the declining <u>popularity of</u>
      A   B

    classical music, others are encouraged that advances in

    electronic reproduction <u>are</u> making classical recordings
                              C

    more accessible <u>than ever</u>. <u>No error</u>
                    D   E

● ANSWERS AND EXPLANATIONS

1. **C** The sentence as written contains a Transitions error. The transition word *however* shows contrast, which is inappropriate in the context of this sentence. The logical relationship between the two independent clauses in this sentence is one of consistency of expectation. The word *similar* is a clue that a transition expressing similarity is needed. The transition word *moreover* in option (C) is correct here. Note that it is correct to use *moreover* after a semicolon separating two independent clauses.

Options (B) and (D), like option (A), incorrectly use transitions that express contrast. Option (E), like option (C), appropriately uses the transition *moreover,* but option (E) introduces an idiomatic error in the phrase *intend on accomplishing.*

2. **C** The first problem you should notice in the sentence as written is a sentence structure error. Two independent clauses may not be joined by just a comma. You should also notice that the underlined part of the sentence includes the wording *the reason is*. This wording should alert you that a cause-and-effect relationship may be present, which, in fact, it is. Option (C) uses the transition word *because*, which shows the logical relationship between the two clauses and also corrects the sentence structure error.

Option (B) is wordy in using the phrasing *the reason why is that*. Option (D) does not contain a transitions error, but it is wordy in using the phrase *their habit of* before *smoking*. Similarly, option (E) is wordy. It is better to use the transition word *because* than the longer phrase *for the reason that*.

3. **B** The underlined word *and* is not the most appropriate conjunction to join the two independent clauses in this sentence. When you see *and* underlined, you should read the sentence carefully to determine whether a specific transition word would be more appropriate. The logical relationship between the two clauses in this sentence is one of contrast. Therefore, the transition *but*, which conveys the idea of contrast, is best here.

Option (C) uses *however,* a transition word that does show contrast. This revision introduces a sentence structure error because when *however* is used to join two independent clauses, it must follow a semicolon, not a comma. Option (D) corrects the transitions error but introduces a verb usage error by substituting *had not been finding* for *did not find*. Option (E), in retaining *and*, fails to correct the transitions error.

4. **A** The underlined phrase correctly uses the transition word *despite* to show the contrast between the dependent and independent clauses in this sentence. The word *surprisingly* in the nonunderlined part of the sentence is a clue that a contrast transition is appropriate here.

Option (B) is incorrect in using the transition word *because*. This transition expresses cause and effect rather than contrast. Option (C) is incorrect because it adds a second transition word, *however*. Option (D) is incorrect because *although* must be used to introduce a clause rather than the noun phrase *the jet lag and my lack of sleep.* Option (E) retains the correct transition, *despite,* but it introduces a less desirable phrasing by substituting *lacking in sleep* for *lack of sleep.*

5. **E** The sentence as written contains a transitions error because the conjunction *yet* repeats the idea of contrast that is already expressed by the transition *though* in the nonunderlined part of the sentence. Option (E) deletes this incorrect use of *yet.*

Option (B) is incorrect because, like option (A), it uses a second transition word, here *but,* which repeats the contrast transition *though* at the beginning of the sentence. Option (C) is wrong because it introduces the transition word *moreover,* which is used to express continuation and so is inappropriate in this sentence that conveys contrast. Option (D) inappropriately rearranges the word order and therefore causes confusion.

6. **C** Option C consists of a noun, followed by a comma, followed by a conjunction. You should consider the conjunction to determine whether it provides an appropriate transition. Think about the logical relationship between the two clauses in this sentence. It is contrast. *The incoming president* wants one thing; *longtime members* want something different. The conjunction *and* does not express contrast. A better word in this context would be *but.*

Option A correctly uses the infinitive form *to shift* following the verb *wants.* Option B correctly uses the singular pronoun *its* to refer to the singular noun *association.* Option D is a correct use of the infinitive *to keep* after the word *prefer.*

7. **C** The word *similarly* is a transition word that shows similarity. The relationship between the clauses in this sentence is one of contrast rather than similarity. The construction *some… others* is clue that contrast is present. The correct transition to express the contrast here is *however.*

Option A is a correct use of the infinitive *to leave* after the verb *want*. Option B correctly uses the plural pronoun *their* to refer to the plural noun *students*. Option D is a correct idiomatic expression.

8. **A**   The word *whereas* can be used to express contrast, but it is not appropriate in this context. The nonunderlined part of the sentence includes the contrast transition *though*. The word *whereas* should be deleted from this sentence.

Option B is a correct use of a third person pronoun *herself* to refer to *Ana*. Option C is a correct idiomatic expression. Option D correctly uses the preposition *in* with the –*ing* verb form *pursuing*.

9. **E**   Option A correctly uses the transition *because* to express the cause and effect relationship between the two classes in this sentence. Option B is a correct use of the past participle *known*. Option C uses correct idiomatic expression in pairing the preposition *from* with the verb *forbid*. Option D is a correct idiomatic expression.

10. **A**   The construction *some...others* used in this sentence is a clue that the relationship between the two clauses is one of contrast. The cause and effect transition word *because* should be changed to a contrast transition such as *while* or *although*.

Option B correctly uses the preposition *of* with the noun *popularity*. Option C correctly uses the plural verb *are* to agree with the plural subject *advances*. Option D is a correct idiomatic expression.

Word Choice

DIFFICULTY: ★ ★

FREQUENCY: ★ ★

SURPRISE FACTOR: ★ ★ ★

● INTRODUCTION TO WORD CHOICE QUESTIONS

Word Choice questions involve selecting the best word or phrase to use in a given context. For one type of Word Choice question, the Diction question, you have to choose one word instead of another. You might have to decide, for example, whether *accept* or *except* is correct in a particular sentence. Another type of Word Choice question, the Idiom question, involves using words in the appropriate combination. Idiom questions often hinge on which preposition is correct in context. Pay attention to the preposition in this sentence:

👎I was *impressed on* the architect's work.

Does this sound funny to you? It should. The correct idiomatic usage in this context doesn't use the preposition *on*. This revision should sound better to you:

👍I was *impressed by* the architect's work.

The verb *impressed* must be used with the preposition *by* here.

Your ear will probably help you recognize word choice errors in many cases. However, since it would be impossible to list every possible idiomatic expression, it can be very easy to be caught off guard by Word Choice questions. Some Word Choice questions are difficult while others are relatively easy.

Characteristics of Word Choice Questions

Word Choice questions can involve all parts of speech and are therefore fairly unpredictable. Some Word Choice questions involve single words only, while others involve words that must be used together in a certain way in order to correctly convey a particular idea. You will find Word Choice questions in all three of the SAT writing categories: Improving Sentences, Identifying Sentence Errors, and Improving Paragraphs. This lesson focuses on Word Choice questions that fall into the first two categories only. For more help with word choice in the Improving Paragraphs questions, review the lesson on transitions.

Most Common Types of Word Choice Questions

The most common Word Choice questions fall into one of the two categories described above: diction and idiom. *Diction* means choosing which word is appropriate in a particular context.

When you read an Identifying Sentence Errors question, notice whether each underlined part of the sentence contains one or more than one word. For parts that contain one word, let the part of speech guide your thinking about possible errors. If the word is a pronoun, you need to think only about the rules for pronouns. If the word is a verb, it's possible that diction is being tested, but it's much more likely that the rules of verb usage are being tested. If, however, a preposition is underlined, either by itself or along with one or more other words, then you'll need to check for correct idiomatic usage. Let's take a look at one of these questions:

<u>Whenever</u> Curtis plays basketball, he <u>finds</u> that <u>he</u> develops a
    A   B   C

severe <u>pain with</u> his knee. <u>No error</u>
        D   E

The correct answer is D. Option A here is a single word, not a verb or pronoun. *Whenever* is used correctly here to introduce a dependent clause. Thus, there is no word choice error in option A. Option B has a single word underlined. Because it is a verb, chances are you should think about the rules for verb usage rather than for diction. In this case, the verb *finds* is in the present tense. It is used correctly here, matching the present tense verb *plays* used earlier in the sentence. Option C also has a single word underlined, the pronoun *he*. Because it's a pronoun, think about the pronoun rules instead of diction issues. *He* is the correct pronoun to refer to Curtis. Look at option D. Two words are underlined, and one of them is a preposition. This is an example of an incorrectly used idiom. The preposition *with* is not the right one to use with the noun *pain*. The correct idiomatic expression here is *pain in*. As in this example, detecting an error in idiom often involves noticing a preposition and the word used immediately before it.

Some SAT questions that test diction are based on students' tendencies to confuse similar sounding words. You can refer to the list in Performance Techniques to review some commonly confused word pairs.

Another kind of diction question involves special forms of adjectives. The *comparative* is the form that usually ends in –*er*, such as *larger* and *greater*. The *superlative* is the form of an adjective that usually ends in –*est*, such as *largest* and *greatest*. The Performance Techniques section includes rules for comparatives and superlatives.

Whereas diction questions generally involve choosing the better of two words, *Idiom* questions test your knowledge of how words are used together. English contains some coordinating expressions, or paired words or phrases that must be used together. If you see one part of a coordinating expression in the nonunderlined part of the sentence, you need to make sure to include the other part as well. See if anything sounds funny in this example:

➥ Isabella is studying *not only* Spanish, *in addition*, Italian.

This sentence should sound strange to you because, in English, whenever the words *not only* appear, correct idiomatic expression demands that the words *but also* appear later in the sentence. Even though the words *in addition* mean something similar to *also*, they are not idiomatically correct here. The sentence must be rewritten:

👍 Isabella is studying *not only* Spanish *but also* Italian.

There are no general rules that apply to all questions of diction and idiom in the way that rules govern the use of verbs and pronouns. There are, however, a limited number of coordinating expressions such as *not only...but also* (the three dots here indicate that other words will appear between *only* and *but),* so the list in the Performance Techniques section of this lesson is definitely something you should become familiar with.

Here are some specific examples of errors involving coordinating expressions. Study these examples carefully to train your ear so that the correct pairings of the coordinating expressions will sound right to you:

👎 *Either* Carlos *and* Juliana will give the speech.
👍 *Either* Carlos *or* Juliana will give the speech.

👎 I will *not only* vote for the candidate *and also* campaign for her.
👍 I will *not only* vote for the candidate *but also* campaign for her.

👎 *Neither* Lily *and* Joseph will be at the party.
👎 *Neither* Lily *or* Joseph will be at the party.
👍 *Neither* Lily *nor* Joseph will be at the party.

👎 Carly *prefers* Brahms *over* Beethoven.
👎 Carly *prefers* Brahms *than* Beethoven.
👍 Carly *prefers* Brahms *to* Beethoven.

👎 I would *rather* see a movie *more than* dine in a pizza parlor.
👎 I would *rather* see a movie *over* dine in a pizza parlor.
👍 I would *rather* see a movie *than* dine in a pizza parlor.

These examples should give you an idea of how these coordinating expressions work. Chances are you will see one or more of these expressions on the test. Remember, if you see the first part of the expression in a sentence, look for the appropriate second part. In Identifying Sentence Errors questions, only the first or the second part of a coordinating expression will be underlined, not both.

Another aspect of training your ear to recognize correct use of coordinating expressions is knowing that *the more* and *the less* may be used interchangeably. Therefore, all four of the following sentences use correct word choice:

👎❙ *The less* you work, *the less* you earn.
👎❙ *The more* I learn, *the more* I forget.
👎❙ *The more* exercise I get, *the less* tired I feel.
👎❙ *The less* exercise I get, *the more* tired I feel.

For many Idiom questions on the SAT, your everyday understanding of the English language is enough to help you recognize whether or not an underlined group of words uses a correct idiomatic expression. Undoubtedly, students whose first language is English will find Idiom questions a bit easier than students for whom English is a second language. However, Idiom questions can be among the most challenging questions for all students. No general rules apply to idioms. Idiomatic expressions are so much a part of the English language that it would be impossible to gather them all together in a list for you to memorize. The performance techniques section includes a list of some idiomatic expressions that you might see on the test, but is it certainly not a complete list.

● **THE TRAP DOOR**
Steering Clear of Word Choice Answer Traps

There is one trap that is you may fall into with Word Choice questions, but you shouldn't think of it as a trap the test maker deliberately sets for you. The trap is encountering a phrase that you think "sounds funny," even though you're not sure why. With many other error types, for example, pronoun case, if something sounds funny to your ear, the sentence almost certainly contains an error. Since word choice is such a broad category with few predictable patterns for you to look for, the criterion of sounding funny is not as useful. An underlined phrase may sound funny because it is indeed incorrectly worded. On the other hand, it may be worded in a perfectly acceptable way and sound funny to you simply because you're not familiar with the particular word or expression. With Word Choice questions, it can be difficult to know when to trust your ear.

Surprisingly, one of the most helpful techniques for avoiding this trap has little to do with word choice. The best strategy here is to develop as much confidence as you possibly can in handling *other* error types on the SAT. Being confident about verb usage, pronouns, sentence structure, modifiers, and parallelism—the issues that are governed by general rules—can help you avoid getting into trouble with the less predictable topic of word choice.

Let's see why this is true. You don't have any way of knowing exactly which idiomatic expressions or which inappropriate word choices will appear on the SAT. On the other hand, you *can* learn to recognize incorrect verb usage, for example, in any context that you're likely to see. If you're working on an Identifying Sentence Errors question and you don't know whether an underlined idiom is used appropriately, check carefully for a more predictable error type. If an underlined part of the sentence contains a verb usage error, that option is the answer to the question. In this case, your uncertainty about whether the idiom is correct doesn't matter. You can still answer the question correctly.

For the Identifying Sentence Errors questions, you should develop a methodical approach to thinking about the four underlined parts of the sentence. If something sounds funny, try to figure out why. The accompanying box provides questions to help you work systematically through the sentence.

Taking a Methodical Approach When Something "Sounds Funny"

Ask yourself: *Learn Your Lines* | *Important Info.!*

1. Does the underlined item include a **verb**? If so, find the verb's subject. Then check for proper subject-verb agreement. Is the tense of the verb correct in the context of any time-related phrases or other verbs in the sentence?

2. Does the underlined item include a **pronoun**? If so, look for its **antecedent.** If you can't find an antecedent, the pronoun may be ambiguous and therefore incorrect. If you do find an antecedent, ask whether the pronoun matches its antecedent in **number.** If the antecedent is plural, then the pronoun must be plural.

3. Does the underlined item include an **adjective**? If so, identify the word it modifies. An adjective can modify only a noun or pronoun, not a verb.

4. If the underlined item is an **adjective,** is it used as part of a comparison? Look for phrases such as *of the two, of everyone,* and *of all,* or for words such as *than, more,* and *less.* These phrasings often indicate that the sentence contains a comparison. If you notice a comparative or superlative adjective, make sure to apply the rules for superlatives and comparatives described in the next section.

5. Do you see a **preposition** anywhere in the sentence? If the sentence includes a preposition that's not underlined, the preposition could be part of a trap for subject-verb agreement. If a preposition is underlined and you haven't spotted any other errors by asking the questions above, this underlined preposition *may* constitute an idiom error. It's still possible that the correct answer to the problem is "No error," but if you've gotten this far through the systematic approach and turned up no previous errors, there's a good chance that the remaining phrase you identified as sounding funny does indeed have an error in word choice. If you can rule out all but two answer choices, your odds of answering this question correctly are 50-50 even if you have no clue about this phrase that sounds funny to you.

● PERFORMANCE TECHNIQUES
Key Formulas and Rules

Except for comparative and superlative adjectives, Word Choice questions do not follow predictable rules. However, there are some words and phrasings that are more likely than others to show up on the SAT. Therefore, this section includes four lists that you should become familiar with: (1) commonly confused word pairs, (2) idiomatic expressions containing prepositions, (3) correctly worded idiomatic expressions, and (4) coordinating expressions, which contain two parts that must be used together.

The words in the two idiom lists are just representative samplings of the kinds of expressions you may see on the SAT, so you certainly don't need to memorize these. However, you should study the commonly confused word pairs and coordinating expressions lists more carefully, because one or more specific expressions on these two lists is likely to show up on the SAT.

Commonly Confused Word Pairs

accept—to receive, to agree with, or to approve of something
  I cannot *accept* that rude behavior.
except—to leave out
  All the sixth graders, *except* five, are serving a detention.
eminent—well-known; respected
  Many people attended the *eminent* man's funeral.
imminent—about to happen
  Dark clouds indicated that a storm was *imminent*.
fewer—is used for items that can be counted
  I eat *fewer* snacks now that I'm in school.
less—is used for aggregate amounts that can't be counted
  I have far *less* money now than I did a year ago.
rise—(for a person) to assume a standing position; (for a thing) to be made to increase
  All please *rise* for the national anthem.
  Gas prices *rise* when the supply is low.
raise—to cause an object to move to a higher position
  Please *raise* your hand if you have a question.
among—is used when three or more things are involved
between—is used when only two things are involved
  It is easier to divide a cookie evenly *between two people* than to divide it *among three people.*

Examples of Idiomatic Expressions Containing Prepositions

acceptable to	keep from
as much by	a lack of
attribute to	long since
committed to	prefer to (*not* than *or* over)
consistent with	prevent from
familiar to	provide for
familiar with	provide with
inaccessible to	speak about
inconsistent with	with which
intolerable to	withhold from
involved in	worry about

Examples of Idioms Worded Correctly for Specific Meanings

count on—is acceptable to mean *rely on*

for the most part—is acceptable to mean *largely* or *primarily*

how long—is acceptable to mean *the length of time that*

in need of—is acceptable to mean *needing* or *who needs*

it is likely—is acceptable to mean *it is possible*

just how—is acceptable as in "*Just how* well the device will work has not been determined."

nearly all—is acceptable to mean *most*

ought—is acceptable to mean *should*

take into account—is acceptable to mean *allow for*

through—is often underlined all by itself when it is used correctly

when—is acceptable to refer only to time, as in "*when* the show stops"

gerund form: *People living in warmer climates* (*living* here is acceptable to mean *who live*)

Coordinating Expressions
(idiomatic constructions that require two parts)

the more…the more	rather…than
the less…the less	prefer…to
neither…nor	not only…but also
either…or	

There are two diction errors that, unlike idiom errors, do follow predictable rules. Whenever you see an adjective in an underlined item, be sure to notice if it is in the **comparative** form (which usually ends in *-er*) or the **superlative** form (which usually ends in *-est*). Examples of comparative adjectives are *higher* and *smaller*. Examples of superlatives are *highest* and *smallest*. Some comparatives and superlatives take slightly different forms. Some examples of these irregular forms are provided in the accompanying box.

Some Frequently Used Irregular Comparatives
and Superlatives

good – better – best	more – more – most
bad – worse – worst	less – lesser – least

Rule 1: Use the *comparative* form of an adjective when comparison is limited to two items.

Rule 2: Use the *superlative* form of an adjective when three or more things are being compared.

Let's look at an example to illustrate these rules. Here is an incorrect use of the superlative: *sound good?*

➥ Of my *two* sisters, Carmella is the *most* athletic.

Because only <u>two people are being compared,</u> it is necessary to replace the superlative *most* with the comparative *more:*

➥ Of my *two* sisters, Carmella is the *more* athletic.

The word *two* is a clue that the comparative is required here.

● **DRESS REHEARSAL**
Sample Questions and Detailed Explanations

Remember to look for the few types of clues that exist for Word Choice questions. For example, the presence of part of a coordinating expression in the nonunderlined part of the sentence is a clue that the question tests word choice. In addition, words and phrases related to number, such as *two*, *both*, *three*, and *of all*, serve as clues that the distinction between comparative and superlative is being tested.

Sample Question 1: The Coordinating Expression "Either... or"

My mother informed <u>us</u> that either my sister <u>~~and I~~</u> would
                        A   B
<u>have to miss</u> the concert because <u>one of us</u> would have to
        C   D
take care of our little nephew. <u>No error</u>
                                        E

The correct answer is B. Option B contains an error in idiomatic construction, but you need to be especially alert to find it. Notice that the nonunderlined portion of the sentence includes the word *either*. *Either* is the first part of the coordinating expression *either...or*. Often when you see the word, *either*, you can expect to see the word *or* later on in the sentence. It is not idiomatically correct to use the word *and* to join two nouns that follow the word *either*. Option A correctly uses the objective form of the pronoun *us*. Option C includes a correct use of the infinitive *to miss*. Option D correctly uses the pronoun *one* to refer to *my sister or I* and correctly uses the pronoun *us* as the object of the preposition *of*.

Sample Question 2: The Coordinating Expression "Prefer... to"

A poll <u>conducted by</u> the student council found that most

     A

seniors, if forced to choose <u>between</u> the two, would prefer . . . ᴛᴏ

         B

<u>attending</u> the prom <u>more than</u> going on the class trip. <u>No error</u>

 C   D   E

The correct answer is D. You should notice that the non-underlined part of the sentence contains the word *prefer*. Remember that this is part of a coordinating expression. When you see the word *prefer* in a sentence, it must be followed by *to*. The expression *prefer...more than* is not idiomatically correct. Refer to the list of coordinating expressions. The word *than* should be paired with *rather,* never with *prefer.* Option A is correct because *conducted by* is a correct idiom. Option B uses correct diction. Because the choice in this sentence is limited to two options, *between* is the correct word. Option C is correct because *attending,* with its –*ing* ending, is parallel to *going,* which appears in the nonunderlined part of the sentence.

Sample Question 3: The Coordinating Expression "Neither...nor"

The <u>principal</u> couldn't believe <u>that</u> neither the students   ...ɴᴏʀ

    A   B

<u>or the teachers</u> expressed a desire <u>to shorten</u> the school day.

     C   D

<u>No error</u>

 E

The correct answer is C. The nonunderlined word *neither* is a clue, because it's the first part of a coordinating expression. Option C should read ***nor*** *the teachers.* It is never correct to use *or* with *neither.* Only *nor* is idiomatically correct. Option A is a correct use of the commonly confused word *principal* for the person. The word *principle* means *idea or belief.* Option B correctly uses *that* to introduce a dependent clause. Option D is a correct use of the infinitive, *to shorten.*

Sample Question 4: An Idiomatic Expression: "Take into account"

When packing for a vacation, <u>you</u> should <u>take an account of</u>
                           A   B

how long you will be gone and <u>whether</u> or not you will have
                                   C

<u>access to</u> laundry facilities. <u>No error</u>
      D   E

The correct answer is B. Depending on your familiarity with the idiom, you may or may not find something funny about the phrasing of option B, *take an account of.* Suppose you read through this sentence and think that the correct answer here may be option E. Before selecting option E as your final answer, you should carefully consider the other answer choices to see if you can spot any of the commonly tested errors. Option A uses the pronoun *you.* This agrees with the pronoun used in the nonunderlined part of the sentence *how long you will be gone,* so it is correct. Option B does include an error in idiom. The correct idiomatic usage here is *take into account,* which is used to mean *consider.* Option C includes the correct use of the word *whether* in the transitional phrase *whether or not.* Option D correctly uses the preposition *to* with the noun *access.* Since you have not found an error in options A, C, or D, you are able to make a 50-50 guess between option B and option E. Having ruled out all other underlined parts of the sentence as potential answers, you should now consider option B more carefully. With a little luck, you will notice that *take an account of* is an incorrect idiom.

Sample Question 5: The Comparative Adjective Used When the Superlative is Required

Of all <u>my teachers</u> this year, Mrs. Currie, <u>who is my</u> history
          A   B

teacher, is <u>the closer</u> <u>to retirement</u>. <u>No error</u>
              C   D   E

The correct answer is C. Option A uses the plural noun *teachers,* which correctly corresponds to the plural pronoun *all* in the nonunderlined part of the sentence. Option B correctly uses the pronoun *who* to introduce the dependent clause *who is my history teacher.* In option C, the word *closer* indicates that a comparison is being made. Whenever you see a clue like this that points to a comparison, consider the issue of comparative vs. superlative. Remember to ask yourself how many items are being compared. Since this sentence contains the word *all,* you know that more than two things are being compared. (If only two things were being compared instead of one, you would see the word *both* here instead of *all.*) Since more than one teacher is being compared, the superlative form *the closest* is required (Rule 2). Notice that option D correctly uses the preposition *to* with the noun *retirement.*

● THE FINAL ACT
Self-Check Quiz

1. <u>Addressing</u> a gathering at my school's annual career day, Dr.
   A
   Patel told <u>us</u> that, <u>for the most part</u>, he had not minded the
   B C
   lack of sleep required <u>of</u> resident doctors during medical
   D
   training. <u>No error</u>
   E

2. John, perhaps my most <u>inquisitive</u> friend, always begins by
   A
   asking <u>me</u> <u>where I'm at</u> whenever he reaches me <u>on my cell</u>
   B C D
   phone. <u>No error</u>
   D E

3. Seeing a Raphael masterpiece for the first time <u>in person</u>, I was
   A
   impressed *with* the artist's <u>remarkable</u> skill in conveying the
   B C
   <u>epic scope</u> of Biblical history. <u>No error</u>
   D E

4. People <u>living in</u> crowded urban areas need to be
   A

   <u>extraordinarily</u> considerate of <u>their</u> neighbors if they hope
   B   C

   to live <u>on</u> harmony together. <u>No error</u>
   D   E

5. Most successful people <u>state</u> that, <u>in order to</u> become
   A   B

   tricky

   <u>imminent</u> in one's field, it is necessary <u>to develop</u> the
   C   D

   qualities of persistence and self-discipline. <u>No error</u>
   E

6. <u>For more than</u> 25 years, Meryl Streep <u>has been acting</u> in a
   A   B

   <u>remarkably</u> wide <u>variation</u> of movies. <u>No error</u>
   C   D   E

7. The director <u>informally</u> polled the choir and found <u>that</u>, of the
   A   B

   entire group, Teresa <u>had been</u> doing choral singing for the
   C

   longest

   <del>longer</del> time. <u>No error</u>
   D   E

   as being both

8. George Lucas is <u>often</u> regarded <u>to be</u> a pioneer in introducing
   A   B

   a new <u>generation of</u> special <u>effects</u> to movie fans. <u>No error</u>
   C   D   E

9. We were <u>fortunate that</u> the area <u>where</u> my family lives was not
   A   B

   tricky

   <u>effected</u> much at all by the catastrophic storm that recently
   C

   swept <u>through</u> much of our home state. <u>No error</u>
   D   E

10. After surviving <u>an amazingly</u> demanding schedule <u>during</u> his
        A   B
    residency, the young doctor <u>was surprised</u> to find that his first
                                          C
    year in practice was even <u>more harder</u>. <u>No error</u>
                              D   E

● ANSWERS AND EXPLANATIONS

1. **E** Option A correctly uses the *–ing* verb form to introduce a modifier that describes *Dr. Patel.* Option B correctly uses the objective pronoun *us* as the object of the verb *told.* Option C, *for the most part,* is a correct idiomatic expression. In the context of this sentence, option D uses the correct preposition to create the idiomatic expression *required of.*

2. **C** The expression *where I'm at,* although you may hear it in everyday conversation, is not idiomatically correct and so should be avoided on the SAT. Option A correctly uses the superlative *most* in a context in which it can be assumed that choice involves more than two friends. Option B correctly uses the objective pronoun *me* as the object of the verb *asking.* Option D is an idiomatically correct expression.

3. **B** To make a correct idiomatic expression, the preposition *at* should be changed to *with* or *by.* Option A correctly uses the idiomatic expression *in person.* Option C correctly uses the adjective *remarkable* to modify the noun *skill.* Option D correctly uses *epic* as an adjective to modify the noun *scope.*

4. **D** The preposition *on* is inappropriate here. The correct idiomatic expression is *in harmony* rather than *on harmony.* Option A correctly uses *living in* to mean *who live in.* Option B correctly uses the adjective *extraordinarily* to modify the adjective *considerate.* Option C correctly uses the plural pronoun *their* to refer to *people.*

5. **C** The use of *imminent* here is a diction error. *Imminent* is used to describe an action that is about to happen. The correct word here is *eminent,* which means well-known. Option A correctly uses the present tense verb *state.* Option B uses a correct

idiomatic expression, *in order to*. Option D correctly uses the infinitive verb form *to develop* after the phrase *it is necessary*.

6. **D** The use of *variation* here is a diction error. The word needed in this context is *variety*. Option A is a correct use of the idiomatic expression *for more than* followed by a time phrase. Option C correctly uses the verb tense *has been acting* to express an action that has happened in the past and continues in the present. Option C correctly uses the adverb *remarkably* to modify the adjective *wide*.

7. **D** The nonunderlined part of the sentence contains the phrase *of the entire group*, indicating that the comparison here involves three or more people. Therefore the comparative form of the adjective, *longer*, is inappropriate. When three or more things are compared, the superlative form of the adjective, in this case, *longest*, is required. Option A correctly uses the adverb *informally* to modify the verb *polled*. Option B is a correct use of the word *that* following *found*. Option C correctly uses the past tense *had been* to describe an action occurring before the poll took place.

8. **B** The nonunderlined part of the sentence contains the clue *regarded*. This is the beginning of the idiomatic expression *regarded as*. It is not correct to say *regarded to be*. Option C is idiomatically correct. Option D correctly uses a plural noun.

9. **C** This is an error in diction. The correct word in this situation is *affected*. Option A is idiomatically correct. Option B correctly uses *where* to refer to a place. Option D is a correct use of the preposition *through*.

10. **D** There is an error with comparative adjectives here. Because *harder* is a comparative adjective, it is incorrect to use *more* with it, because *more* is another comparison word. Option A correctly uses an adverb to modify an adjective. Option B correctly uses the preposition *during*. Option C is a correct use of the past tense.

Wordiness

DIFFICULTY: ★ ★ ★

FREQUENCY: ★ ★

SURPRISE FACTOR: ★ ★ ★

● INTRODUCTION TO WORDINESS QUESTIONS

Wordiness means using more words than necessary to convey an idea. It's easy to be caught off guard by this type of error because a wordiness error often doesn't sound wrong; a wordy sentence may not contain any grammatical errors.

Reducing wordiness can be a bit more complicated than simply applying the grammatical rules that govern the use of verbs and pronouns. With wordiness, you have to make a judgment call. You must first decide if a sentence is wordy and, if it is, then determine how to phrase the sentence as concisely as possible without losing its original meaning.

Wordiness isn't often directly tested, and it appears infrequently in Identifying Sentence Errors questions. In Improving Sentences questions, however, wordiness does show up fairly often in combination with other errors in wrong-answer choices. A big part of the challenge on the SAT Writing section is knowing what error types to expect and where to expect them, so it's important that you become familiar with detecting wordiness.

Characteristics of Wordiness Questions

The most important thing to remember is that a wordy sentence won't necessarily *sound* wrong to you. Wordiness is common in everyday conversation, and it's not necessarily such a bad thing in ordinary speech. On the SAT, however, you need to apply the principles of good *written* language, and these include using a concise, not a wordy, style.

Wordiness errors are less obvious than grammatical errors. Here's an example:

> ⇒I We on the committee have *made a decision* to use the *exact same* procedures *that had been utilized last year.*

Wordy sentences like this may sound vaguely confusing in some way you can't put your finger on. Like this example, though, many wordy sentences don't necessarily contain any *grammatical* errors. The problem is one of style: the sentence is not concise. It's possible to convey the same information in fewer words. See how much easier the sentence is to understand when the unnecessary words are eliminated:

> ⇒I We on the committee have *decided* to use *last year's procedures.*

Remember that, since wordiness appears primarily in the Improving Sentences questions, the correct answer will be right in front of you. You won't have to invent the best wording of the sentence; you will merely have to pick it out from the five choices offered.

Most Common Types of Wordiness Questions

Three types of wordiness errors are described here. Don't worry if you have a hard time telling one type from the other. On the SAT, you never have to *describe* why a particular phrasing is wrong. You simply have to identify that it is wrong or select the best way to revise it. The important thing is that you can detect unnecessary words, not label a phrase as a particular type of wordiness error.

One type of wordiness error is **redundancy.** Redundancy occurs when the same idea is stated by more than one word or phrase. Consider this example:

> ⇒I Marcus *was anticipating* his summer vacation *and looking forward to it* with great excitement.

You should notice that this sentence is not grammatically incorrect, but it is unnecessarily repetitive. The idea of *looking forward* is included in the definition of *anticipating*. So the sentence can be worded more concisely as:

> ▶ Marcus *was anticipating* his summer vacation with great excitement.

Eliminating unnecessary repetition makes the sentence easier to read. Refer to the accompanying box to see a few other examples of redundancy.

Examples of Redundant Phrases

the whole entire thing (*whole* and *entire* mean the same thing)

founded and established (*founded* and *established* mean the same thing)

repeat the idea again (the idea of *again* is included in the meaning of *repeat*)

a pediatrician who works with children (a *pediatrician*, by definition, works with *children*)

look back to the past (the idea of *back* is included in the meaning of *past*)

occurred and took place (*occur* means *take place*)

Redundancy isn't tested frequently on the SAT, but being aware of it as you read will help you become sensitive to wordiness errors. As the examples of redundancy show, wordiness is an issue that requires you to think carefully about the meaning of words in a sentence.

Another kind of wordiness error involves using general words to express an idea that could be stated more directly with fewer words. These errors are called **wordy constructions.** If a sentence contains a wordy construction, you can't simply remove the entire phrase, but you can find a more concise way of expressing its meaning. Look at this example:

> ▶ The attorney and her client *spent time in a lengthy meeting for the purpose of determining which strategy would be the most effective.*

Although this sentence is not grammatically incorrect, you may be able to sense that it contains unnecessary words. See how much stronger and more concise this revision is:

👉 The attorney and her client *met at length to determine the most effective strategy.*

Here, the wordy construction *spent time in a lengthy meeting* is shortened to *met at length.* The wordy construction *which strategy would be the most effective* is shortened to *the most effective strategy.* In addition, the unnecessary phrase *for the purpose of* is deleted. Notice that, even though some words are deleted in the revision, none of the meaning of the original sentence is lost. See the accompanying box for a list of some wordy constructions.

Examples of Wordy Constructions

caused it to happen that—caused
due to the fact that—because
for the reason that—because
go by car—drive
had the feeling of—felt
made an attempt—attempted
made a decision—decided
experienced a great deal of fear—was very afraid
with the intention of accomplishing—intending to

Another type of wordiness error is the **empty phrase**. Empty phrases, also called filler phrases, are words that don't add anything to the meaning of a sentence. A sentence can be improved simply by deleting an empty phrase; no other wording changes are required. In the example above, the original sentence contains the empty phrase *for the purpose of.* You can refer to the accompanying box for other examples of empty phrases.

Examples of Empty Phrases

for the purpose of   this is
it is   which could be
the reason for this is that   which is

● **THE TRAP DOOR**
Steering Clear of Answer Traps

There are only two traps for wordiness errors, and these are traps of your own making, not traps set by the test-maker. The first is simply not being aware that concise language is valued on the SAT.

The second trap is thinking that when it comes to sentence length, shorter is *always* better. While that's *often* true, you can't follow this guideline mindlessly. You have to think about the particular sentence, considering its logic and meaning. Sometimes correcting errors involves using *additional* words to improve the clarity or logical flow of a sentence. Remember the parallelism lesson, which explains the requirement to compare logically similar things? Think about this example:

> 🖐 The *novels of Charles Dickens*, like *Nathaniel Hawthorne*, are frequently included in college English classes.

This sentence compares the novels of one writer to another writer. The comparison must be revised so that the two items being compared are the books of one writer and the books of another writer. Recall from the parallelism lesson that one possible correction for this sentence is:

> 🖐 The *novels of Charles Dickens*, like *those of Nathaniel Hawthorne*, are frequently included in college English classes.

Though this revision adds words to the sentence, the revision doesn't constitute a wordiness error. Rather, the additional words, *those of,* are needed to make the comparison a logical one. The goal in correcting wordiness is to eliminate *unnecessary* words. You sometimes have to carefully consider and compare several answer choices to determine whether additional words are necessary or not.

● PERFORMANCE TECHNIQUES
Key Formulas and Rules

Guideline for Wordiness: Eliminate Unnecessary Words

The above guideline is the only rule for wordiness. It's called a "guideline" instead of a "rule" to remind you that correcting wordiness is not as straightforward as correcting grammatical or usage errors. Handling wordiness requires you to think about the precise meanings of words in a sentence to decide which phrasing is best.

While wordiness can show up in an Improving Sentences question as the only error, you'll often see wordiness in combination with another error type, especially with parallelism and sentence structure errors. Look for the parallelism error in this sentence:

> Many people are drawn to the entertainment industry because they yearn for *fame*, a glamorous *lifestyle*, and *it's possible to earn huge sums of money.*

Parallelism is required here because the object of the preposition *for* is a series. The series is made up of a noun, a noun, and a clause. Rewriting the clause as a noun corrects the parallelism error:

> Many people are drawn to the entertainment industry because they yearn for *fame*, a glamorous *lifestyle*, and the huge earning *potential.*

In this above revision, correcting the parallelism error also makes the sentence shorter.

Sentence structure is another error type that may be associated with wordiness. When these errors occur together, correcting the sentence structure error usually eliminates the wordiness. See if you can find the sentence structure error in this example:

> ⬛▌ Albert Einstein, a famous scientist, *and he* proposed the theory of relativity.

In this sentence, the subject is repeated. *Albert Einstein* and *he* both appear to be subjects of the verb *proposed,* but it is not acceptable to use them both. The sentence structure here could be corrected in two ways. First:

> ⬛▌ Albert Einstein *was* a famous scientist, and he proposed the theory of relativity.

The above revision improves the sentence structure, but the sentence still uses a wordy construction. This revision is even more concise:

> ⬛▌ Albert Einstein, *a famous scientist*, proposed the theory of relativity.

This revision transforms two independent clauses into a single independent clause without losing any of the meaning of the longer sentence.

Remember that wordiness errors show up frequently in wrong answer choices for Improving Sentences questions. Always read through answer choices with an eye for wordiness. Keep in mind, though, that grammatical errors and errors of logic in a sentence take precedence over wordiness. Correct those errors first, even if doing so winds up making the sentence longer. The shortest answer is often, but not always, the best.

● **DRESS REHEARSAL**
Sample Questions and Detailed Explanations

Sample Question 1: Wordiness with Sentence Structure Error

Pioneer women worked industriously to meet the needs of their families, they grew much of their own food and made clothing by hand.

(A) Pioneer women worked industriously to meet the needs of their families, they grew much of their own food and made clothing by hand.

(B) Pioneer women, industriously working to meet the needs of their families, they grew much of their own food and made clothing by hand.

(C) Pioneer women worked very hard to meet the needs of their families, being that they grew much of their own food and made clothing by hand.

(D) Pioneer women worked industriously to meet the needs of their families, although they grew much of their own food and made clothing by hand.

(E) Growing much of their own food and making clothing by hand, pioneer women worked industriously to meet the needs of their families.

The correct answer is (E). The sentence as written consists of two independent clauses that are incorrectly joined by only a comma. The subject of the second clause, *they*, refers to the subject of the first clause, *pioneer women*, so the sentence can be rewritten with one dependent and one independent clause. Option (E) does this.

Option (B) incorrectly uses two subjects, *pioneer women* and *they* with one main verb phrase, *grew...and made*. Option (C) incorrectly introduces a verb error with the phrase *being that*. Option (D) incorrectly uses the contrast transition word *although* in a sentence that doesn't express contrasting ideas.

Sample Question 2: Wordiness with Parallelism Error

Over the summer, Saul plans to practice violin, take a cooking class, <u>and he will be traveling to Italy for two weeks</u>.

(A) and he will be traveling to Italy for two weeks

(B) and travel to Italy for two weeks

(C) being that he will travel to Italy for two weeks

(D) he will also travel to Italy for two weeks

(E) and traveling to Italy for two weeks

The correct answer is (B). This sentence contains a list, a clue that parallelism is required. The first two items in the list, *practice* and *take,* are verbs, while the third is a clause: *he will be traveling.* To correct the parallelism error, this clause must be changed to the verb *travel,* eliminating the unnecessary words *he will be.* Option (B) does this. Correcting the parallelism error here makes the sentence more concise.

Option (C) is incorrect because it adds the unnecessary words *being that* and also does not correct the parallelism error. Option (D) is incorrect because it, like option A, uses a clause rather than a verb for the third item of the series. The words *he will* make this a clause, when only the verb *travel* is needed. Thus, option (D) doesn't correct the parallelism error. Option (E) is incorrect because it uses the *–ing* form *traveling* instead of simply *travel.*

Sample Question 3: Redundancy

<u>Because</u> most of the community's older artisans have passed
    A

away <u>over the last ten years</u>, the <u>declining</u> craft of making
           B   C

quilts <u>is</u> no longer widely practiced. <u>No error</u>
    D   E

The correct answer is (C). This sentence is not grammatically incorrect, but it does contain a wordiness error. It is redundant to use the underlined adjective *declining* to describe *craft* here, because the nonunderlined phrase *no longer widely practiced* means the same thing as *declining.*

Option (A) correctly uses the transition word *because* to express the cause and effect relationship between the two clauses in the sentence. Option B is an idiomatically correct expression. Option (D) correctly uses the singular verb *is* to agree with the singular subject *craft.*

Sample Question 4: Wordy Constructions

Pablo Picasso may be the most famous Cubist painter, but he is not the only painter who worked in the Cubist style.

(A) Pablo Picasso may be the most famous Cubist painter, but he is not the only painter who worked in the Cubist style.

(B) Pablo Picasso is the most famous Cubist painter of all the ones who worked in that style.

(C) Though not the only painter who worked in the Cubist style, Pablo Picasso is the most famous of them all.

(D) Pablo Picasso is the most famous of all the Cubist painters.

(E) Pablo Picasso the most famous of all the Cubist painters.

The correct answer is (D). On a first reading, this sentence may not sound wrong to you. There are no grammatical errors. The transition word *but* correctly expresses contrast, and the two independent clauses are correctly joined by a comma and a FANBOYS word. Still, you should ask yourself whether the sentence is worded in the best way possible. When you see a sentence that is entirely underlined, as this one is, you should suspect a problem with the wording. Notice here that the words *painter* and *Cubist* appear in both clauses of the sentence. Option (D) eliminates this repetition by combining the two clauses into one without compromising the meaning of the original sentence.

Option (B) is a bit less wordy than option (A), but it still uses the wordy construction *of all the ones who worked in that style.* Option (C) is incorrect because it uses the wordy construction *of them all.* Option (E), like option (D), eliminates the wordiness of option (A), but option (E) goes too far in also eliminating the necessary verb *is.*

Sample Question 5: Empty Phrases

The plans that we had made for our vacation fell through when a series of thunderstorms took place.

(A) The plans that we had made for our vacation fell through when a series of thunderstorms took place.

(B) The plans that we had for our vacation fell through in the presence of a series of thunderstorms.

(C) It was a series of thunderstorms that caused our plans for vacation to fall through.

(D) Our plans for our vacation fell through, it was because of a series of thunderstorms.

(E) Our vacation plans fell through because of a series of thunderstorms.

The correct answer is (E). The sentence as written contains no grammatical errors, nor are there any problems with sentence structure. Notice, however, that one choice, option (E), is shorter than all the others. This version retains the meaning of the original and uses correct sentence structure. The shortest answer is the best here. Notice that option (A) contains the empty phrases *that we had made for* and *took place.* Option (E) eliminates these unnecessary phrases. Also note that option (E) introduces the transition word *because,* used in place of option (A)'s *when.* The phrasing *when...took place* in option (A) does describe a cause and effect relationship, and *because* expresses this relationship in fewer words. Don't be afraid to depart from the wording of the original sentence (option (A)) as long as the revision conveys the same meaning in a more correct or concise way.

Option (B) is incorrect because it uses the empty phrase *that we had made for*, and the phrase *in the presence of* is not as precise as the wording *because* used in option (E). Option (C) is incorrect because it uses the empty phrase *it was...that.* Option (D), in addition to being wordy, uses incorrect sentence structure in not using a FANBOYS word with the comma connecting two independent clauses.

● THE FINAL ACT
Self-Check Quiz

1. <u>I mailed my birthday party invitations, started working on party planning and preparation, and continued to do so until the night before the party</u>.

   (A) I mailed my birthday party invitations, started working on party planning and preparation, and continued to do so until the night before the party.

   (B) I worked on party planning and preparation up until the night before the party, as soon as I had mailed my birthday invitations.

   (C) After mailing my birthday party invitations, I worked on planning and preparation until the night before the party.

   (D) Upon mailing my birthday party invitations, the work of party planning and preparation is what occupied me until the night before the party.

   (E) Working on party planning and preparation is what I found myself doing from the time I mailed my birthday invitations until the night before the party was to take place.

2. Over the long weekend, the preschool teacher will <u>prepare a unit on pioneer life, and she will make a bulletin board featuring log cabins</u>.

   (A) prepare a unit on pioneer life, and she will make a bulletin board featuring log cabins

   (B) prepare a unit on pioneer life and she will be in the process of making a bulletin board featuring log cabins

   (C) be preparing a unit on pioneer life and a bulletin board will be featuring log cabins

   (D) prepare a unit on pioneer life and make a bulletin board featuring log cabins

   (E) spend time preparing both a unit on pioneer life and in addition a bulletin board featuring log cabins

3. To do the experiment, the student must heat the solution, add the salt, <u>and then she will have to determine the mass of the resulting precipitate</u>.

   (A) and then she will have to determine the mass of the resulting precipitate

   (B) and determine the mass of the resulting precipitate

   (C) and the mass of the resulting precipitate must be determined

   (D) be determining the mass of the resulting precipitate

   (E) and determine the mass of the precipitate which will result

4. When you are running late to an <u>appointment, this is when you usually encounter bad traffic conditions</u>.

   (A) appointment, this is when you usually encounter bad traffic conditions

   (B) appointment, the result is usually encountering bad traffic conditions

   (C) appointment is usually when you encounter bad traffic conditions

   (D) appointment, it is at this time that you usually encounter bad traffic conditions

   (E) appointment, you usually encounter bad traffic conditions

5. Experts on global warming believe that individual efforts to conserve energy <u>will not be enough to halt the increase in atmospheric gases and counteract the effects of those gases on climate</u>.

   (A) will not be enough to halt the increase in atmospheric gases and counteract the effects of those gases on climate

   (B) will be inadequate for the halting of increases in atmospheric gases and counteracting their effects on climate

   (C) are not likely being enough to halt the increase in atmospheric gases and have a counteracting effect on climate

   (D) is not enough to halt the increasing levels of gases in the atmosphere and counteract the effects the gases are having on the climate

   (E) being inadequate to halt the increases in atmospheric gases and cause a counteracting of their effects on climate.

6. Student drivers must completely understand <u>that the actions done by one person behind the wheel would have a significant impact on other people</u>.

   (A) that the actions done by one person behind the wheel would have a significant impact on other people

   (B) the truth of the fact that one person's actions behind the wheel can have a significant impact on others

   (C) that one person's actions behind the wheel can have a significant effect on others

   (D) the fact that other people would experience significant effects from one person's actions

   (E) the things done by one person when behind the wheel would significantly affect other people

7. To make sure that recess is a good experience for all the children, <u>it is the playground supervisors who must walk around and confront</u> anyone who is bullying another child.

   (A) it is the playground supervisors who must walk around and confront

   (B) the playground supervisors are the ones who must walk around and confront

   (C) the playground supervisors are in the process of having to walk around and also to confront

   (D) it is necessary for the playground supervisors to walk around and be confronting

   (E) the playground supervisors must walk around and confront

8. Many doctors now believe it is their responsibility to serve not only <u>as diagnosticians but also with their intention of serving as health educators</u> for their patients.

   (A) as diagnosticians but also with their intention of serving as health educators

   (B) as professionals who can diagnose but also to provide health education

   (C) as diagnosticians and also to serve as health educators

   (D) as diagnosticians but also as health educators

   (E) in the capacity of diagnostician but also serving as health educators

9. The ancient Greeks are <u>famous for</u> instituting the Olympic
   A
   games as well <u>as</u> for <u>producing</u> serious dramatic plays <u>also</u>.
   B   C   D
   <u>No error</u>
   E

10. Both my brother <u>and I in addition</u> will be available to serve
    A   B
    <u>as caregivers</u> for my great-grandfather while my parents <u>are</u>
    C   D
    away next week. <u>No error</u>
    E

● ANSWERS AND EXPLANATIONS

1. **C** The sentence as written contains the filler words *started* and *continued to do so.* Option (C) eliminates these unnecessary words by restructuring the sentence using the modifier *after mailing my birthday party invitations.*

Option (B) is incorrect because it uses confusing word order by illogically placing the two time references *the night before the party* and *as soon as I had mailed* right next to one another. Option (D) is incorrect because it uses the filler phrases *the work of* and *is what occupied me.* Option (E) is incorrect because it contains the wordy construction *is what I found myself doing.*

2. **D** As often happens with wordiness errors, the shortest version is the best here. The sentence as written is wordy because it is constructed as two independent clauses when, in fact, it would be possible to avoid repetition by restructuring the sentence as a single independent clause with a compound verb. Option (D) does this.

Option (B) is incorrect because it uses the wordy construction *will be in the process of making* instead of *will make.* Option (C) is incorrect because it is wordy in unnecessarily using two independent clauses instead of one independent clause with a compound verb. Option (E) is wordy because it uses the empty phrase *spend time.* Option (E) also contains redundancy because *both* and *in addition* mean the same thing.

3. **B** The sentence as written is wordy because it contains the empty phrase *then she will have to.* Option (B) corrects the wordiness simply by removing the empty phrase. Option (C) is incorrect because it uses the wordy construction *must be determined.* Option (D) is incorrect because it inappropriately uses the verb form *be determining.* Option (E) is incorrect because it is slightly wordier than option (B), using the wordy construction *the precipitate which will result* instead of *the resulting precipitate.*

4. **E** The sentence as written is incorrect because it contains the empty phrase *this is when.* Option (E) simply removes this empty phrase.

Option B is incorrect because it uses the wordy construction *the result is...encountering.* Option (C) is incorrect because it uses the empty phrase *is when.* Option (D) is incorrect because it uses the empty phrase *it is at this time that.*

5. **A** The sentence as written is fairly long and complicated. You may suspect that it's wordy, but when you read through the answer choices, you find that none of them improves upon option (A).

Option (B) is incorrect because it uses the wordy construction *for the halting of.* Also the plural pronoun *their* is ambiguous here because it could refer either to *experts* or to *gases.* Option (C) is incorrect because is uses the incorrect verb form *are not being* and the inappropriate wording *have a counteracting effect on.* Option (D) is incorrect because it contains a subject-verb agreement error. The singular verb *is* does not agree with the plural subject *efforts.* Option (E) is incorrect because of a verb error. The –*ing* verb *being* cannot be used as the main verb in a clause without a helping verb.

6. **C** The sentence as written is incorrect because it uses the wordy construction *actions done by one person.* Option (C) shortens this to *one person's actions* and also eliminates the unnecessary conditional verb *would.*

Option (B) is incorrect because it uses the empty phrase *the truth of the fact that.* Option (D) is incorrect because it uses the filler phrase *the fact that* and the wordy construction *experience significant effects from.* Option (E) is incorrect because it uses the vague and wordy construction *the things done by one person.*

7. **E** The sentence as written is incorrect because it uses the empty phrase *it is the…who.* Option (E) deletes these words.

Option (B) is incorrect because it uses the empty phrase *are the ones who.* Option (C) is incorrect because it uses the wordy and inappropriate construction *are in the process of having to* and unnecessarily uses the word *also.* Option (D) is incorrect because it uses the wordy construction *it is necessary for.* Option (D) also contains a verb error in using the -*ing* form *are having.*

8. **D** The sentence as written is incorrect because it uses the filler phrase *with their intention of serving.* Option (D) simply eliminates this phrase.

Option (B) is incorrect because it uses the wordy construction *professionals who can diagnose.* You should also note that the expression *not only…but also* is a clue that parallelism is required, but parallelism is lacking in option (B). Option (C) is incorrect because it uses the filler words *to serve.* Option (E) is incorrect because it uses the wordy construction *in the capacity of* and also lacks the parallelism required by the construction *not only…but also.*

9. **D** The word *also* is redundant here because it repeats the idea contained in the non-underlined phrase *as well.*

Option (A) correctly uses the preposition *for* with *famous.* Option (B) correctly uses the word *as* to follow the phrase *as well.* Option (C) is a correct use of the –*ing* verb form.

10. **D** The phrase *in addition* is redundant because it repeats the idea already expressed by the nonunderlined word *both.*

Option A correctly uses the subjective form of the pronoun *I* as the subject of the verb *will be.* Option C correctly uses the plural *caregivers* to refer to two people, *my brother and I.* Option D correctly uses the plural verb *are* to agree with the plural subject *parents.*

That's not all, folks.

Don't forget to access more practice online for *Spotlight SAT!*

kaptest.com/booksonline

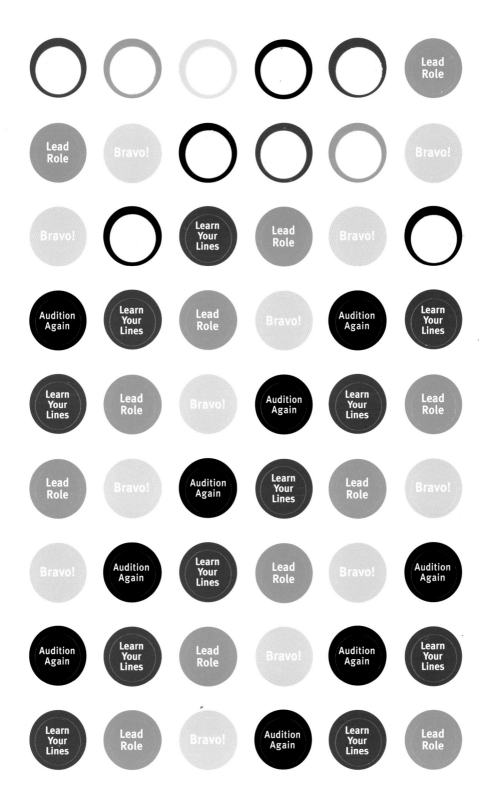

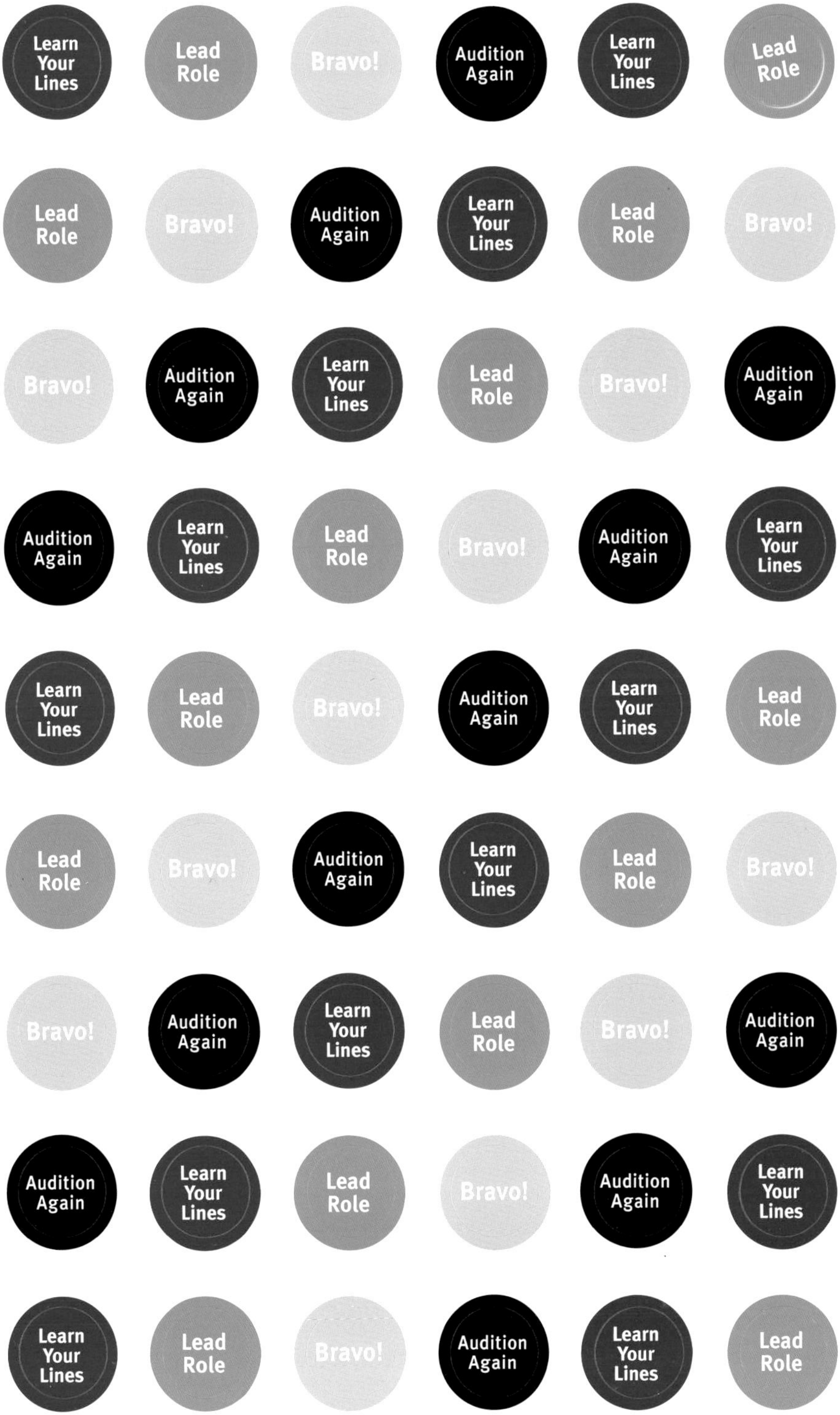
Learn Your Lines
Lead Role
Bravo!
Audition Again
Learn Your Lines
Lead Role
Lead Role
Bravo!
Audition Again
Learn Your Lines
Lead Role
Bravo!
Bravo!
Audition Again
Learn Your Lines
Lead Role
Bravo!
Audition Again
Audition Again
Learn Your Lines
Lead Role
Bravo!
Audition Again
Learn Your Lines
Learn Your Lines
Lead Role
Bravo!
Audition Again
Learn Your Lines
Lead Role
Lead Role
Bravo!
Audition Again
Learn Your Lines
Lead Role
Bravo!
Bravo!
Audition Again
Learn Your Lines
Lead Role
Bravo!
Audition Again
Audition Again
Learn Your Lines
Lead Role
Bravo!
Audition Again
Learn Your Lines
Learn Your Lines
Lead Role
Bravo!
Audition Again
Learn Your Lines
Lead Role

Diet H
a new America